AN ABSTRACT

OF THE

ORIGINAL TITLES OF RECORD

IN THE

GENERAL LAND OFFICE.

WITH AN INTRODUCTION BY
MARY LEWIS ULMER

Southern Historical Press, Inc.
Greenville, South Carolina

Originally printed 1938 by:

New Material Copyright 2022 to:
Southern Historical Press, Inc.

All rights reserved. No part of this publication may be reproduced, stored in a retrieval system or transmitted in any form or by any means without the prior permission of the publisher.

SOUTHERN HISTORICAL PRESS, INC.
PO BOX 1267
Greenville, SC   29601

ISBN #0-89308-849-8

Printed in the United States of America

PREFACE

With the reprinting of "An Abstract of the Original Titles of Record in the General Land Office, Printed in Accordance with a Resolution of the House of Representatives, Passed 24th May, 1838," the Pemberton Press continues to make available to collectors of Texana, material found in few locations. Originals of this volume are extremely rare. Thomas W. Streeter in his *Bibliography of Texas* lists copies held at eight known locations, four of which are outside of Texas. Only three complete copies are available for public use, one at Baylor University, one at the General Land Office and one at the Houston Public Library. The University of Texas has four incomplete copies, however, between them they supply the parts necessary for a complete volume.

Mr. Streeter says "This is one of the fundamental sources of information on the settlement of Texas, mostly for the period ending 1835." The period actually covered is from the Spanish period through the Mexican grants and the opening of Texas to foreign settlement, principally by Anglo-Americans, to the Texas Declaration of Independence. The date of the earliest grant is October 18, 1791 to Edward Murphy, official Indian trader at Nacogdoches and the last one February 27, 1836 to William F. Gray of Austin's Colony.

Land as the source of power and wealth is of interest to most people. In combination with the interesting and varied history of Texas the appeal is increased. This is a source book of facts on early Texans and land.

While collectors of Texana, landsmen and historians will value this book, all Texas genealogists and genealogical libraries will find it especially desirable. It should be the first source checked in the search for Texas ancestors. The original volume is the gem of any Texana collection and this reprint will be a valued addition to all historical and genealogical collections.

March 1, 1964   Mary Lewis Ulmer

AN ABSTRACT

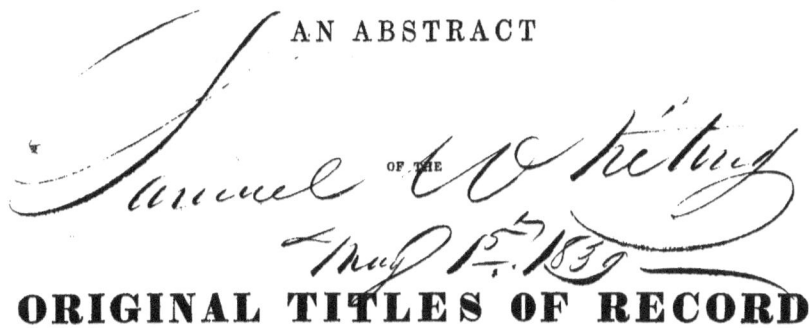

ORIGINAL TITLES OF RECORD

IN THE

GENERAL LAND OFFICE.

PRINTED IN ACCORDANCE WITH A RESOLUTION OF THE
HOUSE OF REPRESENTATIVES, PASSED
24th MAY, 1838.

———*ooooo*O*ooooo*———

HOUSTON:
NATIONAL BANNER OFFICE—NILES & CO., PRINTERS.
1838.

ABSTRACT OF ORIGINAL TITLES

NAMES OF GRANTEES.	DATE OF TITLES.	Leagues.	Labors.
Stephen F. Austin,	May 31, 1828.	5	-
do. do.	" " "	$7\frac{1}{3}$	-
do. do.	" " "	$\frac{1}{3}$	-
do. do.	" " "	$\frac{1}{2}$	-
do. do.	" " "	$\frac{1}{4}$	-
do. do.	" " "	$1\frac{1}{4}$	-
do. do.	" " "	2 1-6	-
do. do.	" " "	3 1-6	-
do. do.	" " "	2	-
do. do.	" " "		3
John Andrews,	July 7, 1824.	1	1
Thos. Alsberry,	" 8, "	2	$1\frac{1}{2}$
Elijah Allcorn,	" 10, "	$1\frac{1}{2}$	1
William Andrews,	" 15, "	1	1
Martin Allen,	" 19, "	1	1
John Austin,	" 21, "	2	
do.	Aug. 21, "		1
Thos. and Wm. Alley,	July 29, "	1	
Ransom Alley,	Aug. 3, "	$1\frac{1}{2}$	
Charles G. H. & Horatio Alsberry,	" " "	$1\frac{1}{2}$	
Simon Asa Anderson,	" 16, "	1	
Samuel T. Angier, George B. Hall & Thos Bradley,	" 16, "	1	
James E. B. Austin,	" 19, "	3	1 & F.
S. T. Angier,	" 24, "		1
John Alley,	May 14, 1827,	1	-
John Alley for the heirs of Wm. Alley,	" 16, "	1	-
James E. B. Austin,	Aug. 24, 1828.	1	-
John Andrews,	May 21, "	1	-
H. F. Armstrong,	March 3, 1831.	$\frac{1}{4}$	-
John H. Allcorn,	" 20, "	$\frac{1}{4}$	-
Miles N. Allen,	May 21, 1827.	$\frac{1}{4}$	-
Richard Andrews,	March 30, 1831.	$\frac{1}{4}$	-
Thomas Alley,	April 4, "	$\frac{1}{4}$	-
William Atkins,	" 18, "	1	-
Patrick Allison,	" 20, "	$\frac{1}{4}$	-
Ephraim Anderson,	" 23, "	1	-
William T. Austin,	" 25, "	1	-
Daniel Arnold,	May 9, "	1	-
Miles N. Allen,	Nov. 29, 1832.	$\frac{3}{4}$	-
D. W. Antony,	Nov. 20, "	$\frac{1}{4}$	-
Richard Andrews,	" 23, "	$\frac{3}{4}$	-
Samuel T. Allen,	Dec. 21, "	$\frac{1}{4}$	-
David Ayers,	Nov. 26, "	1	-
B. T. Archer,	" 18, "	1	-
Elliot Allcorn,	May 31, 1831.	1	-
Amos Alexander,	Oct. 30, 1832.	1	-
Willis Avery,	Nov. 13, "	1	-
Henry Austin,	Oct. 13, 1830.	1	-
Francis Adams,	" 22, "	$\frac{1}{4}$	-
Peter Aldrick,	" " "	$\frac{1}{4}$	-
S. F. Angier,	Dec. 10, "	$\frac{2}{3}$	-
Edmund Andrews,	Nov. 30, "	1	-
Mary Austin,	June 13, 1831.	1	-
Henry Austin,	" 20, "	3	-

WHERE SITUATED.	REMARKS.
On Oyster Cr. and Brazos, 3 leagues from mouth.	
Brazos, W. side, opposite the above, and on Bernard.	
Brazos, W. s., at the mouth; joins Labor No. 6.	
Oyster Cr.; joins Alex. Calvit's league.	
Between Bastrop and Oyster Creek; joins Groce's Hacienda.	
On Chocolate Bayou.	
On E. s. Brazos, between S. Richardson & J. Hall, Nos. 8 & 9.	
Bernard, W. s., Nos. 6, 7, & 8, below Wm. Kincheloe.	
Colorado, E. s., Nos. 2 & 3, above.	
Brazos, W. s., above its mouth.	
Cummins' Cr., joins Hacienda Lab., E. s. Brazos, T. T.	
W. s. Brazos, joins A. Mitchell on s. Lab. opp. 77, below the road No. 18.	
Near Brazos, E. s., joins W. Little's, the ½ league on New Years Creek, the Labor, Brazos, E. s. below the N. Road.	
Brazos, E. s., joins John Foster on the W. Lab. Brazos, W. s. Fort Bend.	
W. s. Peach Creek, joins Kincheloe Lab., W. s. Bra's, below San Felipe, No. 9.	
Buffalo Bayou, at the confluence of principal branches.	
Brazos, W. s. 1½ leagues from mouth.	
Bernard, W. s., 4½ leagues above its mouth.	
Colorado, at the Atascocito Crossing, ½ leag. on W. s., opposite said leag.	
San Bernard, W. s.	
Colorado, E. s., above Atascocito Crossing.	
Chocolate Bayou, W. s., 3 leag. from mouth.	
Brazos, W. s., lab. Brazos, in front of town.	
Brazos, E. s., joining John Fields.	
Navidad, W. s. Atascocito Crossing.	
Colorado, West side.	
W. s. Brazos, 1¼ leagues from mouth.	
Navidad, right bank, joins Kerr.	
Mill Creek, West side E. Fork.	
New Years Creek,	
Eight mile Creek,	
New Years Creek.	
Colorado, W. s., above quarter No. 3.	
San Jacinto Atkins' Creek.	
Navidad, Mul. Creek.	
Mulberry Creek, Navidad, No. 18.	
Big Creek.	
Navasoto.	
Mill Creek.	
Bernard, E. side.	
Colorado A., W. S.	
Brazos A., W. side.	
Yegua, joins J. B. Miller.	
Mouth of Oyster Creek, E. s.	
No. 4., Mill Creek, E. F. E. S.	
Colorado, Wilbarger's Creek.	
do. do.	
Chocolate.	
Navidad.	
Carancahua, West side.	
Gulf and Chocolate.	
Gulf.	
Gulf, Dickinson's Creek.	
Two on Bayou Flores and one on Chocolate below Austin.	

# ABSTRACT OF ORIGINAL TITLES

NAMES OF GRANTEES.	DATE OF TITLES.	QUANTITY.	
		Leagues.	Labors.
William Arnold, - - -	April 15, 1833.	1	- -
John M. Allen, - - -	Dec. 27, 1831.	¼	- -
Henry Austin, - - -	Oct. 6, 1835.	1	- -
S. F. Austin, - - -	Jan. 15, 1830.	4	- -
do. - - -	" " "	1	- -
do. - - -	" " "		2 -
do. - - -	" " "		3 -
do. - - -	Dec. 18, "	2	- -
do. - - -	" " "	1	- -
do. - - -	" " "	1	- -
do. - - -	" " "	1	- -
do. - - -	" " "		2 -
do. - - -	" " "		3 -
do. - - -	Feb. 18, 1832.	1	- -
do. - - -	" " "	1	- -
do. - - -	" " "	1	- -
do. - - -	" " "	1	- -
do. - - -	" " "	1	- -
do. - - -	" " "		3 -
do. - - -	" " "		1 -
do. - - -	" " "		1 -
do. - - -	Dec. 20, 1831.	4	- -
do. - - -	" " "	1	- -
do. - - -	" " "		33 -
do. - - -	" " "	1	- -
do. - - -	" " "	½	- -
do. - - -	" " "	1	- -
do. - - -	" " "		4 -
do. - - -	" " "	1	- -
do. - - -	" " "		9 & F.
do. - - -	" " "		F
John Austin, - - -	May 16, "	1	- -
Henry Austin, - - -	" " "	1	- -
John Austin, - - -	" " "	1	- -
Henry Austin, - - -	" 30, "	5	- -
Robert Armour, - -	Oct. 5, 1835.	1	- -
Dolores Arriola, - -	" 16, "	1	- -
Edward Arriola, - -	" 17, "	1	- -
Lancelot Abbotts, - -	" 29, "	¼	- -
A. M. Alexander, - -	" 5, "	¼	- -
James B. Bailey, - -	July 7, 1824.	1	- -
John Bradley, - -	" 8, "	1	- -
Francis Bingham, - -	" 10, "	1	- -
Thomas Barnet, - -	" " "	1	- -
David Bright, - -	" 15, "	1	- -
do - -	" " "		1 -
Micajah Byrd, - -	" 16, "	1	- -
Wm. B. Bridges, - -	" 21, "	1	- -
Aylet C. Buckner, - -	" 24, "	1	- -
do - -	Aug. 24, "		2 -
C. R. Bostic, & R. Brotherton, P. Burnett, A. S. Sojourner.	July 24, "	1	- -
	" " "	1	- -
Thomas Boatwright, - -	" 27, "	1	- -

Premium Lands.

IN THE GENERAL LAND OFFICE. 5

WHERE SITUATED.	REMARKS.
Carancahua Bay and Keller's Bay.	
Chocolate.	
Bastrop and Oyster Lakes, Chocolate and Bastrop, below 2.	
Forks of Mill Creek, - - - - - - "	
Brazos, above town of San Felipe back of labs. on the W. side.	
Opposite town of San Felipe, No. 4. above, No. 7 below road.	
Below town of San Felipe, No. 8, 1½ between Westall and No. 10, 1¾ between Allen and Newman.	
La Vaca and Navidad, E. s., opposite of Navidad.	
Bay Prairie, Pr. Creek,	
Caney and Bernard, Cedar Lake.	
Gulf, Flores Bayou, joining Patrick's ¼.	
Colorado, E. s., mouth.	
Gulf, Bastrop Creek, joining Groce.	
Brazos, W. s., and joining his Peach Point Tract.	
Brazos, E. s., back of his two leagues, and on the head of Austin's Bayou.	*Premium Lands.*
Gulf, on a Peninsula E. of Brazos and between Oyster Lake & the Gulf, including a small island, at the E. end.	
Gulf, Clear Creek, Dick's Line, opposite J. R. Williams' labor.	
Brazos, E. s. of mouth on Highland Creek, 2½ leag. W. of Galveston Bay.	
Gulf and Galveston Bay, Dollar Point.	
Bernard, E. s., at mouth.	
West of Brazos in Prairie, (Mound) near the mouth.	
Yegua, San Antonio Road.	
La Bahia Road, Yegua, S. s.	
Yegua, La Bahia Road, joining Chriesman and N. Clay.	
Colorado, E. s. above, joins Bastrop and Bowles.	
Colorado, W. s., above Gazley.	
Brazos, W. s., back of labs. below San Felipe and joins town tract.	
Yegua, North of Perry.	
Bernard W. s. and W. fork, and back of his two leagues on Colorado.	
Main Bernard, joins S. Gilbert.	
Brazos A., E. s. below Cooper.	
Navasoto, N. side. - - - - - - - -	Concession.
On Yegua. - - - - - - - - -	"
Brazos, E. s., North of Navasoto. - - - - -	"
Colorado, W. s., joining Pettus and Burnham. - - - -	"
Navasoto E. side.	
Bedais Creek, waters of.	
Bedais Creek,	
Brazos E. s., joins J. Hall, Jr.	
Lake Creek, and joins Ford.	
Brazos, E. s., joins S. Carter.	
" joins Robinson.	
" joins Wm. Pettus on the N.	
" joins W. Little.	
" joins Roark.	
Brazos, W. s., joins W. Harvey above San Felipe.	
W. s. Brazos, joins Lynch & Gates.	
La Vaca, E. s., 5 leagues above mouth.	
Cedar Lake, W. side.	
Bay Prairie on heads of Prairie Creek.	
Bay Prairie, W. of Bernard, Caney.	
Bay Prairie, E. side.	
Brazos, W. s., joins Wm. Harvey.	

NAMES OF GRANTEES.	DATE OF TITLES.	QUANTITY.	
		Leagues.	Labors.
William S. Brown,	July 29, 1824.	1	- -
Benjamin Beason,	Aug. 7, "	1	- -
Enoch Brinson,	" 7, "	1	- -
J. H. Bell,	" " "	1½	- -
William Bloodgood,	" 7, "	1	- -
Edward R. Bradley,	" 10, "	1	- -
James Baird,	" " "	1	- -
Bluford Brooks,	" " "	1	- -
Thomas B. Bell,	" 16, "	1	- -
J. Burnham,	" 16, "	1	- -
"	" 16, "		1 -
Isaac Best,	" 19, "	1	- -
John Brown,	" " "	1	- -
"	" " "		1 -
George Brown & C. Belknap,	May 22, 1827.	1	- -
J. T. Bowman & H. Williams,	Aug. 21, 1824.	1	- -
Charles Brean,	May 24, 1827,	1	- -
Miles M. Battle,	" 31, "	1	- -
W. Barrett &. A. Harris,	June. 4, "	1	- -
Daniel E. Bayles, & I. Vandorn,	April 14, 1828.	1	- -
Solomon Brown,	" 16, "	1	- -
Isham G. Belcher,	May 27, 1828.	¼	- -
Charles Benton,	" " "	¼	- -
Gail Borden,	March 4, 1831.	1	- -
P. P. Borden,	" " "	¼	- -
James H. Bostic,	" 5, "	¼	- -
Thomas H. Borden,	" 12, "	⅓	- -
James Bell,	April 8, "	¼	- -
Gail Borden, Jr.,	March 29, "	1	- -
Thomas Bell,	" 22, "	1	- -
John M. Burton,	" 24, "	¼	- -
Samuel P. Brown,	" 29, "	1	- -
William Burnett,	" 25, "	1	- -
James Beardslee,	" 31, "	1	- -
Alexander Bailey,	" " "	¼	- -
William Barton,	April 4, "	1	- -
Benjamin Barton,	" " "	¼	- -
Elisha W. Barton.	" " "	1	- -
Benjamin Bowles,	" 5, "	1	- -
Edward Burleson,	" 4, "	1	- -
John F. Berry,	" 7, "	1	- -
John S. Black,	" 6, "	1	- -
Marcus D. Black,	" " "	¼	- -
William Burney,	" " "	1	- -
John Bowman,	" " "	1	- -
Jeremiah Brown,	" 18, "	1	- -
Lewis Barksdale,	" 13, "	¼	- -
James Bowie,	" 20, "	1	- -
A. W. Breedlove,	" " "	1	- -
Levi Bostic,	" 23, "	1	- -
George L. Bellon,	" 5, "	1	- -
Jesse Burnham,	" 30, "	1	- -
Peggy Brown,	May 3, "	1	- -
Thomas Bird,	" 7, "	1	- -
William Brookfield,	" 20, "	1	- -
Moses Baine,	" 26, "	1	- -

WHERE SITUATED.	REMARKS.
Brazos, W. s., half above mouth of Navasoto.	
Colorado, W. s., 2 leagues above Atoscocito Crossing.	
Bay of San Jacinto, S. W. side.	
Brazos, W. s., joins Varner.	
Cedar Creek, 5 Leagues above mouth.	
Brazos, E. s., joins A. Robinson.	
Bernard, E. s., below Huff, joins Prater.	
Brazos, W. s., below S. A. Road, joins Curtis.	
West side of the Bernard.	
Colorado, W. side.	
Colorado, joins E. Tumlinson.	
Brazos E. s., between Coshate and La Bahia Roads.	
Buffalo Bayou, N. s., opposite J. R. Harris.	
Brazos E. s., opposite San Felipe de Austin.	
Brazos E. s., back of Allcorn.	
Colorado, E. side, joins S. Betts below.	
Between Bernard and Bay Prairie.	
Brazos, E. side below, and joins Mrs. Wilkins.	
W. side, Brazos, joins J. Polly below.	
Between Bernard and Bay Prairie. - - - - -	{ Claimed by H. M'Guffin.
San Jacinto, W. side, small branch of.	
Mill Creek, E. fork.	
" E. side E. fork.	
" W. side "	
" " "	
" " W. fork.	
Head waters of Mill Creek.	
Navidad, Mulberry fork, N. of Gonzales Road.	
Brazos, W. side, below.	
" back of Boatwright's	
Head of Mill Creek, joins Clokey,	
Cummins and Colorado,	
Mill Creek, W. side W. fork.	
La Bahia Road.	
Mill Creek. E. fork.	
Colorado, W. s., above T. Alley.	
" " "	
Mouth Ten Mile Creek, W. side Colorado.	
Colorado, E. side below, joins S. A. Road.	
Colorado, W. side, joins Decrow.	
Colorado, E. side, joins I. Ingram.	
Holland's Settlement, joins S. W. Groce.	
" joins Gregg & Black.	
" S. of F. Holland.	
Caney Creek, E. of Brazos.	
Navidad Rocky Creek. - - - - - - -	Special Grant.
Colorado, W. side, joins Castleman.	
Navidad, E. side.	
" "	
" " Sandy Creek.	
Buffalo Bayou, joins J. B. Taylor.	
Navidad, N. of road. - - - - - - -	Special Grant.
Colorado, W. side Buckner's Creek.	
Brazos, W. side, N. of Yegua.	
Navidad, high up.	
Navasoto, N. side.	

ABSTRACT OF ORIGINAL TITLES

NAMES OF GRANTEES.	DATE OF TITLES.	QUANTITY.	
		Leagues.	Labors.
Daniel D. D. Baker,	May 2, 1831.	1/4	-
Alexander Brown,	" 17, "	1	-
Crawford Burnett,	June 17, "	1	-
John Bird,	Oct. 14, "	1	-
Charles H. Barnett,	" 16, "	1	-
Charles Baird,	" 17, "	1	-
Jesse Bartlet,	Oct. 19, 1832.	1	-
Charles A. Bettner,	Nov. 20, "	1/4	-
Radford Berry,	" 21, "	1/4	-
John M. Burton,	" " "	1/4	-
David Berry,	" 20, "	1	-
William Bridge,	" " "	1	-
John P. Borden,	" 30, "	1/4	-
Calbert Baker,	" 23, "	1	-
James H. Bostic,	Dec. 5, "	1	-
James W. Bell,	Nov. 30, "	1	-
James Bell,	Dec. 2, "	3/4	-
John Brown,	March 3, 1830.	1	-
Thomas H. Borden,	Nov. 22, "	1/3	-
Edward Baty,	Oct. 21, "	1	-
Josiah H. Bell,	" 27, "	1	-
Silvester Bowen,	" 22, "	1	-
Pumphrey Burnett,	Oct. 14, "	1/2	-
Asa Brigham,	" 30, "	1	-
John Brown,	Dec. 10, "	1/4	-
Peter Burtrand,	Nov. 24, "	1	1
A Bowman & C. K. Reese,	June 20, 1831.	1	-
William Barrett,	Nov. 26, 1832.	1/2	-
Samuel C. Bundick,	" 12, "	1	-
William Baxter,	Feb. 6, 1833.	1	-
James Burleson,	Oct. 29, 1832.	1	-
John Burleson,	" 30, "	1	-
Leman Barker,	" 29, "	1	-
Jesse Barker,	Nov. 13, "	1	-
Benj. Babbit,	" 22, "	1/4	-
Joseph Biegel,	" 29, "	1	-
Thomas H. Barron,	Dec. 1, "	1	-
Jonathan Burleson,	" 4, "	1/4	-
Thomas W. Blakely,	" 16, "	1	-
M'Lin Bracy,	Jan. 7, 1833.	1	-
William Baird,	Oct. 3, 1835.	1	-
James Burleson,	" 3, "	1	-
Benj. Babbit,	" " "	3/4	-
Joseph Baker,	" 5, "	1/4	-
Robert G. Baugh,	" " "	1/4	-
Nathan Brookshire,	" " "	1	-
Joseph Burleson,	" 8, "	1	-
Alexander Blair,	" 10, "	1/4	-
Amaziah Baker,	" 13, "	1	-
Samuel Bowman,	" 16, "	1	-
James Buckhanan,	" 19, "	1	-
Moses Austin Bryan,	" 20, "	1/4	-
Thomas Boatwright,	" " "	1	-
Humphrey Best,	" 21, "	1	-
Friend Boatwright,	" 25, "	1	-
Thos. Barnett, Ad'm of L M'Laughlin,	Sept. 28, "	1	-
Thos. O. Berry,	Oct. 24, "	1	-

WHERE SITUATED.	REMARKS.
Head of Bay Prairie, joins Huff.	
Brazos, E. s., joins J. S. Black.	
N. of Navasoto, joins R. Carter.	
Davidson's Creek and Yegua, joins No. 11.	
Brazos W. side, joins Calvin.	
Navidad, E. side, joins J. S. O'Conner.	
Buckner's Creek, above La Bahia Road.	Part of the lower half granted S. Miller.
San Bernard, E. side.	
Bedais Creek, near San Jacinto Road.	
Cummin's Creek, W. side, joins A. Thompson.	
Colorado, W. s., joins John Castleman.	
Waters of New Years Creek, joins Lessassier,	
Colorado, back of Jones.	
Brazos, E. s., joins Haynes.	
Between Brazos and Colorado, San Antonio Road.	
Davidson's Creek, joins No. 3.	
Brazos, E. side, joins Groce's Retreat.	
Carancahua, W. fork W. side.	
Between Bernard and Caney, middle 3rd of 32.	
Navidad, mouth of Sandy Creek.	
La Vaca, E. side near mouth.	
Navidad, E. side, joins Pettus.	
Trespalacios, E. side.	
Hall's Bayou, E. Brazos.	
Brazos, E. side, joins H. Moss.	
Colorado, E. side, below J. Betts'; labor, No. 5, Brazos, E. s., near mouth.	
Colorado, W. side, joins J. Keller.	Special Grant.
Brazos, W. side, joins J. Phelps.	
Galveston Bay, mouth of Highland Creek.	
Old Caney, E. side, joins H. Curtis.	
Colorado, E. side.	
Colorado, E. side, joins Gililland.	
Colorado, E. side.	
Waters of Wilbarger's Creek, joins Avery.	
Brazos, E. side, joins Groce's Retreat.	
Cummin's Creek, joins F. Lewis.	First granted to F. W. Johnston.
Brazos, E. side, N. Navasoto.	
N. of San Antonio Road, joins Standifer.	
N. of Navasoto, E. of Brazos.	
Brazos, joining James Bell.	
Brazos, E. side, joins M'Lin Bracy.	
Colorado, E. side, Pin Oak Creek,	
Mill Creek, above, and joining Mill Tract.	
Brazos, E. side, joins Denohoe & M'Kenney.	
Cummins' Creek.	
Brazos, joining Cooper & Foster.	
Walnut Creek, E. of Colorado.	
Yegua, waters of.	Known as one-fourth, Leag. 5.
Cummins' Creek.	
La Bahia Road, joins Sims.	
Yegua, N. side.	
Waters of New Years Creek, joins Miller.	
Bedais Creek.	
Yegua.	
Head waters of Yegua.	
Navasoto, N. of.	
Head waters of Navidad.	

ABSTRACT OF ORIGINAL TITLES

NAMES OF GRANTEES.	DATE OF TITLES.	QUANTITY.	
		Leagues.	Labors.
Amy Boatwright,	Oct. 24, 1835.	1	-
Richard Boatwright,	" " "	1	-
William J. Bryan,	Jan. 29, 1836.	$\frac{1}{4}$	-
William Beasley,	" 25, "	1	-
Bernham H. Beaumer,	Feb. 4, 1836.	1	-
Anthony Baudrand,	" 6, "	1	-
Jacob Burlison,	" 9, "	1	-
Joseph C. Bartlett,	" " "	$\frac{1}{4}$	-
James Bradley,	" 15, "	$\frac{1}{4}$	-
Jonathan Burlison,	" 16, "	1	-
Matthew Boren,	" " "	1	-
James B. Blalack,	" 22, "	1	-
James Bell,	" 23, "	$\frac{1}{4}$	-
Thomas H. Bell,	" " "	1	-
Thomas Barnett,	May 26, 1831.	1	-
Jacob Betts,	Aug. 19, 1824.	1	-
M. M. Battle, M. Berry & J. Williams,	" 10, "	1	-
John Byrne,	April 9, 1831.	1	-
Francis Bingham,	July 10, 1824.	1	-
"	" " "		1
James Cummins,	" 7, "	1	-
"	" " "		1
"	" " "	5	-
Silvanus Castleman,	" 7, "	2	-
"	" " "		2
"	" " "	$\frac{1}{2}$	
Sam'l Carter,	" 8, "	1	-
Horatio Chriesman,	" " "	1	2
John C. Clark,	" 16, "	1	-
Merrit M. Coats,	" 19, "	1	-
William Cummins,	" 21, "	1	-
John Cummins,	" " "	1	-
Rebecca Cummins,	" " "	1	-
"	" " "		2
Wm. Cooper & M. Morrison,	" 24, "	1	-
George Cook & Bluford Dewees,	Aug. 3, "	1	-
Morris Callahan & Allen Vince.	" " "	1	-
John Crownover,	" " "	1	-
Alexander Calvit,	" " "		1
"	" " "		1
Hinton Curtis,	" 10, "	1	-
Thomas Cartwright,	" " "	1	1
William Cooper,	" " "	$1\frac{1}{2}$	-
"	" " "		2
James Curtis,	" 19, "	1	-
J. P. Coles,	" " "	$7\frac{1}{2}$	-
"	" " "	$\frac{1}{2}$	-
"	" 19, "	$\frac{1}{2}$	-
Anthony R. Clark,	" 24, "		1
William C. Carson,	May 15, 1827.	1	-
John Cryer,	June 6, "	1	-
Jesse Cartwright,	March 31, 1828.	1	-
"	" " "		1
Peter Conrod.	May 31, 1827.	$\frac{1}{4}$	-
Andrew Castleman,	May 14, 1828,	1	-
John Castleman,	Dec. 21, "	1	-

IN THE GENERAL LAND OFFICE. 11

WHERE SITUATED.	REMARKS.
Head waters of Bedais Creek.	
Middle Bernard.	
Jackson's Creek, and joins Early.	
Head waters of Bedais Creek.	
San Antonio Road, W. of Colorado.	
Waters of Peach Creek, W. of Colorado.	
Waters of Davidson's Creek.	
Brazos, E. side, joins Best, &c.	
Head waters of Buckner's Creek.	
W. of Colorado, near San Antonio Road.	
Bedais Creek.	
Colorado W. side, on San Antonio Road.	Formerly granted to Isaac Marshall.
Waters of Mill Creek.	
Waters of Yegua, joins J. Burleson.	
Brazos, W. side, below La Bahia and Coshate Roads.	Concession.
Colorado, E. side.	
Between San Bernard and Bay Prairie.	
Colorado, W. side, below.	
Colorado, E. side below Kincheloe.	
Brazos, E. side, S. of National Road.	
Colorado, E. side,	
Colorado, W. side opposite League.	
Cummins' Creek, E. side Colorado,	Hacienda.
Colorado, E. side, below Wm. Kincheloe.	
Brazos, West side.	
Colorado, W. side of, one league above La Bahia Crossing.	
Brazos E. side, joins Asa Mitchell, S.	
Brazos, W. side, joins S. Kenedy, labors W. of Brazos, above T. tract.	
Colorado, E. side, joins J. R. Kuykendall.	
Brazos, E. side, 2½ leagues above Coshate Crossing.	
Bernard, E. side, 5 leagues above mouth.	
Bernard, W. side.	
" "	
Brazos, E. side opposite San Felipe,	
Cedar Lake, W. side.	
Colorado, W. side, below Atascocito Crossing.	
Buffalo Bayou, S. side, including Sims' Bayou.	
Colorado, W. side, joins John Cryer.	
Brazos, E. side, between Oyster Creek and Groce.	
Brazos E. side, near the mouth.	
Brazos E. side, opposite town tract, N. of National Road.	
Caney Creek, between Brazos and Bay Prairie.	
Colorado, E. side above, Kincheloe, lab. Brazos, W. s., below T. tract.	
Brazos, E. side, below San Felipe.	
Brazos, W. s. " "	
Brazos, E. side, below San Antonio Road.	
Brazos, W. side, above mouth Yegua.	
Opposite mouth Navasoto, joins Robinson.	
Brazos, E. side, joins Asa Mitchell.	
Brazos, E. side.	
Between Bernard and Bay Prairie.	
Colorado, W. side, joins H. H. League.	
Brazos, E. side joins Jane Wilkins.	
Navidad, E. side, above Atascocito Crossing.	
Bernard, E. side, joins G. Huff.	
Colorado, W. side, above La Bahia Crossing.	
" "	

12 ABSTRACT OF ORIGINAL TITLES

NAMES OF GRANTEES.	DATE OF TITLES.	QUANTITY.	
		Leagues.	Labors.
Henry Cheves,	March 15, 1831.	1	-
Isaac N. Charles,	" 26, "	$\frac{1}{2}$	-
Horatio Chriesman,	" 17, "	1	-
David Chandler,	" 10, "	1	-
James Clark,	" 17, "	1	-
Nestor Clay,	" 18, "	1	-
Susanah Clampitt,	" 25, "	1	-
Silas Clark,	" 21, "	$\frac{1}{4}$	-
Robert Clokey,	" 28, "	1	-
John Cole,	" 24, "	1	-
Joseph B. Chance,	" 26, "	1	-
Ezekiel Clampitt,	" 23, "	1.	-
John Cook,	April 4, "	1	-
Washington Curtis,	" 5, "	$\frac{1}{4}$	-
Sarah Cottle,	" " "	1	-
Elijah Curtis,	" " "	$\frac{1}{4}$	-
John C. Cunningham,	" 6, "	1	-
Elizabeth Campbell,	" 7, "	1	-
Mary Corner,	" 7, "	1	-
W. C. Clark,	" 10, "	1	-
David Colton,	" 21, "	1	-
Aaron Colvin,	" 16, "	1	-
Keziah Cryer,	" 25, "	1	-
Samuel Chane,	May 4, "	$\frac{2}{3}$	-
Jesse H. Cartwright,	April 30, "	$\frac{1}{2}$	-
David Clark,	May 7. "	1	-
Moses Cummins,	" 3, "	1	-
John Corner,	" 10, "	1	-
Richard Carter,	April 30, "	1	-
Philip Coe,	May 4, "	1	-
R. M. Cravens,	" 30, "	1	-
Thomas Corner,	" 28, "	$\frac{1}{4}$	-
Lyman Cronkrite,	June 20, "	1	-
John Cronkrite,	" 21, "	$\frac{1}{4}$	-
James Cooper,	Nov. 19, "	1	-
James Cox,	May 28, 1832.	1	-
J. S. Counsel,	June 22, "	1	-
John S. Cox,	Oct. 16, "	1	-
James Cox,	" 19, "	1	-
Euclid M. Cox,	" " "	$\frac{1}{4}$	-
G. H. Coleman,	Nov. 12, "	1	-
Gabriel Cole,	" 27, "	$\frac{1}{2}$	-
"	" " "	$\frac{3}{4}$	-
Hannah Cornaugh,	Dec. 19, "	1	-
James Cochrane,	April 23, 1833.	$\frac{1}{4}$	-
Thomas Cayce,	" 14, 1830.	1	-
Christopher G. Cox.	" " "	1	-
Nicholas Clopper,	Dec. 18, "	1	-
Thomas Cox,	Oct. 30, "	1	-
Maria Cummins,	Nov. 20, "	1	-
Young Coleman,	Oct. 22, "	1	-
Abram M. Clare,	Dec. 9, "	1	-
Nestor Clay,	" 10, "	1	-
Goodwin B. N. Cotton,	" 15, "	1	-
Frederick J. Calvit,	" 8; "	1	-
Wm. C. Clapp,	June 23, 1831.	$\frac{1}{4}$	-

WHERE SITUATED.	REMARKS.
Mill Creek, W. fork, E. side.	Special Grant.
Brazos, Below, E. side. Part of 1¼ leagues granted to N. F. Roberts.	
Yegua, at La Bahia Road.	Special Grant.
Caney Creek, waters of.	
New Years Creek, joins E. Allcorn.	
La Bahia, near Cole's Mill.	Special Grant.
Yegua, waters of; joins J. P. Cole's.	
Caney Creek, joins F. Grimes' Fourth.	
Mill Creek, La Bahia Road.	
New Years Creek, N. side.	
Yegua, joins Mrs. Clampit.	
Brazos, W. side, joins P. & W. Kerr & Singleton.	
Colorado N. side, joins A. Casterman.	
Colorado, E. side.	
Colorado, E. side, joins L. Woods.	
" joins S. Cottle.	
Colorado, E. side.	
"	
San Jacinto, W. side, joins Pevehouse.	
San Jacinto, W. side.	
Cummins' Creek.	Special Grant.
Yegua, N. side, S. of Bexar Road.	
Navidad, W. fork.	
Navidad, E. side, opposite Hardy.	
Cummins Creek, N. side joins J. R. Philips.	
Brazos, W. side, North of Yegua.	
" N. side, and N. of Yegua, joins J. P. Cole's.	
San Jacinto, Atkins' Creek.	
Navasoto, Saline Creek.	
Mill Creek, E. fork, E. side.	
Colorado, W. side, back of heirs of Alley.	
Little Lake Creek, joins Shannon and Atkins.	
Mustang Creek, high up.	
San Jacinto, joins Clark & Corner.	
Mill Creek, E. fork E. side.	
Bowman's Creek, E. side Brazos.	
Navidad, waters of.	
Brazos, joins Bennett.	
Yegua, waters of, joins Clokey.	
Colorado, W. side, joins Joshua Parker's half.	
Navasoto, North of, joins Baine & Lee.	
Bernard, E. side, joins J. J. Powell.	
Bernard, Back of Powell & Co.	
Navasoto, E. side, joins R. Ray.	
Peach Creek, W. side.	{ Originally granted to B. Sims.
Colorado, W. side, joins H. H. League.	
" No. 6., below League.	
" below League.	
La Vaca Bay, mouth of.	
Bay Prairie, Cedar Island.	
Caraucahua, W. side, No. 10.	
" W. fork, joins Coleman,	
Navidad, W. side, above E. M'Nutt.	
Colorado, W. side, between Cox & Keller.	Special Grant.
Oyster Creek, mouth of, W. side.	
Trespalacios, W. side.	

ABSTRACT OF ORIGINAL TITLES

NAMES OF GRANTEES.	DATE OF TITLES.	Leagues.	Labors.
John Caldwell,	June 8, 1831.	1	-
John T. Criswell,	" 15, "	1	-
Thomas Choate,	Jan. 18, 1832.	1	-
Tacitus Clay,	March 25, 1833.	$\frac{1}{4}$	-
Thomas Christian,	Oct. 29, 1832.	1	-
Isaac Casner,	" 30, "	1	-
Hugh M. Childress,	" " "	1	-
James Crawford,	Nov. 13, "	1	-
James Campbell,	" 27, "	1	-
Jacob Casner,	" " "	1	-
Robert Cunningham,	March 4, 1833.	1	-
John Crownover, Sr,	Oct. 8, 1835.	1	-
Arter Crownover	" " "	1	-
Silvanus Cottle,	" " "	$\frac{1}{4}$	-
Isaiah Curd,	" 12, "	1	-
Hugh Chandler,	" 16, "	$\frac{1}{4}$	-
John H. Callahan,	" 19, "	1	-
Noah Carnes,	" 20, "	1	-
John G. Conner,	" 22, "	1	-
Cyrus Campbell,	" " "	1	-
John Chesney,	" 30, "	1	-
Thomas Cannon,	Jan. 27, 1836.	$\frac{1}{4}$	-
James Cochrane,	" 29, "	$\frac{3}{4}$	-
Mariano Cavero,	Feb. 6, "	$\frac{1}{4}$	-
Tho. Cochrane,	" 21, "	1	-
James Cummins,	Nov. 18, 1831.	1	-
"	" " "	1	-
James Curtis, (Padre,)	Aug. 3, 1824.	1	-
John Cook & Isaac Hughs,	" 24, "	1	-
James Cummins, son of R. Cummins,	" 16, "	6	-
Patrick Clopper & Co.,	Dec. 16, 1828.	3	-
William H. Carson,	Nov. 22, 1832.	$\frac{1}{4}$	-
Tho. Caruthers,	" " "	1	-
John Crownover,	Aug. 3, 1824.	1	-
"	" " "		1
Joseph Duty,	July 19, "	1	-
George Duty,	" " "	1	-
Thomas M. Duke,	" 24, "	1	-
Peter Demoss,	" " "	1	-
Charles Demoss,	Aug. 3, "	1	-
Bluford Dewees & George Cook,	" " "	1	-
Clement C. Dyer,	" 10, "	1	-
"	" 24, "		$1\frac{1}{2}$
Nicholas Dillard,	" 16, "	1	-
John Dickinson,	" 19, "	1	-
Bryant Dottery,	March 7, 1831,	1	-
Joseph Davis,	" 16, "	1	-
Abraham Dillard,	" 20, "	$\frac{1}{4}$	-
William Dever,	" 31, "	$\frac{1}{4}$	-
Thomas Decrow,	April 5, "	$\frac{1}{4}$	-
William Dever,	" 16, "	1	-
William B. Dewees,	" 28, "	$\frac{1}{2}$	-
Charles Denehoe,	" 12, "	1	-
Jesse Denson,	May 4, "	1	-
Lemuel Dickinson,	" 7, "	1	-
Abraham Durst,	" 6, "	1	-
Elizabeth Devers,	June 21, "	1	-

IN THE GENERAL LAND OFFICE. 15

WHERE SITUATED.	REMARKS.
Colorado, W. side, joins W. Pettus.	
Colorado, W. side, below H. League.	
Turkey Creek, Clear Creek, joins J. R. Williams.	
Navidad, E. side, joins E. Mercer.	
Colorado, 6 Leagues N. of Bastrop.	
San Antonio Road, above; joins Christian.	
Wilbarger's Creek, waters of.	
" " "	
La Vaca, E. side Gonzales Road, joins Ponton.	
Wilbarger's Creek, waters of.	
Skull Creek, joins D. Gilliland.	
Bear Creek, (Trinity.)	
Bedais Creek.	
Pin Oak Creek, E. Colorado.	
Navasoto, N. side.	
Navasoto, E. side.	
Cypress Bayou, N. Branch, joins Simmons.	
Navidad and Buckner's Creek, head of.	
Between Navasoto and San Jacinto.	
" " "	
Yegua.	
Yegua, joins Guild	
Brazos, West side; Caney Creek.	
Colorado, W. side—Buckner's Creek, waters of.	
Colorado, E. side.	
Northern part of his Hacienda Tract. - - - - -	Concession.
Southern part of his Hacienda Tract. - - - - -	"
Brazos, W. side near San Antonio Road.	
Galveston Bay, W. side, joins Johnson Hunter.	
Bernard, E. side, below J. H. Bell, and 5 leagues on Mill Creek.	
Buffalo Bayou, joins J. Brown & J. Austin.	
Colorado, E. side, joins J. H. Moore's half league.	
Brazos, E. side; Navasoto, Saline Creek.	
Colorado, W. side, joins Crier.	
Brazos, W. s., below Town Tract—below & adjoining Jno. Rabb's lab.	
Colorado, E. side, between La Bahia and Atas. Roads.	
Colorado, E. side, joins Anderson.	
Bay Prairie, E. side.	
Between San Bernard and Bay Prairie.	
Bay Prairie, E. side, West Bernard	
Colorado, W. side.	
Colorado, E. side, above W. Kincheloe.	
Brazos, E. side, South of National Road.	
Cedar Lake, E. side.	
Clear Creek, W. Galveston Bay, joins J. R. Williams.	
Mill Creek, W. side, W. fork.	
Yegua Creek, joins Sam'l Gates.	
Doe Run, " "	
" joins W. Gates & Westall.	
Colorado, E. side.	
Between Navasoto and Brazos, joins W. Sutherland.	
Colorado, W. side, joins E. Tumlinson.	
Brazos, E. side, Fish Pond Creek.	
Spring Creek, San Jacinto. - - - - - - -	Special Grant.
Brazos, W. side, N. of Yegua.	
Mound League Bernard.	
Buckner's Creek, joins Curate.	

ABSTRACT OF ORIGINAL TITLES

NAMES OF GRANTEES.	DATE OF TITLES.	QUANTITY.	
		Leagues.	Labors.
Kincheloe W. Davis,	May 28, 1832,	1	
Williamson Daniels,	Oct. 17, "	1	
J. J. Dewitt,	" 20, "	1	
Samuel C. Douglass,	" " "	1	
John H. Dabney,	Nov. 19, "	1	
Daniel T. Donalson,	" 21, "	$\frac{1}{4}$	
John Densmore,	April 23, 1833.	$\frac{1}{4}$	
Felipe Dewitt,	Dec. 24, 1829.	$1\frac{1}{4}$	
John Denton,	Oct. 23, 1830.	$\frac{1}{4}$	
Jeremiah Dwyer,	Nov. 10, "	1	
F. W. Dempsey,	Dec. 18, "	1	
John Davis,	" 10, "	1	
John J. Dillard,	" " "	1	
Thomas M. Duke,	Nov. 29, "	1	
Erasmus D. Downer,	Jan. 18, 1832.	$\frac{1}{4}$	
Silas Dinsmore,	Oct. 18, 1832.	1	
Sarah Deel,	Nov. 20, "	1	
William Dobie,	" 19, "	$\frac{1}{4}$	
Matthew Duty,	Oct. 29, "	$\frac{1}{2}$	
S. Duty, (heirs of,)	" 30, "	$\frac{1}{2}$	
Joseph Duty,	" " "	$\frac{1}{2}$	
Samuel Denton,		1	
Sixto Dominguez,	Oct. 9, 1835.		9
James C. Duff,	Feb. 5, 1836.	1	
Gerrit Damker,	" " "	$\frac{1}{4}$	
Mortimer Donahoe,	" 8, "	$\frac{1}{4}$	
Isaac Donahoe,	" " "	$\frac{1}{4}$	
John Dorsey,	" 9, "	$\frac{1}{4}$	
Juan Delgado,	" 10, "	1	
Socrates Darling,	" 13, "	1	
Delaplain,	" 17, "	1	
Thomas K. Davis,	" 19, "	1	
John Dzickanski,	May 3, 1831.	$\frac{1}{4}$	
Samuel Davidson,	July 21, 1824.	1	
Bazil Derbin,	Oct. 22, 1830.	$\frac{1}{4}$	
Thomas Earle,	July 7, 1824.	1	1
John Elam,	Aug. 7, "	1	
Gustavus E. Edwards,	" 19, "	1	
Robert Elder,	" 24, "		1
Benjamin Eaton,	May 16, 1827.	1	
Mary Anna Earle,	March 29, 1831.	$\frac{1}{4}$	
Frederick Ernst,	April 16, "	1	
Holden Evans,	" 11, "	1	
John H. Edwards,	" 13, "	1	
John T. Edwards,	" 16, "	$\frac{1}{4}$	
Charles Edwards,	" 30, "	1	
John Eblin,	June 10, "	1	
Felix B. Ernest,	Oct. 22, 1830.	$\frac{1}{4}$	
George Ewing,	Nov. 10, "	1	
William J. Eaton,	Jan. 25, 1832.	$\frac{1}{4}$	
Jacob Ebberly,	Nov. 7, "	1	
Alexander Ewing,	Oct. 3, 1835.	$\frac{1}{4}$	
Musgrove Evans,	Feb. 13, 1836.	1	
Vincent L. Evans,	" 14, "	1	
Nicholas Eastland,		1	
W. H. Eastland,	" " "	1	
John S. Evans,	April 6, 1831.	1	

IN THE GENERAL LAND OFFICE. 17

WHERE SITUATED.	REMARKS.
Brazos, W. side, joins Edward Robinson.	
La Vaca, E. side, Gonzales Crossing.	
Yegua and Davidson's Creeks, joins J. F. Perry.	
Mill Creek and Bernard. - - - - - -	Superceded.
Colorado, Skull Creek, joins No. 3.	
Navidad, W. Fork, joins Hensley.	
Peach Creek, W. side. - - - - - - -	Originally granted B. Sims.
La Vaca, E. side, Bowling-green Creek, joins Cox.	
Carancahua, W. side, joins Brown.	
Prairie Creek, W. of Caney.	
Colorado, E. side, below J. Betts.	
Mustang Creek, above mouth.	
" E. side.	
Prairie Creek. - - - - - - - -	Special Grant.
Colorado, W. side, at the mouth.	
Lake Austin, Bay Prairie.	
Clear Lake, W. side, joins Wilson & Murphy. . - - -	Special Grant.
Middle Creek, E. Brazos, joins J. Routh,	
Colorado, E. side, joins Webber. - - - - -	Special Grant.
Colorado, E. side, joins M. Wells.	
Colorado, E. side, joins Hornsby.	
Davidson's Creek, N. W. of I. Long.	
W. of Brazos, and joins Cummins' Hacienda.	
Navidad, Mulberry Fork.	
Colorado, W. side.	
Brazos, E. side, joins M·Lin Bracy.	
" " joins Solomon Renfellett.	
San Jacinto, W. side, joins Clark.	
San Bernard, E. side, joins Mancha.	
Colorado, W. side, joins S. F. Austin & Steward.	
Peach Creek, waters of.	
Between Brazos and Bernard.	
Big Creek, N. side.	
Brazos, W. side, joins W. M'Williams.	
Navidad, W. side, third above Smith.	
Oyster, S. side Buffalo Bayou; labor on Green's Bayou.	
Brazos, W. side, between Coshate and La Bahia Roads.	
Bay Prairie, E. side.	
Brazos, E. side, S. of National Road, joins Allsberry.	
Mill Creek, W. side, W. fork.	
Jackson's Creek, joins J. Harbor.	
Mill Creek, W. fork, W. side.	
Between Navasoto and Brazos, joins Whitesides.	
Spring Creek, San Jacinto.	
Fort Bend.	
Pin Oak Creek, Colorado.	
Colorado, W. side, joins J. H. Moore's half league.	
Navidad, W. side, joins H. Smith.	
La Vaca, E. side.	
Colorado, nearly opposite Matagorda.	
Wilbarger's Creek, waters of, joins Avery.	
Cummins' Creek, W. side, joins Kensly & Peebles.	
Colorado, W. side.	
Colorado, W. side, joins Evans.	
Colorado, Sandy Creek.	
" W. side Sandy Creek,	
" W. side.	

NAMES OF GRANTEES.	DATE OF TITLES.	QUANTITY. Leagues.	Labors.
Amos Edwards,	Nov. 14, 1830.	1	-
David Fitzgerald,	July 10, 1824.	1	-
John Foster,	" 15, "	2½	-
"	" " "		3
Churchill Fulchear,	" 16, "	1	-
Randolph Foster,	" " "	1	-
Isaiah Flanikin,	" " "		2
Elisha Flowers,	" 19, "	1	1
James Fisher,	" " "	1	-
David Fenter,	" 29, "	1	-
Isaac Foster,	Aug. 10, "	1	-
Charles Fallenash,	" 19, "	1	-
John F. Fields,	" 24, "		1
John Fitzgibbons,	Dec. 11, 1828.	½	-
Joshua Fletcher,	Feb. 26, 1831.	1	-
Gehu Furnash,	March 30, 1831.	¼	-
Samuel Fulton,	April 9, "	1	-
Philo Fairchilds,	" 4, "	1	-
James Ford,	" 11, "	1	-
Elisha Flack,	" 13, "	¼	-
Samuel Fuller,	" 20, "	1	-
Charles Fodhran,	May 18, "	¼	-
Moses A. Foster,	June 22, 1832.	1	-
Wm. W. Ford,	Oct. 17, "	¼	-
David Frost,	Nov. 21, "	¼	-
S. Rhodes Fisher,	Dec. 2, 1830.	1	-
Alexander Farmer,	Nov. 23, 1831.	1	-
S. Rhodes Fisher,	Oct. 29, 1832.	1	-
John R. Foster,	Nov. 26, "	¼	-
S. Rhodes Fisher,	Oct. 29, "	¾	-
"	" " "	¼	-
James Foster, Senr.,	Nov. 22, "	1	-
Daniel B. Fryer,	" 27, "	1	-
Peter H. Fullenwider,	Oct. 20, 1835.	1	-
Marcus F. Fulton,	" 24, "	¼	-
Reuben Fisher,	Feb. 10, 1836.	1	-
Eli Fan,	" " "	1	-
Wm. Fitzgibbons,	April 6, 1831.	1	-
Freeman George,	July 7, 1824.	1	-
"	" " "		1
Samuel Gates,	" 8, "	½	-
"	" " "	½	-
Charles Garrett,	" 15, "	1	-
"	" " "		1
Wm. Gates,	" 16, "	1	-
"	" " "	1	-
Robert Guthrie,	" 19, "	1	-
Chester S. Gorbit,	" " "	1	-
Jerod E. Groce,	" 29, "	5	-
"	" " "	2	-
"	" " "	3	-
Daniel Gilliland,	Aug. 3, "		1
Tho. Gray & J. H. Moore,	" 16, "	1	-
" "	" " "		1
Mitchell Gouldrick,	" 24, "		1
Sarah Gilbert,	May 11, 1827.	1	-
Preston Gilbert,	June 4, "	1	-

IN THE GENERAL LAND OFFICE. 19

WHERE SITUATED.	REMARKS.
Galveston Bay, W. side, Jack Davis's Point.	
Brazos, E. side, joins W. Hall & Tho. Barnett,	
" " joins Penning & Randon.	
" W. side, opposite his two leagues and a half.	
" E. side, joins John Randon.	
" " 3 leagues below town tract.	
" W. side, above town tract.	
Bay Prairie, E. side, W. of South Bernard; lab. Colorado, W. s., No 7.	
Brazos, E. side, near mouth Yegua, above.	
Colorado, E. side, below Kincheloe,	
Between S. Bernard and Bay Prairie.	
Brazos, W. Side, between La Bahia and San Antonio Roads.	
Brazos, E. side, near the mouth.	
Mill Creek, E. side, E. fork.	
Mill Creek, W. fork, joins G. Borden.	Special Grant.
Back of and joining E. Robins.	
Brazos, E. side, joins J. E. Groce.	
Big Creek, S. side, joins Lippincot.	
San Jacinto, above the junction.	
Bay Prairie, joins Sil. Castleman.	
Navidad, W. side.	
Colorado, E. side, joining J. Duty.	
Navasoto, N. of.	
Lake Creek, San Jacinto, joins Griffith.	
Yegua, joins Lassassier & J. P. Coles.	
Prairie Creek.	
Dickinson's Creek, mouth of.	Special Grant.
Prairie Creek, joins J. B. Jaques.	
Carancahua, E. fork, W. side, joins R. Moore.	
Colorado, W. side, mouth of.	
Peninsula, joins H. N. Gove.	
Davidson's Creek, joins J. W. Bell.	
Yegua, waters of, joins A. R. Stevens.	
Between Navasoto and Bedais Creeks.	
San Antonio Road.	
Colorado, W. side, joins Cook, Woods & Alley.	
Navasoto, E. side S. Antonio Road,	
Eight Mile Creek, Navasoto.	
Between San Bernard and Bay Prairie.	
Brazos, E. side, opposite San Felipe.	
Brazos, W. side.	
Jackson's Creek.	
Bernard, W. side, below Kincheloe.	
Brazos, E. side, S. of National Road.	
" W. side, joins Byrd & S. Gates.	
" " half league below the above.	
La Vaca, E. side.	
Brazos, E. side.	
Oyster and Bastrop Creeks.	
Brazos, E. side, at Coshate Crossing.	
Between La Bahia and Coshate.	
Brazos, W. side, joining Boatwright.	
San Bernard, W. side.	
Colorado, W. side, above E. Tumlinson.	
Clear Creek, W. of Galveston Bay.	
Peach Creek, E. side.	
Colorado, W. side.	

ABSTRACT OF ORIGINAL TITLES

NAMES OF GRANTEES.	DATE OF TITLES.	QUANTITY.	
		Leagues.	Labors.
Edward Gallaher,	May 21, 1827,	$\frac{1}{4}$	
C. C. Givens,	Dec. 11, 1828,	$\frac{1}{4}$	
Thos. J. Gazley,	March 1, 1831.	1	
Fred. Grimes,	" 9, "	$\frac{1}{4}$	
Heirs of Gillet,	" 27, "	1	
George Grimes,	" 16, "	1	
F. W. Grasmeyer,	April 4, "	$\frac{1}{4}$	
Darius Gregg,	" 6, "	$\frac{1}{4}$	
Jesse Grimes,	" " "	1	
F. Greenwood,	" 7, "	1	
J. P. Gill,	May 13, "	$\frac{1}{4}$	
Elizabeth Gordon,	April 11, "	1	
L. W. Groce,	" 21, "	1	
Noah Griffith,	" 11, "	1	
S. Gates,	May 7, "	1	
Daniel Gilliland,	" 26, "	1	
Henry Griffith,	" 10, "	1	
George Galbraith,	" 13, "	$\frac{1}{4}$	
Joel Greenwood,	" " "	1	
Tho. Gay,	July 8, "	$\frac{1}{4}$	
Andrew Graham,	Nov. 19, 1832.	1	
William Gorham,	" 21, "	$\frac{1}{4}$	
Thomas Gay,	" 24, "	$\frac{1}{4}$	
Claiborne Garrett,	Dec. 3, "	$\frac{1}{4}$	
Heirs of R. Graves,	Nov. 15, 1830.	1	
Peter W. Grayson,	July 22, 1831.	1	
Patrick Green,	Jan. 8, 1833.	1	
James Gilliland,	Oct. 15, 1832.	1	
Alfred R. Guild,	Feb. 6, 1833.	$\frac{1}{4}$	
Moses Gage,	Oct. 8, 1835.	1	
Alfred Gee,	" 19, "	1	
Benjamin Greenville,	" 23, "	1	
Benjamin Green,	" 27, "	1	
Jerod E. Groce, Jr.,	Jan. 29, 1836.	1	
Thomas Gray,	Feb. 4, "		
Daniel Gray,	" " "	1	
Joshua Gray,	" 5, "	$\frac{1}{4}$	
William F. Gray,	" 27, "	1	
Humphrey N. Gove,	Dec. 15, 1832.	$\frac{1}{4}$	
Elizabeth Greenwood,	May 7, 1831.	1	
M. F. Grantham,	Dec. 6, 1832.	$\frac{1}{4}$	
Mayberry B. Gray,	Oct. 13, 1835.	$\frac{1}{4}$	
John Hall,	July 10, 1824.	1	
"	" " "	1	
"	" " "		2
William Hall,	" 10, "	1	
John Huff,	" " "	1	
James Hope,	" " "	1	
"	" " "	$\frac{1}{4}$	
"	" " "		2
William Harvey,	" 20, "	1	
William J. Harris,	" 21, "		1
Eli Hunter,	" 24, "	1	
Charles S. Hudson,	" 29, "	1	
John Haddin,	" " "	1	
James Hensley,	Aug. 3, "	1	1
William Holland,	" 10, "	1	

WHERE SITUATED.	REMARKS.
Colorado, W. side, joins Kincheloe.	
Mill Creek, joins Little.	
Colorado, W. side.	
Caney Creek, joins Stevenson.	
Bedais Bayou, Branch of San Jacinto.	
Mill Creek, E. fork W. side, joins B. Eaton.	
Colorado, W. side, joins W. Barton.	
Holland's Settlement, joins Holland.	
" joins M'Intire,	
San Jacinto, waters of.	
Mill Creek, W. fork W. side.	
New Year's Creek, Waters of,	
Holland's Settlement, joins Holland.	Special Grant.
San Jacinto, Lake Creek.	
Brazos, W. side, joins San Antonio Road.	
Colorado, W. side, joins Dewees.	
Colorado, Jones's Creek.	
Spring Creek, joins Miller.	
Brazos, E. side, joins F. Greenwood.	
Bernard, joins G. Huff & Moore.	
Buckner's Creek.	
Navidad, Mulberry Fork.	
Cummins' Creek, W. side.	
Brazos, E. side; San Jacinto, joins A. Brown.	
Trespalacios, joins H. Harrison.	
Carancahua, E. fork, E. side.	Special Grant.
" E. side, joining P. W. Grayson.	
Colorado, E. side, joins Tolson.	
Davidson's Creek, N. E. of I. Long,	
Plumb Creek, W. of Colorado.	
Bedais Creek, head of.	
Cummins' Creek, waters of.	
Navidad and Buckner's Creek, head of.	
Brazos, E. side, joins heirs of Whiteside.	
Colorado, W. side Walnut Creek.	
" " "	
Navidad, W. side.	
Peninsula, Matagorda Grove and Oyster Creek.	
Brazos, W. side, N. of Yegua.	
" " mouth of Caney, joins T. Bell.	
Jackson's Creek, joins Jackson.	
Brazos, E. side, joins A. Robinson.	
" " joins his first league and S. F. Austin.	
" " opposite San Felipe.	
" " joins W. Pettus.	
Bernard and Peach Creek.	
Brazos, E. side.	
" " between Sutherland and Davidson.	
" " joins his league on S. E.	
" W. side, joins W. White.	
San Jacinto, W. side, joins A. M'Cormick,	
Peach Creek, W. side.	
Colorado, E. side, Below Kincheloe.	
" " joins Ally.	
Bernard, E. side, below Huff; lab. W. side Brazos, below T. T. No. 12.	
Navasoto, 10 Mile Creek.	

ABSTRACT OF ORIGINAL TITLES

NAMES OF GRANTEES.	DATE OF TITLES.	QUANTITY.	
		Leagues.	Labors.
Fras. Holland,	Aug. 10, 1824.	1	
Kinchen Holliman,	" " "	1	
Johnson Hunter,	" " "	1	
George Harrison,	" 16, "	1	
John R. Harris,	" " "	1	
Thos. S. Haynes,	" " "	1	
Samuel C. Haddy,	" 19, "	1	
George Huff,	" " "	1½	
David Harris,	" " "	1	
David Hamilton,	May 9, 1827.	1	
Abner Harris & Wm. Barrett,	June 4, "	1	
Joseph Harbor,	Dec. 11, 1828.	1	
Harmon Hensley,	March 16, 1831.	1	
Arribella Harrington,	" 23, "	1	
John Hodge,	" 21, "	1	
Obediah Hudson,	" 31, "	1	
Samuel Hinch,	" " "	1	
Abijah Highsmith,	April 5, "	1	
Josiah F. Halliton,	" 6, "	1	
James Hodge,	" 8, "	1	
Archibald Hodge,	" " "	1	
Jacob Hays,	" " "	1	
James Holland,	" 7, "	¼	
Joseph House,	" 13, "	1	
William Hardy,	" 16, "	1	
Samuel H. Hardin,	" 25, "	½	
Heirs of Wm. Hodge,	" 23, "	1	
John Hall,	" 25, "	¼	
James Hall, Jr.,	" 26, "	1	
William R. Hensley,	April 20, "	1	
William Hardin,	" 23, "	1	
James Hall, 3rd,	May 7, "	1	
Edward St. John Hawkins,	" 16, "	¼	
Walter Hamilton,	April 30, "	1	
Joshua Hadley,	May 7, "	1	
Thos. Hill,	July 14, "	1	
Robert Hodge,	" " "	1	
James Hollinsworth,	Oct. 28, "	¼	
William R. Hunt,	Feb. 23, 1832.	1	
John Harris,	Oct. 16, "	¼	
Isaac K. Hawkins,	" 18, "	¼	
Francis Henderson,	Nov. 12, "	1	
John M. Hensley,	" 10, "	1	
Wm. W. Hawkins,	" 20, "	¼	
Johnson Hunter,	" 28, "		1
Caiaphas K. Ham,	" 23, "	¼	
Silvanus Hatch,	March 3, 1830.	1	
William Harris,	Dec. 18, "	⅔	
Henry Harrison	Nov. 2, "	¼	
Samuel Hoit,	" 15, "	1	
Elisha Hall,	" 12, "	1	
William Heard,	" 24, "	1	
Jemima Heard,	" 29, "	1	
W. D. C. Hall,	Dec. 2, "	1	
John M. Heard,	" 10, "	1	
Thomas H. P. Heard,	" " "	1	
Henry Harrison,	" 16, "	½	

WHERE SITUATED.	REMARKS.
Branch of Navasoto, near La Bahia Road.	
Brazos, W. side, joins John Rabb.	
San Jacinto, mouth of.	
Cedar Lake.	
Buffalo Bayou, S. side Bray's Bayou.	
Cedar Creek, between Navasoto and Brazos.	
Brazos, E. side, joins M'Farland.	
Bernard and Peach Creek, joins J. Teel.	
San Jacinto, W. side, mouth of Branch.	
Peach Creek and Bernard.	
Brazos, W. side, joins J. Polly.	
New Year's Creek,	
Mill Creek. E. fork, W. side, joins S. M. Williams.	
New Year's Creek, joins James Clark.	Altered by Act of Congress from Robert Hodge.
Mill Creek, E. fork, W. side.	
La Bahia Road.	
La Bahia Road, S. of Yegua.	
Colorado, E. side, joins Curtis.	
San Bernard, W. side, joins T. Slaughter.	
San Jacinto, W. side.	
" "	
" waters of, N. of Mrs. M'Intire.	
Holland's Settlement, Ten Mile Creek.	
Spring Creek, S. of San Jacinto.	
Navidad, W. side, joins J. Alley.	
Half-way Bayou, between Retreat and lower place.	
San Jacinto, above the junction.	
Brazos, E. side, joins J. Best.	
" " joins Mouser & Best.	
Navidad, Rocky Creek.	
Buffalo Bayou, joins Richardson.	
Brazos, W. side, San Antonio Road.	
Buckner's Creek, joins J. Castleman.	
" above La Bahia Road, joins Cook.	
Holland's Settlement, joins Black.	
Mill Creek, W. fork W. side, below Dotery.	
San Bernard, E. side, joins Nos. 1, 2, and 3.	
Yegua, Mound Prairie, joins J. P. Coles.	
Colorado, E. side.	
San Jacinto, joins J. Hadley.	
Yegua, joins No. 1, belonging to J. F. Perry.	
San Antonio Road, Brazos, E. side, joins Coleman.	
Cummins' Creek, W. side, joins Peebles.	
Yegua, and joins J. F. Perry.	
Brazos, E. side Iron's Creek, joins labors 9 and 16.	
Mill Creek, W. side.	
La Vaca, E. side, joins E. M'Nutt.	
Chocolate Bayou, E. side, joins S. F. Austin.	
Colorado, W. side, below Cayce.	
Matagorda Bay, Live Oak-street Creek.	
Colorado, E. side, below Betts.	
Navidad, W. side.	
" E. side.	
Brazos, E. side, joins J. W. Hall.	
Mustang Creek, W. side.	
Sandy Creek, W. side, joins Batty.	
1st ¼ joins Cayce's, 2d ¼ joining below the former, Colorado, W. side,	

ABSTRACT OF ORIGINAL TITLES

NAMES OF GRANTEES.	DATE OF TITLES.	Leagues.	Labors.
Derrill F. M. Hunter,	July 20, 1831.	$\frac{1}{4}$	-
W. D. C. Hall,	June 24, "	1	-
Samuel C. Hiroms,	July 25, "	1	-
H. H. Hunt,	Oct. 22, "	$\frac{1}{4}$	-
George House,	Nov. 22, "	1	-
James Hughson,	Jan. 17, 1832.	1	-
W. P. Harris & Robert Wilson.	" 13, "	1	-
David A. Huffman,	March 3, "	1	-
David Harris,	Oct. 20, "	1	-
William P. Harris,	Dec. 10, "	1	-
Mauricio Henry,	" 13, "	$\frac{1}{4}$	-
Samuel Houston,	Jan. 9, 1833.	1	-
Isaac Harris,	June 25, 1832.	1	-
Reuben Hornsby,	Oct. 30, "	1	-
William A. Hall,	Dec. 3, "	1	-
Jesse Holderman,	" 3, "	$\frac{1}{4}$	-
Burd L. Hanks,	" 24, "	1	-
Pascal B. Hamlin,	Oct. 11, 1835.	1	-
W. P. Huff,	" 10, "	1	-
Samuel Hayslett,	" 19, "	1	-
John D. Holcomb,	" 20, "	$\frac{1}{4}$	-
B. M. Hatfield,	" 23, "	1	-
W. C. J. Hill,	Jan. 25, 1836.	1	-
Solomon Hall,	Feb. 5, "	1	-
Ezra Hill,	" 12, "	1	-
Antonio Houija,	" 15, "	$\frac{1}{4}$	-
William Harris,	July 10, 1824.	1	-
William J. Harris & D. Carpenter,	Aug. 16, "	1	-
Alexander Hodge,	April 12, 1828.	1	-
Prosper & Adol. Hope,	Dec. 11, "	$\frac{1}{2}$	-
Harris & Wilson,	June 13, 1832.	2	-
John Hinkson,	Nov. 13, 1836.	$\frac{1}{4}$	-
John Hibbins,		1	-
Samuel Isaacs,	July 15, 1824.	1	-
"	" " "	-	1
Seth Ingram,	" 29, "	2	-
"	" " "	-	1
John Ingram,	May 29, 1827.	$\frac{1}{4}$	-
Perry B. Isles,	April 6, 1831,	1	-
Amasa Ives,	May 16, "	1	-
Ira Ingram,	Nov. 13, 1830,	1	-
Seth Ingram,	" " "	1	-
John Irons,	July 16, 1824,	1	-
John Ijams,	Aug. 7, "	1	-
Ira Ingram,	" 24, "		1
Henry Jones,	July 8, "	1	-
Randal Jones,	" 15, "	$\frac{1}{2}$	-
"	" " "	$\frac{1}{2}$	-
"	" " "		1
Alexander Jackson,	" 16, "	2	-
H. W. Johnson, T. H. Walker & T. H. Borden,	" 29, "	1	-
Isaac Jackson,	Aug. 7, "	1	-
Oliver Jones,	" 10, "	1	-
"	" " "		1
James Jones,	" " "	1	1
Humphrey Jackson,	" 16, "	1	-
"	" " "		1

IN THE GENERAL LAND OFFICE. 25

WHERE SITUATED.	REMARKS.
Clear Creek.	
Clear Creek, above, joining J. F. Perry.	Special Grant.
Green's Bayou, N. side, between Vince and Shipman.	
Navidad, W. side, above H. Smith.	
Mustang Creek, joining Heard & Dillard.	
Carancahua Bay, E. side, mouth of.	
Buffalo Bayou, N. side, mouth of Green's Bayou.	Special Grant.
La Vaca, E. side, between Ewing and Morgan.	
Middle Creek, E. side, near Galveston Bay.	Originally granted to J. Cook & S. Hughs.
Galveston Bay, Red Bluffs.	Special Grant.
Brazos, E. side, joins A. and T. J. Calvit.	
Carancahua, W. side, E. of Keller's Bay.	
Colorado, E. side, above Bastrop.	
Colorado, E. side.	
Navidad, waters of, above B. Perry.	
Mill Creek, joins M'Lain, Clokey & Cox.	
Yegua, waters of, joining S. M. Williams.	
Lake Creek,	
Yegua, waters of.	
Peach Creek, Waters of.	
Navasoto.	
Yegua, waters of.	
Bedais Creek.	
Peach Creek, W. side Colorado.	
Navidad, East side.	First granted N. F. Roberts, secondly J. N. Charles.
Brazos, E. side, Joins N. F. Roberts.	
" " joins Richardson.	
Buffalo Bayou, N. side, near mouth.	
Brazos, E. side, and joins Battle below.	
New Year's Creek, joins James Walker.	Out of 3 leagues granted to Clopper & Co.
Buffalo Bayou.	
Carancahua, E. fork, joins J. K. Looney.	
La Vaca, E. side, below James Campbell.	
Brazos, E. side, joins Knight & White.	
" W. side, 500 varas above Botts' spring.	
Bernard, W. side,	
Brazos, W. side, above Town Tract, Mill Creek.	
Colorado, E. side, above.	
" "	
Spring Creek, joins T. Bell & Stephenson.	
Matagorda Bay, joins E. R. Wightman.	
Bay Prairie, near Bay.	Special Grant.
Brazos, E. side, above; Labors opposite Town Tract.	
San Jacinto Bay, mouth of Cedar Bayou.	
Brazos, E. s., S. of National Road, and 1 out lot in T. T. of San Felipe.	
" W. side, joins A. Kuykendall.	
" E. side, joins Knight & White.	
Colorado, E. side, joins Kincheloe.	
Brazos, W. side, in Fort Bend.	
Colorado, E. side; Peach Creek and Bernard.	
Between San Bernard and Bay Prairie.	
Brazos, E. side, below La Bahia Road.	
Between Bernard and Bay Prairie.	
Mill Creek,	
Colorado, E. s., above Kincheloe. Lab. Fort Bend, near Tho. Borden.	
San Jacinto, E. side.	
" "	

ABSTRACT OF ORIGINAL TITLES

NAMES OF GRANTEES.	DATE OF TITLES.	Leagues.	Labors.
John Jones,	May 31, 1827.	¼	-
Wm. H. Jack,	March 19, 1831.	1	-
Isaac Jackson,	" " "	1	-
"	" 21, "	1	-
Elisha D. Jackson,	March 21, 1831.	1	-
Edward Jenkins,	April 4, "	1	-
Patrick C. Jack,	" 6, "	¼	-
Isaac Jameison,	" 7, "	1	-
John Jones,	" 16, "	1	-
Stephen Jones,	" 19, "	1	-
Edward Jeffrey,	" 28, "	¼	-
Angus J. James,	May 5, "	¼	-
Silas Jones,	June 15, "	1	-
John H. Jones,	Oct. 17, 1832.	1	-
Spencer H. Jack,	April 20, "	¼	-
Benjamin F. Jaques,	Oct. 29, 1830.	1	-
Thomas Jameson,	Nov. 29, "	½	-
William H. Jack,	Oct. 3, 1835.	1	-
Thomas James,	" 16, "	1	-
Simon Jones,	" 20, "	1	-
Timothy Jones,	" 24, "	1	-
F. W. Johnson,	March 28, 1831.	1	-
Samuel Kennedy,	July 7, 1824.	1	-
"	" " "	-	1
Abner Kuykendull,	" 7, "	1	-
"	" " "	½	-
Jose Kuykendall,	" 8, "	1	-
Abner Kuykandall,	" " "	-	2
William Kincheloe,	" 8, "	1	-
"	" " "	1	-
James Knight & W. C. White,	July 15, "	1	-
" "	" " "	-	1
Robert Kuykendall,	" 16, "	1	-
"	" " "	1	-
John Kelly,	" 19 "	-	2
Alfred Kennon,	" " "	1	-
Imla Keep,	" 24, "	1	-
Brazilla Kuykendall,	Aug. 7, "	-	1
Wm. Kerr & Peter Kerr,	" 10, "	1	-
James Kerr,	May 6, 1827.	1	-
Wm. Kingston & P. Powell,	" 8, "	1	-
John Keller,	June 4, "	1	-
Gibson Kuykendall,	May 27, 1828.	¼	-
Elizabeth Kuykendall,	" 1, "	1	-
Brazilla Kuykendall,	April 27, "	¼	-
William Kuykendall,	" 29, "	¼	-
John Kelly,	March 5, 1831.	1	-
James Kegans,	" 23, "	1	-
John Kincade,	" 31, "	¼	-
James Knight & W. C. White,	April 4, "	1	-
Sarah Kennedy,	" 25, "	1	-
Samuel Kennelly,	" 28, "	1	-
Abner Kuykendall,	" 24, "	1	-
"	May 9, "	1	-
F. G. Keller,	" 6, "	1	-
Lucy Kerr,	June 21, 1832.	1	-
Anthony D. Kinniard,	Nov. 22, "	1	-

WHERE SITUATED.	REMARKS.
Brazos, back of H. Jones.	
Cummins' Creek, south side.	
New Year's Creek, waters of, joins S. Miller.	
Jackson's Creek, joins Newman & Harbour.	
La Bahia Road, Coles' Creek.	
Colarado, W. side.	
Holland's Settlement, N. of F. Holland.	
Mill Creek, E. side.	
Cummins' Creek, No 2.	
Brazos, E. side, above, joins J. Hope's labors.	
Brazos, W. side, back of H. Jones.	
Big Creek.	
Colorado, W. side, below La Bahia Road.	
Brazos, E. side, joins White—now Stephen Jones.	
Navidad, E. side, above Hardy's.	
Prairie Creek, joins A. C. Peyton.	
Trespalacios, E. side.	Upper half of No. 27.
Highland Creek, head of.	Special Grant.
Navasoto, N. side.	
Bedais Creek, head waters of.	
Brazos, near Mrs. Anderson.	
Between Cummins' Creek and Colorado.	Concession.
Brazos, W. margin.	
" "	
" W. side.	
New Year's Creek, S. La Bahia Road.	
Brazos, W. side, joins A. Kuykendall.	
Brazos, W. side.	
Colorado, E. side, joins A. Jackson.	
" W. side, above his 1st.	
Brazos, E. side, joins S. Isaacs.	
Brazos, W. side, in front of Rapids, old Fort.	
Colorado, E. side, joins J. Clark.	
" " W. side, opposite A. Jackson.	
Navasoto, Millican's League.	
Brazos, W. side, below M'Williams.	
San Bernard, W. side.	
Brazos, W. side.	
" " joins Wm. S. Brown.	
La Vaca, E. side.	
Cedar Creek.	
Colorado, W. side, below Jennings's Camp.	
Mill Creek, E. side.	
" W. side, E. fork.	
" E. side, E. fork.	
" " "	
Brazos, E. side, joins labors and J. Padilla.	
New Year's Creek, S. E. of Miller.	
Joins Furnash and J. P. Coles.	
Colorado W. side, joins Jinkins, San Antonio Road.	
Brazos, W. side, below No. 3.	
Colorado, W. side, below No. 4.	
Yegua and San Antonio Road.	Special Grant.
Brazos, W. side; Yegua, N. side, on San Antonio Road.	
La Vaca, E. side, above Kerr.	
Cummins' Creek, W. side.	
Joins Black & Hadley.	

NAMES OF GRANTEES.	DATE OF TITLES.	QUANTITY.	
		Leagues.	Labors.
G. B. King,	March 5, 1833.	1	-
Lewis Kincheloe,	Oct. 5, 1835.	$\frac{1}{4}$	-
S. F. Knight,	Oct. 19, "	1	-
John B. Klekamp,	Feb. 3, 1836.	1	-
T. P. Kuykendall,	" 5, "	$\frac{1}{4}$	-
Brazilla Kuykendall,	" " "	$\frac{3}{4}$	-
Maria Kegans,	Dec. 3, 1832.	1	-
Gibson Kuykendall,	May 27, 1828.	$\frac{3}{4}$	-
Francis Keller,	March 3, 1830.	1	-
William Little,	July 10, 1824,	1	-
"	" " "		1
James Lynch,	" 16, "	1	-
Nathl. Lynch,	Aug. 19, "	1	-
Benjamin Lindsay,	" " "	1	-
Jane H. Long,	April 30, 1827.	1	-
"	May 1, "		1
H. H. League,	" 25, "	1	-
Joel Lakey,	" 28, "	1	-
John Little,	" 21, "	1	-
"	" " "		1
Elizabeth Lippincott,	" 19, "	1	-
David Lawrence,	March 4, 1831.	1	-
Adam Lawrence,	" 10, "	$\frac{1}{4}$	-
Allen Larison,	" 12, "	$\frac{1}{4}$	-
Isaac Lee,	" 13, "	1	-
Hirom Lee,	" 16, "	$\frac{1}{4}$	-
Josiah D. Lester,	" 15, "	1	-
Joel Lakey,	April 2, "	1	-
William D. Lacy,	March 28, "	$\frac{1}{4}$	-
Franklin Lewis,	" 29, "	1	-
Samuel Lawrence,	" 26, "	1	-
Richard Lawrence,	April 4, "	$\frac{1}{4}$	-
W. T. Lightfoot,	" " "	$\frac{1}{4}$	-
William Laughlin,	" 11, "	$\frac{1}{4}$	-
Zachariah Landrum,	" 10 "	1	-
William Landrum,	" " "	1	-
John Landrum,	" " "	1	-
John Logan,	" 16, "	1	-
Joel Lakey,	" 23, "	$\frac{1}{2}$	-
Luke Lasassier,	" 13, "	1	-
Eleanor Leving,	Dec. 8, "	1	-
Abner Lea, Jr.,	June 2, 1832.	1	-
Jacob Long,	Nov. 23, "	1	-
Abner Lea, Sr.,	" " "	1	-
Henry K. Lewis,	" 28, "		5
Luke Lasassier,	Oct. 29, 1830.	1	-
Jos. K. Looney,	Nov. 10, "	$\frac{1}{4}$	-
Henry K. Lewis,	" 8, "		$1\frac{1}{3}$
James Lindsay,	" 29, "	$\frac{1}{4}$	-
Samuel Love,	July 23, 1831.	1	-
Ira R. Lewis,	June 5, "	1	-
Greenberry Logan,	Dec. 22, "	$\frac{1}{4}$	-
John W. Lytle,	Jan. 23, 1833.	1	-
Mary Lawrence, (Widow,)	Dec. 11, 1832.	1	-
John E. Lewis,	Nov. 22, "	$\frac{1}{4}$	-
Enoch Latham,	Oct. 6, 1835.	$\frac{1}{4}$	-
Lubbe Levering,	Feb. 3, 1836.	1	-

WHERE SITUATED.	REMARKS.
Navasoto, E. side, joins John Woodruff.	
Dry Creek, N. of Cummins' Hacienda, and joins D. Styer on the West.	
Navidad, head waters of.	
Peach Creek, W. of Colorado.	
Between the head of Yegua and Pin Oak.	
" " " "	
Brazos, E. side, N. of Navasoto.	Augmentation for marrying.
Caney Creek, back of Lakey.	
Carancahua Bay.	
Brazos, E. side, joins Thos. Barnett.	
" W. side, Fort Bend.	
" " joins A. Robinson.	
San Jacinto, E. side, near mouth.	Forfeited and redeeded to J. F. Perry.
Between Bernard and Bay Prairie.	
Brazos, W. side, near Fort Bend.	
Opposite town of San Felipe, No. 12, and S. of National Road.	
Colorado, W. side, Jennings' Camp.	
Brazos, W. side; Caney Creek, joins J. Elam.	
Brazos, W. side, joins labors below Town Tract.	
Brazos, W. side, in Fort Bend.	
Big Creek, W. of the Brazos.	
Cedar Creek, branch of Caney Creek.	
New Year's Creek, joins Miller & K.	
Mill Creek, E. fork, joins C. Benton.	
New Year's Creek, joins J. Walker.	
" joins S. Woodward.	
Mill Creek, E. fork, W. side.	
Caney, or Lakey Creek.	
Mulberry Fork, Navidad.	
La Bahia Road, W. Cummins' Creek.	Special Grant.
Brazos, W. side, joins John P Cole & Colvin.	
Colorado, W. side.	
" " joins Knight & White.	
Holland's Settlement, joins F. Holland.	
Bedais Creek, joins League.	
" San Jacinto.	
Little Dry Creek, joins F. Greenwood.	
Cummins' Creek, joins W. H. Jack.	
Caney Creek, joins his league.	Special Grant.
New Year's Creek and Yegua.	"
Navidad, W. side, joins Whitehead.	
Brazos, E. side, joins S. A. Road.	
Davidson's Creek, joins J. J. Dewitt.	
Navasoto, N. side.	
Buffalo Bayou, below W. Hardin.	
Colorado, E. side, below Betts.	
Carancahua, W. fork, E. side.	
San Jacinto. (Island.)	
Middle Creek, right side, branch of Clear Creek.	
Peninsula, Matagorda.	
Dickinson's Creek, Brazos, E. side.	
Chocolate Bayou, head of.	
Galveston Bay, mouth of Dickinson's Creek.	
Cedar Creek, E. Brazos.	
Buckner's Creek, W. side.	
Brazos, E. side, joins Rawdon.	
Colorado, W. side, San Antonio Road.	

30 ABSTRACT OF ORIGINAL TITLES

NAMES OF GRANTEES.	DATE OF TITLES.	QUANTITY.	
		Leagues.	Labors.
M. B. Lawrence,	Feb. 6, 1836.	1	-
William Latham,	" 13, "	¼	-
Jacob Lance,	" 15, "	1	-
Joseph La Flore,	April 15, 1833,	¼	-
Samuel Lawrence,	Jan. 28, 1836.	1	-
James Lastley,	Oct. 12, 1835.	1	-
Chas. W. Lhomideu,	June 23, 1831.	¼	-
Lewis Lomas,	May 30, 1831.	1	-
Asa Mitchell,	July 7, 1824.	½	-
"	" 7, "	1	-
Shubal Marsh,	" 8, "	1	-
William Morton,	" 15, "	1½	-
"	" " "		[-
Robert Millican,	" 16, "	2½	-
William Millican,	" " "	1	-
James D. Millican,	" " "	1	-
William Matthis,	" 19, "	1	-
Moses Morrison & Wm. Cooper,	" 24, "	1	-
Wiley Martin,	July 29,	1	-
John M'Neel,	Aug. 3,	1	-
Luke Moore,	" " "	1	-
Daniel M'Neel,	" 3, "	1	-
Pleasant D. M'Neel,	" 7, "	1	-
Simon Miller,	" " "	1	-
G. W. & J. G. M'Neel,	" 10, "	½	-
" "	" " "	½	-
John M'Farland,	" " "	1¼	-
"	" 10, "		1
John Monks,	" 16, "	1	-
J. H. Moore & Thos. Gray,	" " "	1	-
" "	" " "		1
John M'Closkey,	" " "	1	-
"	" " "		1
Thos. F. M'Kinney,	" " "	1	-
Sterling M'Neel,	" 19, "	1	-
David Mouser,	" " "	1	-
S. R. Miller,	" " "	1	-
Samuel Miller,	" " "	1	-
Joseph Mims,	" " "	1	-
Asa Mitchell,	Aug. 24, "		1
David H. Milburn,	May 27, 1828.	¼	-
Andrew Miller,	March 7, 1831.	1	-
Edward R. Miller,	" 10, "	1	-
Elliot Millican,	" 26, "	1	-
Alexander M'Coy,	" 18, "	¼	-
Simon Miller.	" 20, "	¼	-
James M'Cain,	" 23, "	1	-
James Miles,	" " "	1	-
William Munson,	" 28, "	1	-
John H. Money,	" 31, "	¼	-
Thos. H. Mays,	April 4, "	¼	-
J. D. Morris,	" 6, "	¼	-
Margaret M'Intire,	" 5, "	1	-
John W. Mitchell,	" 12, "	¼	-
Joseph Miller,	" 16, "	1	-
Elisha Moore,	" 19, "	1	-
John Moore,	" 15, "	1	-

WHERE SITUATED.	REMARKS.

Brazos, W. side, head of Yegua.
Buckner's Creek, waters of, joins Evans.
Walnut Creek.
Dickson's Creek.
Brazos, W. side; Yegua, S. side, marked S.
Yegua, N. side.
Dickenson's Creek.
Colorado, W. side, joins Gazley.
Brazos, E. side, joins Carter.
Oyster Creek, both sides.
Brazos, E. side, joins W. Parker & Robinson.
   "   " joins R. Jones.
   "   W. side, at the mouth of a ravine.
   "   E. side, joins J. Millican.
   "   " between it and Navasoto.
   "   " joins Millican.
   "   " at the San Antonio Crossing.
Cedar Creek, W. side; W. of Bernard.
Bernard E. side, below G. Huff.
Bernard, E. side,
Bray's Bayou, branch of Buffalo Bayou.
Bernard, W. side.
   "   E. side.
   "   "
Brazos, W. side, near mouth, joins S. F. Austin,
Bernard E. side, joins S. M'Neel.
Brazos, E. side, joins Cooper.
   "   " opposite Town Tract.
Between Bernard and Bay Pr.
Bernard, W. side.
Colorado, "
Cedar Lake, E. side.
Below Town Tract, W. side Brazos.
Brazos, E. side, below San Antonio Road.
Bernard, E. side.
Brazos, E. side.
New Year's Creek; Brazos W. side.
Brazos, W. side, between Coshate and La Bahia Roads.
Bernard, W. side.
Brazos, E. side, at its mouth.
Brazos, W. side, joins Joseph, mouth Big Creek.
Doe Run, La Bahia Road, joins Gates.
New Year's Creek, W. side, joins Munson.
Brazos, E. side, N. of Navasoto, joins Whitesides.
Mill Creek, W. fork, E. side, joins Borden.
Cedar Creek, joins G. Kuykendall.
La Bahia Road, joins R. Clokey.
Cummins' Creek, joins J. Andrews.
New Year's Creek, waters of.
   "   " joins Clark.
Colorado, W. side.
   "   E. side, mouth of Burlison's Creek.
Big Dry Creek, San Jacinto, Holland's Settlement.
Between La Bahia and San Antonio Roads, joins Rawley.
Spring Creek, San Jacinto.
Bernard and Peach Creek.
Holland's Settlement, joins Whitesides.

NAMES OF GRANTEES.	DATE OF TITLES.	QUANTITY. Leagues.	Labors.
James B. Miller, - - -	April 23, 1831,	1	- -
John W. Moore, - -	" 28, "	¼	- -
" - - -	" " "	¾	- -
William Montgomery, - -	May 4, "	1	- -
Wiley Martin, - - -	" 7, "	1	- -
William S. Martin, - -	" 13, "	¼	-
John F. Martin, - - -	" 11, "	¼	- -
Robert Matthews, - -	" 8, "	¼	- -
John H. Moore, - - -	" 17, "	½	- -
Isaac Maden, - -	June 16, "	¼	- -
Lawrence Martin, - - -	Nov. 8, "	¼	- -
Joshua W. Martin, - - -	Jan. 17, 1832.	¼	- -
Jos. M'Cormick, - -	June 22, "	1	- -
Isaac Marshall, - - -	Oct. 18, "	¼	- -
Samuel Millet, - -	Nov. 20, "	1	- -
James Murphy, - - -	Dec. 29, "	¼	- -
Ruth Mackey, - -	" 8, "	1	- -
Antonio Mancha, - - -	" 22, "		14 -
Miguel Muldoon, - -	May 16, 1831.	2	- -
" - - -	" 31, "	2	- -
" - -	Feb. 28, "	2	- -
" - - -	" " "	2	- -
" - -	" " "	1	- -
John M'Croskey, - - -	Oct. 29, "	1	- -
Francis Moore, - -	March 3, 1830.	1	- -
Eli Mercer, - - -	Dec. ,13 "	1	- -
Dugald M'Farland, - -	" 29, "	1	- -
James Moore, - - -	Oct. 22, "	1	- -
Eliakien P. Myrick, - -	" 27, "	1	- -
Henry W. Munson, - -	" 2, "	1	- -
William Menifee, - -	Nov. 24, "	1	- -
Thomas Menifee, - - -	Dec. 4, "	1	- -
Shubal Marsh, - -	" 14, "	½	- -
John Matthis, - - -	" 11, "	¼	- -
Louisa Anna Morton, - -	Nov. 27, 1831,	1	- -
Nancy A. M'Farland, - -	Dec. 17, 1830.	1	- -
William Murphy, - -	Jan. 17, 1831.	¼	- -
Francis Menifee, - - -	June 23, "	1	- -
Robt. D. Moore, - -	" 22, "	1	- -
George B. M'Kinstry, - -	Nov. 24, 1830.	1	- -
John M'Neel, - -	July 7, 1831.		1 -
Hugh M'Guffin, - - -	Nov. 22, "	1	- -
James Morgan, - -	" 19, "	1	- -
Miguel Muldoon, - - -	Dec. 15, "	2	- -
Eli Mitchell, - -	March 2, 1832.	¼	- -
Sylvester Murphy, - -	Oct. 25, "	1	- -
Ritson Morris, - -	Nov. 14, "	1	- -
T. F. M'Kinney, - - -	" 20, "		1 -
Philip M'Elroy, - -	Oct. 30, "	1	- -
Elizabeth S. M'Kenzie, - -	"	1	- -
William Medford, - -	Oct. 5, 1835.	1	- -
Daniel M'Mahan, - - -	" 16, "	1	- -
M. M'Dowell, - -	" 17, "	1	- -
Joseph M'Allister, - - -	" 20, "	¼	- -
James W. Moore, - -	" " "	1	- -
N. C. Moffitt, - - -	Feb. 5, 1836.	1	- -
Andrew Mayo, - -	" 12, "	1	- -

WHERE SITUATED.	REMARKS.
Mill Creek, head of, and La Bahia Road. - - -	Special Grant.
Brazos, W. side, joins Knight & White. - - -	"
Bernard, W. side, joins Thomas Slaughter, - - -	"
San Jacinto, waters of, joins Landrum.	
Brazos, W. side, joins A. & J. Kuykendall. - - -	Special Grant.
Brazos, E. side, and S. E. of San Antonio Road.	
Navasoto, between it and San Antonio Road,	
Branch of Navasoto, Boiling Spring Creek.	
Colorado, E. side, La Bahia Crossing.	
Navidad, E. side, below Atascocito Crossing.	
" Rocky Creek.	
Colorado, E. side, in Main Prairie, near Ross.	
San Bernard, joins M'Gary.	
Mill Creek, joins Thomas Hill. - - -	{ Re-granted to Jas. Bell, Feb. 23, 1836.
Buckner's Creek, head of.	
Colorado, W. side, joins E. Gallaher. - - -	{ Originally granted to R. Wright.
Colorado, E. side, Pin Oak Creek.	
Eight Mile Point, joins Allen & Richardson.	
San Bernard, W. fork, joins A. Jackson. - -	Concession,
Buckner's Creek, above La Bahia Road. - - -	"
Navidad and Rocky Creek. - - -	"
" E. side, below Gonzales Road. - - -	"
" " joins the above two leagues. - - -	"
Colorado, E. side, and joins R. Ally. - - -	"
Chocolate Bayou, joins Harris & Angier.	
Navidad, E. side.	
Colorado, E. side, below Betts,	
" " "	
Bayou Austin, E. side,	
Navidad, W. side, joins E. M'Nutt,	
" " W. of Mustang Creek.	
Navidad, W. side.	{ Special Grant. Forfeited by John M'Cormic.
Brazos, E. side, above Bolivar. - - -	
Mustang Creek, W. side Colorado.	
Bayou Austin, left side. - - -	{ Louisa Anna Morton is Widow Kenny.
Carancahua, near the mouth.	
La Vaca, E. side, joins James Kerr, above.	
Mustang, E. side.	
Carancahua, joins F. Stack.	
Brazos, E. side, Middle Creek, - - -	Special Grant.
" below J. G. & G. W. M'Neel's half league.	
La Vaca, E. side, joins J. H. Bell.	
" " "	
Clear Creek Lake, joins S. F. Austin.	{ This ¼ includes 2 lubs., Nos. 9 & 10, at mouth Brazos, E. s.
Brazos. E. side, near mouth - - -	
Middle Creek, Clear Creek.	
Galveston Bay, E. of Clear Lake.	
Brazos, W. side, joins S. F. Austin.	
Colorado, E. S., joins Hornsby.	
West Bernard, W. side.	
Colorado, W. side, joins Gazley and Barton.	
Between head waters of Navasoto and Bedais Creeks.	
Bedais Creek.	
Buckner's Creek, head waters of.	
Bedais Bayou, waters of	
Colorado, W. side, joins heirs of Ally.	
" " Walnut Creek.	

34 ABSTRACT OF ORIGINAL TITLES

NAMES OF GRANTEES.	DATE OF TITLES.	QUANTITY.	
		Leagues.	Labors.
Amanda M'Cracken, - -	Feb. 19, 1836.	1	-
Achilles M'Farland, - -	July 10, 1824,	1	-
William M'Williams, - -	" 19, "	1	-
Elizabeth M'Nutt, - -	" 21, "	1	-
David M'Cormick, - - -	" " "	1	-
Thos. M'Coy & D. Deckro, -	" 24, "	1	-
M'Lain & M'Nair, - - -	" " "	1	-
John M'Cormick, Shelby & Frazier,	" " "	1	-
Thos. Davis & D. H. Milburn, -	" " "	1	-
Arthur M'Cormick, - -	Aug. 10, "	1	-
David H. Milburn, - - -	May 27, "	¼	-
John Martin, - -	" 19, 1828.	¼	-
William M'Intire, - - -	April 6, 1831,	¼	-
Isaac M'Gary, - -	March 29, "	1	-
J. B. M'Nealy, - -	April 11, "	1	-
William M'Farland, - -	" 6, "	1	-
Samuel M'Early, - - -	May 14, "	1	-
Howard M'Elroy, - -	Oct. 16, 1832.	1	-
N. A. M'Faddin, - -	" 20, "	1	-
William M'Guffin, - -	Nov. 12, "	1	-
Andrew Millican, - -	Dec. 13, "	1	-
John M'Guffin, - -	Oct. 23, 1830.	¼	-
Philip M'Elroy, - -	" 30, 1832.	1	-
Tho. M'Donald, - - -	" 3, 1835.	1	-
James Nelson, - -	Aug. 7, 1824.	1	-
Joseph Newman, - - -	" 10, "	1¼	1
William Neel, - -	June 4, 1827.	¼	-
Jonathan Newman, - -	March 21, 1831.	1	-
John Nichols, - -	Oct. 20, 1832.	1	-
Joshua Nelson, - - -	June 23, 1831.	¼	-
George W. Nexan, - -	" 23, "	1	-
John D. Newell, - - -	Oct. 23, 1832.	1	-
M. B. Nuckolls, - -	Aug. 3, 1824.	1	1
Andrew Northington, - -	May 28, 1831.	1	-
William New, - -	Nov. 10, 1830.	¼	-
James C. Neil, - - -	" 26, 1832.	1	-
James Orrick, - -	Aug. 10, 1824.		1
Jeremiah S. O'Connor, - -	April 9, 1831.	1	-
Greenberry Overton, - -	Feb. 3, 1836.	1	-
James G. O. Farrell, - -	May 20, 1831.	1	-
Heirs of Osburn, - -	Nov. 8, 1832.	1	-
William Parker, - - -	July 8, 1824.	1	1
William Pettus, - -	" 10, "	1	-
" - - -	" " "	1	-
" - -	" " "		1
William Prater, - - -	" 19, "	1	-
" - - -	" " "		1
Zeno Philips, - - -	" " "	1	-
Pamelia Pickett, - - -	" 21, "	1	1
Joshua Parker & W. Park, -	July 24, "	1	-
Pleasant Pruit, - -	" " "	1	-
Joseph Polly & S. Chance, -	" 27, "	1	-
Freeman Pettus, - -	Aug. 3, "	1	-
" - -	" " "		1
" - - -	" " "	1	-
John Petty, - - -	" 10, "	1	-
James E. Phelps, - -	" 16, "	1	-

WHERE SITUATED.	REMARKS.

Yegua, Waters of, joins Sparks.
Brazos, E. side, joins Frs. Biggum.
Brazos, W. side, joins Kinnon.
Navidad and La Vaca, near the confluence.
San Bernard, W. side.
Cedar Lake, W. side, W. of Bernard.
Colorado, E. side, above Kincheloe.
Brazos, W. side, above place called Fort Bend.
" " joins M'Cormick & Shelby.
San Jacinto, S. W. side.
Brazos, W. side, joining Joseph.
Mill Creek, E. side, E. fork.
Big Dry Creek, joins Mrs. M'Intire.
Bernard, E. side, joins Mrs. Powell.
Ten Mile Creek, E. of Brazos.
Colorado, W. side, below.
Spring Creek, joins A. Roberts.
Cummins' Creek, joins J. Andrews.
Yegua, joins Cox and Mitchell,
Holland's Settlement, joins Kinnard,
Brazos, E. side, N. of Navasoto,
La Vaca, E. side, joins Hatch.
Colorado, E. side, joins Hornsby.
Brazos, E. side.
Colorado, E. s., above Kincheloe.
" " " Lab. Brazos, W. s., below T. Tract.
Brazos, E. side, back of David Bright.
Jackson's Creek, Waters of, joins Mrs. Early.
Piney Creek, joins Ives and Stevenson.
Colorado, E. side, between Wightman and Lesassier.
Carancahua, E. fork, E. side.
" " "
Between S. Bernard & Bay Prairie, labs. No. 10, W. s., Brazos, at mouth.
San Bernard,
Carancahua W. Fork, E. side.
Yegua, Waters of, joins A. R. Stephens,
Brazos, W. side, above Town Tract.
" E. side.
Colorado, W. side, on San Antonio Road.
Navidad, joins Burnham.
Wilbarger's Creek, joining Wells and Duty.
Brazos, E. s., joins Richardson, or Richinson, lab. opposite S. Felipe.
Brazos, E. side.
Colorado, W. side.
Brazos, E. side, N. of National Road.
Bernard, E. side.
Brazos, W. side, above Town Tract, below Kuykendall.
Bernard W. side.
Bay Prairie, E. s., W. of Bernard. Lab. Brazos, W. s., above S. Felipe.
Peach Creek, W. side, 4 leagues of Kincheloe.
Bay Prairie, E. side, and W. of Bernard.
Between Bernard and Bay Prairie.
Colorado. W. side, 8 leagues above Atascocito Crossing.
Colorado, E. side, above Tumlinson.
Between San Bernard and Bay Prairie.
Colorado, E. side, between La Bahia and Atascocito.
Brazos, W. side, joins T. Allsbury.

ABSTRACT OF ORIGINAL TITLES

NAMES OF GRANTEES.	DATE OF TITLES.	Leagues.	Labors.
James E. Phelps,	Aug. 16, 1824.	2	-
Joseph H. Polly,	" " "	1	-
William Prior,	" 24, "	-	1
Isham B. Philips,	May 9, 1827.	1	-
Jonathan C. Peyton,	" 27, "	1	-
William Pryor,	" 21, 1828.	1	-
Joshua Parker,	" 30, "	$\frac{1}{2}$	-
Robert Peebles,	March 22, 1831.	1	-
Elizabeth Powell,	" 21, "	1	-
Mary Phelps,	" 28, "	1	-
James Pevehouse,	April 7, "	1	-
John Peterson,	" 2, "	1	-
Joseph Powell,	May 2, "	$\frac{1}{4}$	-
Samuel Pharr,	April 27, "	$\frac{1}{4}$	-
James R. Phillips,	" 23, "	1	-
Beverley A. Porter,	" 30, "	1	-
Burril Perry,	May 16, "	1	-
Spencer Pugh,	" 6, "	1	-
John F. Pettus,	" 11, "	1	-
Samuel O. Pettus,	Jan. 21, 1832.	1	-
James Price,	Feb. 22, "	1	-
William Ponton,	Nov. 27, "	1	-
James Perry,	" 6, "	1	-
Juan Antonio Padilla,	April 6, 1830,	2	-
Robt. Peebles,	June 27, 1831.	1	-
James F. Perry,	Oct. 28, "	1	-
"	Nov. 3, "	2	-
Zeno Philips,	Feb. 24, 1832.	1	-
Maria D. Pierce,	Oct. 30, 1830.	$\frac{1}{4}$	-
George M. Patrick,	Nov. 13, "	$\frac{1}{4}$	-
James F. Perry,	Aug. 25, 1831.	5	-
"	" " "	2	-
"	" " "	1	-
John Parton,	Feb. 8, 1832.	1	-
Henry Parker,	" 5, 1833.	1	-
Henry B. Prentiss,	April 20, "	1	-
John Peski,	" 15, "	$\frac{1}{4}$	-
William Parks,	Jan. 17, "	$\frac{1}{4}$	-
John G. W. Pierson,	1832.		
Richardson Perry,	Oct. 10, 1835.	1	-
Orville Perry,	" 12, "	1	-
Eliza Peak,	" 16, "	1	-
James W. Pankey,	" 19, "	1	-
Thos. O. Berry,	" 24, "	1	-
Heirs of Obidiah Pitts,	" 29, "	1	-
Elisha M. Pease.	Feb. 3, 1836.	$\frac{1}{4}$	-
Polly Perry, (Wife of James Day,)	" 9, "	1	-
Peter Pieper,	" 11, "	1	-
Lawrence W. Perry,	" 12, "	1	-
John Powell,	" 17, "	1	-
James Powell,	" 22, "	$\frac{1}{4}$	-
George S. Penticost,	Aug. 19, 1824.	1	-
John Paine,	Oct. 16, 1835.	1	-
Daniel Parker,	April 29, 1833.	1	-
Frederick Rankin,	July 7, 1824.	1	-
"	" " "	-	1

WHERE SITUATED.	REMARKS.
Brazos, E. side, 3 leagues above its mouth.	
" W. side, joins K. Halliman.	
" E. side, S. of National Road.	
On Peach Creek, E. side, and W. of Bernard.	
In Bay Prairie, on Small Creek, W. of Live Oak.	
Mill Creek, W. side, E. fork.	
Colorado, W. side, joins Westall.	
Cummins' Creek, West side.	
Bernard and Turkey Creek.	
La Bahia Road, S. of Yegua.	
San Jacinto, W. side, below base line.	
Holland's Settlement, South of, and joins Holland.	
Bernard, E. side.	
Big Creek, opposite to E. Lippincot.	
Cummins' Creek, W. side, - - - -	Special Grant.
Brazos, W. side, joins Curtis; N. of Yegua.	
Navidad, W. of Gonzales Road, 24.	
Colorado, W. side, joins Burnham.	
Mill Creek, W. side, W. fork, - - -	Special Grant.
" " " joins Dottery.	
San Antonio Road, W. of Brazos.	
La Vaca, below Gonzales Road, E. side.	
Yegua, Davidson's Creek.	
Brazos, E. side, joining Iron's, opposite Town T'tract, - -	{ Title with S. F. Austin's Premium Lands
" W. side, joins J. Rabb & J. H. Polly, - -	Concession.
Between San Bernard and Bay Prairie, - - -	"
Yegua, S. side, and joins N. Clay, - - -	"
Brazos, E. side. N. of Navasoto, joins Jno. Austin.	
Caney, E. side.	
Flore's Bayou, right side.	
Chocolate Bayou.	
Dickinson's Creek, E. side.	
Clear Creek, near the mouth.	
Trespalacios, E. side, joins T. Jameson.	
" near road leading to League's Crossing.	
Sims' Bayou, Buffalo Bayou, joins J. R. Harris.	
Chocolate Bayou, joins G. Lagan, above.	
Trespalacios, W. side, including mouth of P. O. Bayou.	
Buckner's Creek, head of.	
Navasoto, N. side.	
Yegua, N. side,	
" and joins James Cox.	
Bedais, head of.	
Navidad, head waters of.	
Brazos, E. side, and joins Babbitt.	
Colorado, W. side, waters of Buckner's Creek.	
" " Buckner's Creek,	
Cummins' Creek, E. side, joins Cummins.	
Brazos, E. side, joins M'Kenzie and others.	
Navidad, W. side, below Gonzales' Crossing.	
Bedais Creek.	
Between Bernard and Bay Prairie.	
Between Navasoto and Bedais Creek.	
East of Navasoto, and on San Antonio Road.	
San Jacinto, E. side, at Atascocito Crossing.	
At the head of a creek, E. side Cedro.	

ABSTRACT OF ORIGINAL TITLES

NAMES OF GRANTEES.	DATE OF TITLES.	Leagues.	Labors.
John Rabb,	July 8, 1824.	1	2
George Robinson,	" " "	1	-
William Roberts,	" " "	1	-
Andrew Robinson,	" 10, "	½	-
Stephen Richardson,	" " "	1	-
Andrew Robinson,	" " "	½	-
"	" " "	-	1
Elijah Roark,	" " "	1	-
"	" " "	-	1
Noel F. Roberts,	" 15, "	1¼	-
James Ross,	" 19, "	1	-
Early Robbins,	" " "	-	1
William Robins,	" " "	1	-
"	" " "	-	1
William Rabb,	" " "	3	-
"	" " "	2	-
"	Aug. 24, "	-	2
Amos Rawls,	July 24, "	1	-
Daniel Rawls,	" " "	1¼	-
Thomas Rabb,	" " "	1	-
Benj. Rawls & Owen H. Stout,	Aug. 3, "	1	-
David Randon & J. Pennington,	" " "	1	-
Andrew Rabb,	" 10, "	1½	-
William Raleigh,	" 16, "	1	-
John Randon,	" 19, "	1	-
Patrick Reels & J. Frobough,	April 30, 1827,	1	-
Andrew Roberts,	May 11, "	1	-
Lawrence Raiway,	" 23, "	1	-
Edward Robertson,	March 31, 1828.	1	-
Early Robbins,	April 27, "	¼	-
Abraham Roberts,	March 24, 1831.	1	-
Moses Rosseau,	April 4, "	1	-
Robert Ray,	" 9, "	¼	-
William Robinson,	" 6, "	1	-
William Rankin,	" 10, "	1	-
Benjamin Rigby,	" 14, "	1	-
Wm. J. Russell,	" 23, "	1	-
Allen C. Reynolds,	" " "	1	-
Jacob Reed,	May 9, "	1	-
Raleigh Rogers,	" 6, "	1	-
Andrew Rea,	June 18, "	¼	-
Patrick Reels,	Oct. 14, "	½	-
Morgan Rector,	June 19, 1832.	1	-
James Ryan,	Nov. 20, "	1	-
Joseph Rees,	April 14, 1830.	1	-
Samuel Rogers,	Nov. 15, "	1	-
Joseph Rector,	Dec. 6, "	1	-
Richard R. Royall,	" 10, "	1	-
Thomas J. Reed,	" " "	1	-
Albert G. Reynolds,	June 19, 1831.	1	-
John Raney,	Dec. 16, "	1	-
William J. Russel,	Nov. 16, 1832.		1
James Ruth,	" 19, "	¼	-
J. E. Robertson,	" " "	1	-
Joseph Rogers,	Oct. 30, "	1	-
George F. Richardson,	Dec. 17, "	¼	-
Jesse Richards,	Oct. 10, 1835.	1	1

WHERE SITUATED.	REMARKS.
Brazos, W. s., joins Samuel Kennedy. Labs. below Town Tract.	
Brazos, E. side, joins Marsh and Bradley.	
" " joins James Bailey.	
" " joins E. R. Bradley.	
" " joins Wm. Harris.	
" W. side, in front of the mouth of Navasoto.	
" E. side, opposite San Felipe, and S. of National Road.	
Near Brazos, E. side, joins W. Little,	
Brazos, E. side, N. of the National Road.	
" " joins John Randon.	
Colorado, E. side, above Kincheloe.	
Brazos, W. side. above Town Tract.	
San Bernard, E. side.	
Brazos, W. side, above Town Tract.	
Colorado, E. side, 1 league above La Bahia Road.	
Bay Prairie, E. side.	
Colorado, W. side, above La Bahia Road.	
Bay Prairie, E. side, W. of Bernard.	
" " " between Foster and Cummins.	
Colorado, E. side, above Kincheloe.	
Bay Prairie, E. side.	
Brazos, E. side, joins Fulcher & Foster.	
Colorado, E. side, above Kincheloe.	
Brazos, W. side, between La Bahia and San Antonio Roads.	
" E. side, joins N. F. Roberts.	
Green's Bayou.	
Brazos, E. side, and joins Thomas Westall.	
Between Bernard and Bay Prairie.	
Brazos, W. side, joins Barrett & Harris.	
Mill Creek, E. side.	
Spring Creek, San Jacinto, joins S. Brown.	
Colorado, W. side, joins San Antonio Road.	
Ten Mile Creek, E. of Brazos.	
Colorado, W. side, below.	
Lake Creek, San Jacinto.	
Bedais Creek, joins Z. Landrum.	
Cummins' Creek. - - - - -	Special Grant.
Buffalo Bayou, W. side, joins J. Austin,	
Brazos, W. side, San Antonio Road.	
San Jacinto, waters of, joins Z. Landrum.	
" " "	
Eagle Lake, joins M'Nair; E. of Colorado.	
Brazos, E. side, N. of. Navasoto.	
Navidad, E. side, joins Muldoon.	
Colorado, E. side, below J. Betts.	
Sandy, E. side, Branch of Navidad, joins Wm. Menifee.	
Navidad, W. side, joining H. W. Munson.	
Carancahua, W. side, joins J. Brown.	
Sandy, 2 leagues from the mouth.	
Brazos, E. side, Hall's Bayou.	
Colorado, W. side, below H. H. League.	
Bailey's Prairie, joins Samuel Carter.	
Middle Creek, joins S. Murphy.	
Matagorda Bay, W. of Colorado, marked S. H. J.	
Colorado, E. side, joining Wilbarger's	
Rocky Creek.	
Between Navidad and La Bahia.	

ABSTRACT OF ORIGINAL TITLES

NAMES OF GRANTEES.	DATE OF TITLES.	Leagues.	Labors.
Antonio del Rios,	Oct. 16, 1835.	1	-
Zoraster Robertson,	" " "	1	-
R. J. W. Reel,	" 21, "	1	-
William Roberts,	Feb. 9, 1836.	1	-
John G. Robinson,	" 12, "	1	-
Solomon Rumfeldt,	" " "	1	-
John D. Ragsdale,	" 16, "	1	-
Stephen Richardson,	April 23, 1831.	$\frac{1}{3}$	-
David Randon,	Dec. 5, 1832.	$\frac{1}{2}$	-
William Smithers,	July 16, 1824.	1	-
Christian Smith,	" 19, "	1	-
Moses Shipman,	" " "	1	1
David Shelby, Jas. Frasier and J. M'Cormic,	" 24, "	1	-
Owen H. Stout,	Aug. 3 "	1	-
John Smith & Hugh M'Kenzie,	" " "	1	-
Robert Scoby,	" " "	1	-
Gabriel Straw Snyder,	" 7, "	1	-
Thomas Stevens,	" " "	1	-
Bartlett Sims,	" " "	1	-
Cornelius Smith,	" 10, "	1	-
William Selkirk,	" " "	1	-
Walter Sutherland,	" " "	1	-
William Stafford,	" 16, "	$1\frac{1}{2}$	-
"	" " "		1
Philip Singleton,	" 19, "	1	-
Nancy Spencer,	" " "	1	-
William Scott,	" " "	1	-
"	" " "	1	-
"	" " "		1
James Strange,	" 24, "	1	-
George W. Singleton,	May 14, 1827.	1	-
Daniel Shipman & J. N. Charles,	" 21, "	1	-
Thomas Slaughter,	" " "	1	-
James Stevenson,	March 7, 1831.	1	-
James Stevens,	" 8, "	1	-
James Schrier,	" 22, "	1	-
William Sutherland,	" " "	1	-
Thomas S. Saul,	" 29, "	1	-
Nelson Smith,	" 30, "	1	-
Joseph Smith,	" 31, "	$\frac{1}{4}$	-
John Shaw,	" " "	1	-
David Shelby,	" 28, "	$\frac{3}{4}$	-
Lancelot Smithers,	April 4, "	$\frac{1}{4}$	-
Samuel Sawyer,	" " "	$\frac{1}{4}$	-
John Shannon,	" 8, "	1	-
Owen Shannon,	" " "	1	-
Wm. B. D. Smith,	April 5, "	$\frac{1}{4}$	-
James P. Stevenson,	" 9, "	1	-
Henry Scott,	" 8, "	1	-
Jno. & James Steward,	" 9, "	1	-
William W. Shepperd,	" 16, "	1	-
Willis Stanley,	" 23, "	1	-
Marmaduke Sandifer,	" 18, "	1	-
Jacob Stevens,	May 4, "	1	-
George W. & W. H. Scott,	April 30, "	1	-
Charles D. Sayre,	May 4, "	1	-
Francis Smith,	" 7, "	1	-

WHERE SITUATED.	REMARKS.

La Bahia Road, E. side Navasoto.
Bedais Creek, joins Sims.
Yegua.
Bernard, W. side, joins E. M'Kenzie.
Cummins' Creek, W. side.
Half-Way Bayou, East side Brazos.
Navidad, E. side.
Brazos, W. side, below San Felipe.
" E. side, joins N. F. Roberts.
" W. side, joins W. C. White.
Cedar Creek, E. side San Jacinto.
Bra's, E. s. joins W. Little & T. Burnett, lab. No. 1. on W. s. Bra's, at mouth.
Brazos, W. side, 6 leagues above Fort Bend.
Bay Prairie, East side.
Colorado, E. side, below Kincheloe.
Bay Prairie, E. side.
Colorado, E. side, joins R. Ally.
Brazos, E. side, joins J. Best & J. E. Groce.
Peach Creek, W. side, No. 2.
Oyster Creek, Brazos, E. side joins J. Bailey.
On an island near mouth of Colorado, below Raft.
Brazos E. side, 4 leagues above La Bahia Road.
" " back of W. Little.
" " above town of San Felipe de Austin.
" W. side, mouth of Yegua.
" " opposite Randon & Pennington.
San Jacinto, E. side, joins Strange.
" " Cedar Creek.
" " between the said two leagues of his.
" " between Scott and Lynch.
West Bernard, joins Phillips & Kincheloe.
Bernard, W. side.
" "
Caney Creek,
" joins James Stevenson.
Mill Creek, E. fork, W. side.
" W. side.
Yegua, joins. J. P. Coles.
Mill Creek, E. fork, E. side.
Jackson's Creek, joins Mrs. Early above; New Year's Creek.
Cummins' Creek, N. side.
Mill Creek, joining Sutherland,
Back of Henry Jones, joining John Jones.
Colorado, W. side.
San Jacinto, W. side, first above the Junction.
Little Lake Creek, joins John Corner.
San Jacinto, Bedais Creek.
Piney Creek.
Brazos, W. side, below.
Colorado, W. side, above. - - - - } Petitioned for by Jas. Curtis.
Cummins' Creek, N. side, joins Logan and Jones.
Caney Creek, joins Lakey & Stevenson.
Navidad, W. side, Gonzales' Crossing.
San Bernard.
Navidad, W. side, joins Sandifer. - - " Special Grant.
Big Creek, joins W. T. Austin.
Brazos, W. side, N. of Yegua.

ABSTRACT OF ORIGINAL TITLES

NAMES OF GRANTEES.	DATE OF TITLES.	QUANTITY.	
		Leagues.	Labors.
Ebemileck Swearingen,	May 7, 1831.	1	-
Jasper Sergeant,	" 20, "	1	-
Peyton R. Splane,	April 30, "	1	-
Emilus Savage,	" " "	1	-
Jacob Shannon,	" " "	1	-
Heirs of Jonathan Scott,	" 29, "	1	-
Elizabeth Smith,	May 13, "	1	-
James Smith,	" " "	¼	-
Charles B. Stewart,	" 17, "	¼	-
Joseph Sanpierre,	June 15, "	1	-
Thomas M. Splane,	" 20, 1832.	1	-
George W. Singleton,	Oct. 15, "	1	-
Robert Stevenson,	Nov. 19, "	1	-
Ashley R. Stevens,	" 22, "	1	-
Joseph E. Scott,	" " "	1	-
James W. Scott,	" 23, "	1	-
Alexander Somerville,	April 29, 1833.	¼	-
Heirs of Smally,	" 12, 1830.	1	-
Florence Stack,	Oct. 29, "	¼	-
Henry Smith,	" 22, "	1	-
John H. Scott,	Dec. 22, "	¼	-
Patrick Scott,	Oct. 22, "	1	-
George Sutherland,	Nov. 24, "	1	-
James Small,	" 29, "	¼	-
Edward Shipman,	Dec. 14, "	¼	-
Albert Silsby,	Aug. 16, 1831.	¼	-
Thos. S. Sutherland,	April 17, 1833.	¼	-
William Simpson,	Feb. 25, "	1	-
James Standifer,	Nov. 8, 1832.	1	-
Elizabeth Standifer,	" " "	1	-
James Smith,	" " "	1	-
William C. Sparks,	" 21, "	1	-
Michael Scanlan,	Dec. 20, "	¼	-
John F. Stevenson,	1832.	1	-
Matthew Sparks,	Oct. 3, 1835.	1	-
Samuel Swearingen,	" " "	1	-
Richard Smith,	" 12, "	1	-
Charles S. Smith,	" 14, "	1	-
Ignatius Sims,	" 26, "	1	-
Daniel Sayre,	" 29, "	¼	-
Nimrod Stiffler,	Feb. 5, 1836.	¼	-
J. W. Stoddard,	" 6, "	1	-
William Sweeny,	" 16, "	1	-
Isaac B. Shipler,	" 18, "	¼	-
Washington T. Shuff,	" 22, "	1	-
Joseph San Pierrie,	Aug. 24, 1824.		1
Reuben P. F. Stone,	Oct. 22, 1832.	¼	-
James Scott,	Aug. 7, 1834.	1	-
Wm. D. Sutherland,	April 17, 1833.	¼	-
Thomas J. Tone & Jamison,	July 24, 1824.	1	-
George Teel,	Aug. 3, "	1	-
Jesse Thompson,	" 7, "	1	-
John D. Taylor,	" 10, "	1	-
David Talley,	" 16, "	1	-
"	" " "		1
Elizabeth Tumlinson,	" " "	1	-
"	" " "		1

IN THE GENERAL LAND OFFICE. 43

WHERE SITUATED.	REMARKS.
Brazos, W. side, N. of Yegua.	
Navidad, N. of Gonzales' Road.	
Colorado, E. side, joins J. Tumlinson,	
Colorado, W. side, above.	
Big Dry Creek, San Jacinto.	
San Bernard, W. side.	
Willow Creek, branch Spring Crek; Brazos, E. side.	
San Jacinto, joins W. C. Clark.	
Big Creek, joins Asa Wixen.	
Navidad, E. side, below Atascocito Road.	
N. of Navasoto.	
Brazos, E. side, San Antonio Road.	
Navasoto, N. side.	
Yegua, joins Fryer & Luster.	
Brazos, E. side, Navasoto.	
" " " joins R. Carter.	
Bernard, W. side, Matagorda Crossing.	
Colorado, below Jacob Betts.	
Carancahua, W. fork, E. side,	
Navidad, W. side, joins Job Williams.	
Trespalacios, joins W. C. Clapp.	
Navidad, E. side, near the mouth.	
Mustang, mouth of.	
Carancahua, E. side, joins Stack.	
Green's Bayou, N. side.	
S. of, and joining Hinton Curtis, Cedar Lake.	
Bowling-green, Huisatcha Bay, joins P. Dimitt.	
Matagorda Bay, joins I. & S. Ingram.	
Five leagues N. of Bastrop, joins 21.	
Colorado, E. side, joins J. Standifer.	
" " joins Childress.	
Brazos, E. side, N. of Navasoto.	
Peach Creek, back of R. Kuykendall.	
W. Bernard, E. side.	
Yegua, waters of.	
" "	
Navidad, head waters of.	
Walnut Creek, W. side Colorado.	
Bedais Bayou, where La Bahia Road crosses it.	
Brazos, W. side, joins Cummins & J. P. Stevenson.	
Peach Creek, W. side of Colorado.	
Navasoto, E. side on La Bahia Road.	
Navidad, E. side.	
Colorado, W. side, joins Graham.	
Waters of the Yegua. - - - -	{ Originally granted Hinch.
Back of No. 4, belonging to Jno. Randon, E. of Brazos.	
Colorado, E. side, between Bowman and Williams.	
San Bernard, E. side, S. of G. Huff.	
Mustang Creek, E. side, joins F. Menifee on the N. E.	
Between Bernard and Bay Prairie.	
Bernard, E. side, below George Huff.	
Bernard, E. side.	
Buffalo Bayou, Piney Point Tract.	
Brazos, E. side, joins Gorbit.	
" W. side, below Town Tract.	
Colorado, W. side, joins B. Beason.	
" W. side, joins Jesse Burnham's labor	

ABSTRACT OF ORIGINAL TITLES

NAMES OF GRANTEES.	DATE OF TITLES.	QUANTITY.	
		Leagues.	Labors.
J. F. Tong,	Aug. 19, 1824.	1	-
Ezekiel Thomas,	" " "	1	-
James Tumlinson,	" " "	1	-
"	" " "	½	-
"	" " "	-	1
Jacob Thomas,	" 24, "	-	1
Samuel Toy,	May 7, 1827.	1	-
Nathaniel Townsend,	March 28, 1831.	1	-
John Townsend,	" 30, "	¼	-
William S. Townsend,	" " "	¼	-
W. H. Taylor,	April 4, "	1	-
Thomas Thompson,	" 5, "	¼	-
Isaac F. Tinsley,	" 6, "	¼	-
John A. Thompson,	" 5, "	¼	-
Robert Taylor, Jr.,	" 20, "	¼	-
Thomas Taylor,	" 27, "	1	-
W. W. W. Thompson,	" 20, "	1	-
Jacob Thomas,	May 19, "	¼	-
Alexander Thompson,	June 20, 1832.	1	-
Henry Thierweistar,	Oct. 18, "	¼	-
Thomas Thompson,	Nov. 19, "	¾	-
Joseph Thompson,	" 16, "	1	-
George Tennille,	April 5, 1830.	1	-
Josiah Tilley,	Jan. 23, 1832.	1	-
Thomas Tolson,	" " "	¼	-
Jesse C. Tannehill,	Oct. 29, "	1	-
Wm. H. Toy,	" 12, 1835.	1	-
William Townsend,	" 20, "	1	-
Daniel Tyler,	" 22, "	¼	-
Charles Tapp,	Feb. 15, 1836.	¼	-
Joseph Thompson,	" 23, "	1	-
Title of the Town of San Felipe,	July 1, 1824.	4	-
Title of the Town of Bastrop,	June 8, 1832.	4	-
Joseph Urban,	Jan. 29, 1836.	1	-
Ammon Underwood,	July 25, "	¼	-
Martin Varner,	" 8, 1824.	1	-
"	" " "	-	1
William Vince,	" 21, "	1	-
Richard & Robert Vince,	Aug. 21, "	1	-
Jesse Vance,	June 4, 1827.	¼	-
John Vince,	May 4, 1831.	¼	-
Allen Vince,	" 30, "	½	-
Susan Vince,	" 3, "	¼	-
Jonathan Vest,	" 28, "	1	-
Robert Vince,	Nov. 16, 1832.	½	-
Lewis L. Veder,	Oct. 29, 1830.	¼	-
Cornelius H. Vandever,	Nov. 26, "	1	-
William Vince,	Dec. 14, 1832.	-	1
Isaac Votan,	Oct. 12, 1835.	1	-
John D. G. Varrelman,	" 20, "	1	-
John Vanderwerts,	Feb. 23, 1836.	1	-
Isaac Van Dorn & D. E. Bayles,	April 14, 1828.	1	-
James Whitesides,	July 16, 1824.	1	-
"	" " "	-	1
Heirs of Wm. Whitesides,	" 19, "	1	-
Thomas Westall,	" " "	1	-
"	" " "	-	2

IN THE GENERAL LAND OFFICE. 45

WHERE SITUATED.	REMARKS.
Bernard, W. side.	
Buffalo Bayou, 5 leagues from its mouth.	
Colorado, E. side, 5 leagues above Atascocito.	
Colorado, E. side; is the lower half of No. 1, below Kincheloe.	
Colorado, E. side, above his league,	
Opposite the town of Austin, N. of National Road.	
Brazos, W. side, 3 leagues below town of Austin.	
Cummins' Creek, W. side.	
Mill Creek and Cummins' Creek, joins W. H. Jack.	
" " " "	
Colorado, W. side, joins John Castleman.	
" E. side.	
" joins Cunningham.	
" E. side.	
N. W. of Abner Kuykendall's half league on New Year's Creek.	
Navidad, Mulberry Fork.	
" E. side, Gonzales' Crossing.	
Bray's Bayou, S. side, near Luke Moore.	
Cummins' Creek W. side, joins Nos. 12 and 13.	
Bray's Bayou, joins Luke Moore.	
Buckner's Creek, head of, joins A. Graham.	
Navidad, E. side, Gonzales' Road.	
Joining and W. of M. Varner & J. B. Austin.	
Trespalacios, W. side J. W. E. Wallace.	
Colorado, E. side, joins Webber.	
" " joins Burlinson.	
La Bahia Road, head waters of Navidad.	
Bedais Creek.	
Brazos, E. side, and joins Whitesides.	
Walnut Creek, head waters of, W. of Colorado.	
Yegua, joins Wallace.	
Colorado, E. side, on San Antonio Road.	
San Bernard, W side.	
Davidson's Creek, E. side.	
Brazos, W. side.	
Opposite San Felipe de Austin.	
Buffalo Bayou, S. side.	
Buffalo and Green's Bayous.	
Bernard, E. side, joins Beard.	
San Jacinto, Atkin's Creek, joins Clark.	
" and Lake Creek.	
" W. side.	
Navidad, W. side, joins J. Ally & J. Andrews.	
Buffalo Bayou, joins J. Taylor.	Concession.
Bay Prairie, joins J. C. Peyton.	
Colorado, W. side.	
Green's Bayou, mouth of, joins Harris.	
Navasoto, E. side, on San Antonio Road.	
Yegua, waters of.	
Cummins' Creek, waters of.	
Between Bernard and Bay Prairie.	{ Once claimed by Hugh M'Guffin.
Brazos, E. side, mouth of Navasoto,	
" " joins Martin Varner's labor.	
" " one league above Coshatte Crossing.	
" " joins N. F. Roberts.	
Colorado, W. s., joins Wm. Pettus. Labs. Brazos, W. s., below T. T.	

ABSTRACT OF ORIGINAL TITLES

NAMES OF GRANTEES.	DATE OF TITLES.	Leagues.	Labors.
Francis F. Wells,	July 21, 1824.	1	-
"	" " "	-	1
James Walker,	" " "	1	-
Nath'l Whiting & Nathan Osburn,	" 24, "	1	-
John R. Williams,	" 29, "	1	-
"	" " "	-	1
Solomon Williams,	Aug. 7, "	1	-
"	" " "	-	1
Samuel M. Williams,	" 10, "	1	-
"	" " "	1	-
"	" " "	-	1
"	" " "	-	1
"	" " "	-	1
Henry & B. Whitesides,	" 10, "	1	-
Joseph White,	" 12, "	1	-
Thomas Williams,	" 16, "	1	-
William Whitlock,	" " "	1	-
Amy White,	" 16, "	1	-
Reuben White,	" " "	1	-
George F. Williams,	" 19, "	1	-
Robert H. Williams,	" " "	1	-
William C. White,	" " "	1	-
John Williams, (Minor,)	" 24, "		1
Zedock Woods.	May 15, 1827.	1	-
Elias R. Wightman,	" 25, "	1	-
Jane Wilkins,	" 26, "	1	-
Caleb Wallace.	" 14, 1828.	1	-
James Westall,	" 21, 1827.	¼	-
Ralph Wright,	June 4, "	¼	-
Samuel M. Williams,	May 11, 1828.	1	-
"	" " "	1	-
"	" " "	1	-
"	" " "	1	-
Sandford Woodward,	March 11, 1831.	1	-
William Williamson,	" 21, "	1	-
James Winn,	" 31, "	1	-
Norman Woods,	April 4, "	¼	-
Montreville Woods,	" " "	1	-
Leander Woods,	" " "	¼	-
James Wallace,	" 9, "	1	-
Barnabas Wixon,	" 4, "	1	-
Robert M. Williamson,	" 23, "	1	-
Tandy Walker,	" 27, "	1	-
Asa Wixon,	April 23, 1831.	¼	-
James G. Wright,	" 16, "	1	-
Archibald S. White.	May 5, "	1	-
Anna White,	" 12, "	1	-
William Whitaker,	" 18, "	1	-
D. J. White,	" 31, "	1	-
Ephraim Whitehead,	Nov. 14, "	1	-
Joel Wheaton,	" 24, "	1	-
Thos. J. Wooton,	Feb. 14, 1832.	1	-
John Woodruff,	Oct. 20, "	1	-
Nicholas Whitehead,	Nov. 18, "	¼	-
Augustus Williams,	" 19, "	1	-
John T. Whitesides,	" 20, "	1	-
George W. Whitesides,	" 23, "	1	-

WHERE SITUATED.	REMARKS.
Near the confluence of Navidad and La Vaca.	
Brazos, W. side, below J. G. & G. W. M'Neel.	
New Year's Creek, joins S. R. Miller.	
Colorado, W. side, below Atascocito.	
Clear Creek, W. of Galveston Bay.	
Clear Creek, N. side.	
Bay Prairie, E. side, joins A. C. Buckner.	
Brazos, E. side, S. of National Road.	
Bernard, E. side, below Huff.	
Bernard, W. side, joins John Cummings.	
Brazos, W. side, above Town Tract.	
Opposite Town Tract, S. of National Road.	
Brazos, W. side, near the mouth.	
Brazos, E. side, near mouth of Navasoto, above.	
Bernard, W. side.	
Cedar Bayou, W. side.	
On San Jacinto, above Atascocito Crossing.	
San Jacinto, W. side.	
San Jacinto, E. side, joins H. Jackson.	
Trespalacios Bayou, 4 leagues from its mouth.	
Between San Bernard and Bay Prairie.	
Brazos, W. side, Coshate Crossing.	
In front of San Felipe, S. of National Road.	
Between Bernard and Bay Prairie.	
Colorado, E. side, at its mouth, fronts on Matagorda Bay.	
Brazos, E. side, joins W. Morton.	
" " joins Groce's Retreat.	
New Year's Creek, Doe Run.	
Colorado, W. side, joins Galliher.	
Brazos, E. side, joins Brown & Allcorn.	
Buffalo Bayou, joins Harris Moore & Austin.	
Mill Creek, W. fork.	
" "	
Caney Creek, waters of, joins D. Lawrence.	
Cummins' Creek, W side.	
" " joins Wm. H. Jack.	
Colorado, W. side, joins J. Cook.	
" " above Thos. Alley.	
" E. side.	
Brazos, " joins J. E. Groce & Isaac Jackson.	
Big Creek, joins E. Lippincot.	
Brazos, W. side, joins Little.	Special Grant.
Brazos, E. side, joins J. E. Groce.	
Big Creek, joins Nos. 5 & 6.	
Cyprus Bay, San Jacinto, E. side of said Bayou.	
Navidad, E. side, joins Jesse Cartwright.	
Lake Creek, Branch of San Jacinto.	
Navidad, opposite John Andrews.	
Brazos, E. side, joins Caleb Wallace.	
Navidad, W. side, joins Samuel Fuller.	
Buffalo Bayou, above Pine Point.	
Brazos, E. side, joins John Jones.	
Navasoto, E. side.	
Wolf Creek, Yegua.	
Navasoto, N. side.	
Buckner's Creek, head of.	
Colorado, E. side, Pin Oak Creek, joins Mrs. Campbell.	

ABSTRACT OF ORIGINAL TITLES

NAMES OF GRANTEES.	DATE OF TITLES.	QUANTITY.	
		Leagues.	Labors.
Reuben D. Woods,	Nov. 24, 1832.	1	- -
Sam'l M. Williams,	Dec. 28, 1831.	1	- -
"	" " "	1	- -
"	" " "	1	- -
"	" " "	2	- -
"	" " "	1	- -
"	" " "	1	- -
Matthew R. Williams,	Oct. 29, 1830.	1	- -
Peter White,	" 22, "	1	- -
Job Williams,	" " "	1	- -
Margaret Wightman,	" 30, "	¼	- -
Joseph W. E. Wallace,	Dec. 28, "	1	- -
Heirs of B. Wightman,	Oct. 28, "	1	- -
Jesse White,	Nov. 15, "	1	- -
Thos. J. Winston,	" 20, "	1	- -
Benj. J. White,	" 24, "	1	- -
Robert Wilson,	Dec. 10, "	1	- -
Edward Walker,	July 20, 1831.	1	- -
William Wroe,	Jan. 18, 1832.	1	- -
Parker Williams,	Dec. 13, "	¼	- -
John H. Wade,	Jan. 17, 1833.	¼	- -
Josiah Wilbarger,	" 22, 1832.	1	- -
John F. Webber,	" " "	½	- -
Martin Wells,	Oct. 29, "	1	- -
John B. Waters,	" " "	½	- -
James Waddlington,	Dec. 3, 1832.	¼	- -
John B. Waters,	Nov. 21, 1832.	½	- -
M'Henry Winburn,	Oct. 3, 1835.	¼	- -
Edward P. Whitehead,	" 7, "	¼	- -
John Y. Wallace,	" 8, "	1	- -
James D. Wilkinson,	" 14, "	1	- -
David Wade,	" 18, "	1	- -
Abner W. Woodsey,	" 29, "	¼	- -
Thos. M. Whittington,	Jan. 25, 1836.	1	- -
Jacob Watters,	Feb. 3, "	1	- -
Bernhard Witle,	" 6, "	¼	- -
Sam'l Wolfenbarger,	" 12, "	1	- -
Ann Wooldrige,	" 20, "	1	- -
Felix Wright,	" 22, "	¼	- -
Alvin B. Woodward,	" 23, "	¼	- -
John J Whitesides,	Oct. 14, 1831.	1	-
Samuel Young,	April 21, 1831.	¼	- -
Michael Young,	May 5, "	1	- -
Asa Yeamans,	July 8, "	1	- -
Abraham Zubar.	March 4, 1833,	1	- -

IN THE GENERAL LAND OFFICE.   49

WHERE SITUATED.	REMARKS.
San Bernard, E. side, below, and joins Huff.	Origin'ly granted Geo. Teel.
Opposite Town Tract.	Concession.
La Bahia Road, joins H. Chriesman.	"
Brazos, W. of San Antonio Road.	"
Buckner's Creek, W. of Colorado.	"
Colorado, E. side, above San Antonio Road.	"
" W. side, between La Bahia and Bexar Roads.	"
" E. side, below J. Betts.	Special Grant.
Navidad, E. side, joins S. Bowen.	
" W. side, opposite mouth of Sandy.	
Caney, W. side.	
Trespalacios, W. side.	
Caney, mouth of, and Peninsula.	
Navidad, E. side.	
Mustang Creek.	
Carancahua, N. W. side.	
Clear Creek, joins J. Dickinson.	
Brazos, E. side, joins Groce & Mitchell.	
Trespalacios, E. side.	
Bernard, W. side, mouth of.	
Trespalacios, W. side, joins J. H. Scott & Wallace.	
Colorado, E. side.	
" " joins M. Duty.	Special Grant,
" "	
" "	
Heads of Pin Oak and Rabb's Creeks.	
North of San Antonio Road.	
Yegua, Waters of, joins Fryer, Miller & Holderman.	
Brazos, E. side, below Isaac's	
Yegua.	
Head waters of Cummins' Creek.	
Peach Creek, and joins leagues 3 & 4.	
Buckner's Creek.	
Yegua, joins Fryer.	
Colorado, W. side, San Antonio Road.	
Waters of Buckner's Creek.	
Walnut Creek, W. side Colorado.	
Yegua, waters of.	
Mill Creek, waters of.	
" " joins Pryer & Armstrong.	
Holland's Settlement, joins Caleb Wallace.	
Navidad, W. Fork.	
Big Creek, N. side.	
Dry Creek, N. side.	
San Jacinto, waters of; Lake Creek, joins A. Ray.	

ABSTRACT OF ORIGINAL TITLES

SOLD BY THE STATE OF

NAMES OF GRANTEES.	DATE OF TITLES.	QUANTITY.	
		Leagues.	Labors.
Jose Maria de Aguirre,	Oct. 4, 1833.	11	-
Rafael de Aguirre,	" " "	11	-
"	" 22, "	11	-
Jose Juan Acosta,	Sept. 30, "	11	-
Gregorio Basquez,	Oct. 19, "	11	-
Miguel Davilla,	" 18, "	11	-
Santiago del Valle,	June 12, 1832.	10	-
Ignacio Galindo,	April 13, 1833.	11	-
Justo Lienda,	Aug. 5, 22, Oct. 5, 23, '33	10	-
Francisco Ruis,	Aug. 31, 1833.	9	-
Jose Antonio Manchaca,	Sept. 27, "	11	-
Thomas de la Vega,	Oct. 4, "	11	-
Maximo Moreno,	" 8, "	11	-
Jose Antonio de Péña,	" " "	11	-
Pedro Zarza,	" 17, "	11	-
David Jose Sanches,	" 3, "	10	-
Jose Leal,	" 26, "	6	-
Marcelino Martinez,	" 18, "	3	-
Carlos O'Campo,	" 19, "	5	-
Jose Maria Sanchez,	" 19, "	5	-
Fernando Rodriguez,	" 29, "	2	12
Antonio Manchaca,	Nov. 2, "	11	-
Marcelino Martinez,		1	-
Atanacio de la Sarda,		11	-

COAHUILA AND TEXAS.

WHERE SITUATED.	REMARKS.
Blank, land not designated.	
Brazos, W. side, mouth of Bush Creek,	
San Gabriel and Williamson, joins Davilla & Sarza, & on Cow Bayou.	
On San Andres and Brazos, including the town of Tenoxticlan.	
On E. side Brazos, joins Antonio Manchaca, and crosses Isaac's Creek.	
South side San Andres, Buffalo and Donoho's Creeks, and head of Alligator Creek.	
Between Colorado and Onion Creek, W. side of Colorado.	
Brazos, both sides, mouth of Bear Creek and Turtle Bayou.	
Brushy Creek, and San Gabriel, W. side Brazos and San Antonio Road, joins A. Kuykendall; and E. Brazos, joins Iron's.	
On both sides of Brazos, mouth of San Andres, Tenoxticlan.	
Brazos, both sides, mouth of Cow and Tahuacano Bayous.	
Waco Village, E. side, joins Manchaca.	
San Andres, left side, below Lampassus Creek.	
" " Jose de Sanchez.	
Brazos, both sides, and San Gabriel, mouth of Willamson's Creek.	
" E. side, mouth of Turtle Bayou, and N. side San Gabriel.	
San Andres, S. side.	
Both sides Brazos, joining Ignacio Galindo & Gregorio Basquez.	
Brazos, W. side, mouth of Waco Creek, below Waco Village, joins Austin.	
Brazos, E. side, between G. Basquez, Antonio Sarda and Brazos, W. s., and Davidson's Creek.	
Brazos, W. side, near mouth of San Andres, and joins V. Blanco.	
San Andres, S. side.	
Brazos, E. side, below and adjoining Antonio Manchaca.	
Brazos, E. side, old bed of River.	

A

LIST OF TITLES

ISSUED BY

TALBOT CHAMBERS,

COMMISSIONER

FOR MILAM'S COLONY.

ABSTRACT OF ORIGINAL TITLES

NAMES OF GRANTEES.	DATE OF TITLES.	QUANTITY.	
		Leagues.	Labors.
Thomas Anderson,	March 14, 1835.	1	-
Phillip J. Allen,	May 23, "	1	-
Theodore Bissell,	March 19, "	1	-
John W. Bunton,	April 8, "	¼	-
Hiram Beals,	May 23, "	¼	-
Martha Barker,	June 12, "	1	-
Henry Brown,	May 20, "	1	-
William Cannon,	March 29, "	1	-
L. C. Cunningham,	Aug. 1, "	¼	-
James Curtis,	Feb. 20, "	¼	-
James Dojle,	July 31, "	1	-
Andrew Dunn,	March 30, "	1	-
William Duty,	June 26, "	¼	-
Isaac Decker,	March 17, "	1	-
Horatio Egglestone,	July 16, "	1	-
S. P. R. Eggleston,	Feb. 21, "	1	-
Rebwen Gage,	Sept. 25, "	1	-
Sinclair D. Garvis,	March 26, "	1	-
Atarcas Garcia,	" 23, "	¼	-
Edward Gritten,	July 28, "	¼	-
"	" " "	1	-
Henry P. Hill,	" 14, "	1	-
James Haggard,	May 21, "	1	-
William H. Haggard,	" 23, "	1	-
David Holderman,	" 25, "	1	-
Thomas R. Jackson,	March 28, "	1	-
Edward S. Keeps,	Feb. 20, "	1	-
Mary Ann Lindsey,	April 22, "	1	-
Addison Litten,	March 23, "	1	-
Bartholemew Manlove,	April 22, "	1	-
Noel Mixon,	July 23, "	1	-
Martin M'Carven,	Feb. 21, "	1	-
Jesse L. M'Crooklin,	June 18, "	1	-
Ezeriah Moore,	" 21, "	¼	-
Thomas G. M'Geehe,	Feb. 19, "	1	-
John G. M'Geehe,	April 5, "	1	-
Benj. F. Mims,	May 22, "	¼	-
James Northcross,	April 22, "	1	-
James C. Neill,	June 1, "	1	-
Daniel L. Richardson,	Sept. 20, "	1	-
Mary Sweargert,	March 24, "	¼	-
Thomas F. Slaughter,	Feb. 23, "	1	-
Wilkinson Sparks,	July 21, "	¼	-
James Stewart,	" 17, "	1	-
John Stewart,	Sept. 20, "	1	-
Benjamin Tennel.	June 1, "	1	-
William Barret Travis,	April 10, "	1	-
Richards Vaughan,	June 17, "	¼	-
Walker Wilson,	March 12, "	1	-
Amelia Wilson,	April 21, "	1	-
Seaborn J. Whatley,	March 30, "	1	-
Benjamin Williams,	July 27, "	1	-
Freelove Woody,	March 30, "	1	-

IN THE GENERAL LAND OFFICE. 55

WHERE SITUATED.	REMARKS.
On Onion Creek.	
Joins No. 5, description not given.	
On Williamson's Creek.	
On the San Antonio Road, joins ¼ No. 1.	
On Cedar Creek, joins No. 7.	
On the N. side San Antonio Road.	
On the E. side Guadaloupe, on the San Antonio Road.	
On Williamson's Creek branch of Onion Creek,	
On San Antonio Road, joins No. 3 on the N. E.	
On the W. side St. Marks, on the San Antonio Road.	
On the San Antonio Road, 10 miles from Bastrop.	
On Onion Creek, joins No. 5.	
On Colorado, above mouth Cedar Creek, joins Manlove.	
On the W. side Colorado, on Williamson's Creek, joins 10 league grant.	
On the Rio Blanco.	
On the waters of Onion Creek, includes a spring.	
On the waters of Cedar Creek, joins A. Litton,	
On Onion Creek, joins No. 5.	
On Cedar Creek and San Antonio Road,	
On Cedar Creek, and joins Doyle on the E.	
On Purdinalla's Creek, 4000 varas wide.	
On Colorado, mouth of Spring Creek.	
On W. side Colorado, about ten miles N. of San Antonio Road.	
On the waters of Onion Creek.	Calls for 1 leag., should be ¼.
On the Colorado, 1200 varas wide.	
On Onion Creek and Jackson's Creek.	
On York's Creek, on San Antonio Road.	
On Colorado, below the mouth of Onion Creek.	
On San Antonio Road, includes the mouth Cedar Creek.	
On Colorado, includes the mouth of Cedar Creek.	
On the waters of the Rio Blanco.	
On Onion Creek, joins Allen on the N.	
On the waters of the Rio Blanco.	
On San Antonio Road, joins Gritten.	
On the St. Marks and San Antonio Road Crossing.	
On Bear Creek, Slaughter's Fork.	
On Onion Creek, joins Jackson on the S.	
On the Colorado and Cedar Creek.	
" below the mouth of Onion Creek.	
On the waters of the Guadaloupe.	
On the San Antonio Road, joins A. Litten on the E.	
On Onion Creek.	
On the Colorado.	
In the vicinity of San Antonio Road.	
Plumb Creek.	
On the Colorado.	
On Onion Creek.	
"	
On Onion Creek and the Rio Blanco.	
On the Rio Blanco.	
"	
On Onion Creek.	

A

LIST OF TITLES

ISSUED BY

JOSE ANTONIO NAVARRO,

IN

GREEN DE WITT'S COLONY.

ABSTRACT OF ORIGINAL TITLES

NAMES OF GRANTEES.	DATE OF TITLES.	Leagues.	Labors.
Caleb P. Alexander,	May 5, 1831.	1	-
George Allen,	June 2, "	1	-
John M. Ashby,	July 18, "	1	-
William W. Arrington,	June 16, 1832.	$\frac{1}{4}$	-
Simeon Bateman,	April 23, 1831.	1	-
Caleb Brock,	May 5, "	1	-
Francis Berry,	" 15, "		24
"	Aug. 24, "		1
Moses Baker,	June 22, "	1	-
Arthur Burns,	July 9, "	1	-
Squire Burns,	" 10, "	$\frac{1}{4}$	-
Kimber W. Barton,	" 11, "	1	-
Esther Berry,	" 20, "		24
"	" " "		1
Valentine Bennet,	Nov. 8, "	$\frac{1}{4}$	-
Humphreys Branch,	" 20, "		24
"	" 29, "		1
David W. Brand,	" 25, "	$\frac{1}{4}$	-
George Blair,	Dec. 1, "		24
"	June 28, "		1
David Burgett,	May 10, 1832.		24
"	Nov. 26, 1831.		1
Jose R. Bedford,	June 6, 1832.	$\frac{1}{4}$	-
Isaac Baker,	" 14, "	$\frac{1}{4}$	-
Harriet Cottle,	May 1, 1831.	1	-
Jonathan Cottle,	" " "	1	-
William Cobbey,	" 5, "	$\frac{1}{4}$	-
Matthew Caldwell,	" 22, "	1	-
Almond Cottle,	July 13, 1831.	$\frac{1}{4}$	-
William Chase,	Aug. 17, "	1	-
Cyrus Campbell & Sons,	" 24, "	1	-
Richard A. Chrisholm,	Sept. 7, "	1	-
Joseph D. Clements,	Nov. 6, "	1	-
George W. Cottle,	Sept. 12, 1832.	1	-
Benjamin Duncan,	June 28, 1831.	$\frac{1}{4}$	-
James C. Davis,	" 30, "	$\frac{1}{4}$	-
Zachariah Davis,	July 19, "	1	-
Patrick Dowlearn,	" 25, "	$\frac{1}{4}$	-
Miles G. Dikes,	Aug. 23, "	$\frac{1}{4}$	-
George W. Davis,	Sept. 6, "	1	-
John Davis,	Oct. 28, "	$\frac{1}{4}$	-
William Dearduff,	Nov. 5, "	$\frac{1}{4}$	-
Edward Dickinson,	" 26, "	$\frac{1}{4}$	-
Abraham Denton,	May 12, 1832.	$\frac{1}{4}$	-
Jesse N. Davis,	" 15, "	$\frac{1}{4}$	-
Jacob C. Darst,	April 24, 1831.		24
"	July 1, "		1
Daniel Davis,	May 1, "	1	-
Almerion Dickinson,	" 5, "	1	-
Eliza De Witt,	April 15, "	1	-
Graves Fulcher,	" 24, "	$\frac{1}{4}$	-
Churchill Fulcher,	" " "	1	-
Benjamin Fulcher,	" " "	$\frac{1}{4}$	-
George Foley,	July 10, "	$\frac{1}{4}$	-
Benjamin Fugua,	June 14, 1832.	$\frac{1}{4}$	-
Silas Fugua,	" 16, "	1	-
John Fennell,	Sept. 13, "	$\frac{1}{4}$	-

WHERE SITUATED.	REMARKS.
On Plum Creek.	By his Attorney, B. Fletcher.
On San Marcus, S. W. side.	
On the La Vaca, Below the La Bahia Road.	
On the Guadalupe, above Gonzales.	
" below Gonzales.	
On Plum Creek,	
On a branch of a creek, flowing from the N. E. into St. Marcos.	
On the Guadalupe below Gonzales.	
" "	
" above Gonzales.	
Quarter No. 19, in Class No. 1	
On the Guadalupe.	
On a branch of Plum Creek.	
On the Guadalupe, below Gonzales.	
" "	
" above Gonzales.	
" "	
" below Gonzales.	
On the San Felipe Road.	
On the Guadalupe, below Gonzales.	
On the La Vaca and Tejocotes Creek.	
On the Guadalupe, below Gonzales.	
Five miles from Guadalupe, on a creek, N. E. side.	
On the Guadalupe, above Gonzales.	
San Marcos, above Gonzales.	
On the Guadalupe, below Gonzales,	
On Plum Creek.	
On La Vaca Creek.	
On the Guadalupe.	
On the La Vaca, above the San Felipe Road.	
On the St. Marcos, above Gonzales.	
On the Guadalupe.	
"	
On the Tejocotes Creek and La Vaca, 28 miles from Gonzales.	
On the San Marcos.	
On the La Vaca River.	
On the La Vaca, E. of the La Bahia Road.	
On the Guadalupe.	
Plum Creek.	
On the Guadalupe.	
On the La Vaca.	
On a Sandy Creek.	
On the Guadalupe, above Gonzales.	
On the Tejocotes Creek.	
On the Guadalupe, above Gonzales.	
" "	
On a Creek which empties into the La Vaca.	
On the Guadalupe, below Gonzales.	
On the San Marcos, below the old Bexar Road.	
On the Guadalupe, above Gonzales.	
" below Gonzales.	
" "	
" "	
On the La Vaca, above the Atascocito Road.	
On the San Marcos,	
"	
On the Carizo Creek, S. W. of the Guadalupe.	

ABSTRACT OF ORIGINAL TITLES

NAMES OF GRANTEES.	DATE OF TITLES.	Leagues.	Labors.
John E. Garwin,	May 5, 1831.	¼	-
Michael Gillan,	June 22, "	1	-
James George,	" 28, "	1	-
James Gibson,	" 12, "		24
"	" " "		1
Samuel Highsmith,	April 1, "		24
"	Aug. 3, "		1
John Henry,	May 5, "	1	-
George Hinds,	" 10, "	1	-
James Hinds,	" 25, "	1	-
Eben Haven,	June 24, "	1	-
William House,	July 6, "	¼	-
William Hill,	Aug. 11, "	1	-
James Hughes,	June 6, 1832.	¼	-
Edward Hughart,	" 21, "	¼	-
Richard Heath,	May 24, "	¼	-
Thomas Jackson,	" 1, 1831.		24
"	" 10, "		1
Phineas James,	" 1, "	1	-
John Jones,	July 10, "	¼	-
John G. King,	April 24, "	1	-
Andrew Kent,	June 28, "	1	-
George C. Kimble,	Nov. 28, "	¼	-
Joseph Kent,	June 10, 1832.	¼	-
Frederick Kistler,	July 11, "	1	-
Byrd Lockhart,	April 30, 1831.	1	-
Charles Lockhart,	May 10, "	1	-
Byrd B. Lockhart,	" 25, "	¼	-
Samuel Lockhart,	July 9, "	1	-
Washington Lockhart,	Sept. 10, "	¼	-
Andrew Lockhart,	" 14, "	1	-
John B. Lockhart,	Dec. 2, "	¼	-
William Leach,	June 12, 1832.	¼	-
Joseph P. Lawler,	Sept. 13, "	¼	-
William B. Lockhart,	" 17, "	¼	-
John M'Coy,	April 24, 1831.	1	-
Jesse M'Coy,	" " "	¼	-
Joseph M'Coy,	May 1, "	1	-
George F. Managhan,	" " "	¼	-
William A. Matthews,	" 5, "	¼	-
John M'Coy, Jr.	" " "	1	-
Silas M. Morris,	June 22, "	1	-
Spencer Morris,	" 25, "	1	-
Samuel M'Coy,	July 9, "	¼	-
Stephen B. Morrison,	June 22, "	1	-
Abraham O. M'Clure,	July 6, "	¼	-
John M'Crabb,	" 13, "	¼	-
Bartholomew M'Clure,	Sept. 6, "		24
"	" 12, "		1
Samuel Middleton,	" " "	¼	-
Robert Mills,	" 13, "	¼	-
Thomas R. Miller,	" 20, "	¼	-
Bethel Morris,	June 1, 1832.	¼	-
Daniel M'Coy,	" 18, "	1	-
Joseph M'Coy, Jr.,	July 11, "	¼	-
John Morris,	Sept. 16, "	¼	-
Elihu Moss,	Nov. 25, 1831.	1	-

WHERE SITUATED.	REMARKS.
On the Guadalupe below Gonzales.	
On the San Marcos, below the Bexar Road.	
On Plum Creek.	
On Tejocotes Creek.	
On the Guadalupe.	
On the San Marcos, above Gonzales.	
On the Guadalupe.	
On the San Marcos, below the Bexar Road.	
On Plum Creek,	
"	
On the Guadalupe.	
On Plum Creek.	
On Tejocotes Creek.	
On the Guadalupe, below Gonzales.	
On Tejocotes Creek.	
On the La Vaca.	
On the Guadalupe, below Gonzales,	
" "	
" above Gonzales.	
On the La Vaca.	
On the Guadalupe, above Gonzales.	
On the La Vaca River, above the Atascocito Road.	
On the San Marcos.	
On the Guajalote Creek.	
On the Tejocotes Creek.	
On the Guadalupe, below Gonzales.	
On the Guadalupe.	
" above the La Bahia Road.	
" below Gonzales.	
"	
"	
" above Gonzales.	
" "	
On the Tejocotes Creek.	
On the Guadalupe, below Gonzales.	
" "	
" "	
" above Gonzales.	
On the San Marcos, "	
On the Guadalupe.	
On a Creek running into the La Vaca.	
On the San Marcos, above Gonzales.	
On the Guadalupe. - - - - -	{ By his Attorney, James M'Coy.
On the San Marcos, below the Bexar Road.	
On a Creek running into the San Marcos.	
On the Guadalupe.	
On a branch of Tejocotes Creek.	
"	
On the Guadalupe, below Gonzales,	
" "	
" "	
On the Tejocotes Creek.	
On the E. side of Tejocotes Creek.	
On Tejocotes Creek.	
On the La Vaca.	
On the Guadalupe.	

ABSTRACT OF ORIGINAL TITLES

NAMES OF GRANTEES.	DATE OF TITLES.	QUANTITY.	
		Leagues.	Labors.
David G. Mills, - - -	June 15, 1832.	¼	- -
Ira Nash, - -	May 1, 1831.	1	- -
John A. Neil, - -	June 20, "	1	- -
John Oliver, - -	May 1, "		24 -
" - -	July 27, "		1 -
Alexander Porter, - "	June 22, "	1	- -
William l'age, - -	Aug. 24, "	¼	- -
James B. Patrick, -	Sept. 3, "	1	- -
Philander Priestly, - -	Dec. 10, "	¼	- -
Andrew Ponton, - -	June 18, 1832.	¼	- -
Jesse Robinson, - -	May 5, 1831.	¼	- -
Edwin Richeson, -	Sept. 15, "	1	- -
James Roney, -	June 11, 1832.	¼	- -
John Roe, - -	July 10, "	¼	- -
Stephen Smith, - -	April 15, 1831.	1	- -
Claiborne Stinnet, - - -	" " "	¼	- -
John Sowell, - -	May 5, "		24 -
" - -	July 1, "		1 -
Samuel Sharpe, - -	May 5, "	¼	- -
Robert Smith, - -	" "	1	- -
William A. Sowell, - -	June 22, "	¼	- -
Lewis D. Sowell, - - -	" 25, "	¼	- -
Solomon Seals, - -	July 1, "	1	- -
William P. Stapp, - - -	" 9, "	¼	- -
Jonathan Scott, - -	" " "	¼	- -
Elijah Stapp, - -	" 16, "	1	- -
Darwin M. Stapp, - - -	" 19, "	¼	- -
Stephen F. Sanders, -	Nov. 22, "	¼	- -
John Smeathers, - -	May 8, 1832.	1	- -
William St. John, - - -	June 12, "	¼	- -
William Strode, - -	" 15, "	1	- -
James Shaw, - - -	" 16, "	¼	- -
Winslow Turner, -	April 15, 1831.	1	- -
James Thompson, - -	" 24, "	1	- -
Felix Taylor, - -	May 1, "	1	- -
Winslow Turner, Jr., - -	" " "	¼	- -
Elijah Tate, - -	" 5, "	¼	- -
Peter Teal, - - -	" 29, "	¼	- -
John J. Tumlinson, - -	June 15, "	1	- -
Hepsebeth Taylor, -	July 26, "	1	- -
Joseph Tumlinson, - -	Aug. 8, "	¼	- -
William Taylor, - -	" " "	1	- -
Littleton Tumlinson, -	Dec. 7, "	¼	- -
James Tumlinson, - -	" 8, "	¼	- -
David C. Tumlinson, - -	" 15, "	¼	- -
Alnbrose Tinney, - -	June 22, 1832.	1	- -
Ezekiel Williams, - -	May 1, 1831.	¼	- -
Byrum Wickson, - -	" " "	¼	- -
James F. Wood, - - -	June 22, "	1	- -
Isaac Weldon, - - -	" 30, "	¼	- -
Russel Ward, - -	July 20, "	¼	- ▲
Malkijah Williams, -	Nov. 20, "	¼	- -
Allam B. Williams, - -	May 10, 1832.	1	- -
Tobias Wintworth, -	" 15, "	¼	- -
Samuel Williams, - -	June 15, "	¼	- -
Maria Ann Williams, - -	Sept. 16, "	1	- -
Christopher Williams, - -	May 12, "	¼	- -

WHERE SITUATED.	REMARKS.
On the Guadalupe.	
" above Gonzales.	
On Plum Creek.	
On the Guadalupe, above Gonzales.	
On the Guadalupe.	
On the La Vaca, above the La Bahia Road.	
On Tejocotes Creek,	
On the Guadalupe, above Gonzales.	
E. of Gonzales, N. of the San Felipe Road.	
" La Vaca, No. 30, Class 4.	
San Marcos, above Gonzales.	
On the La Vaca.	
On Tejocotes Creek.	
"	
On the San Marcos, above Gonzales.	
On the Guadalupe, "	
" "	
" "	
On Plum Creek.	
On the San Marcos, below the old Bexar Road.	
On the Guadalupe, above Gonzales.	
" "	
On the San Marcos.	
N. of San Felipe Road.	
On a Creek which runs into the La Vaca.	
On the Guadalupe, below Gonzales.	
" above Gonzales,	
On the San Marcos, "	
On a Creek which runs into the La Vaca.	
On a branch of Tejocotes Creek.	
On Tejocotes and La Vaca.	
At the Falls of Tejocotes Creek,	
On the San Marcos, above Gonzales.	
On the Guadalupe, below Gonzales.	
" "	
" "	
On the San Marcos, above Gonzales.	
On the Guadalupe, above the La Bahia Road.	
" above Gonzales.	
" above the La Bahia Road.	
On the Guadalupe.	
On the La Vaca.	
On Tejocotes Creek.	
"	
"	
At the foot of a hill, dividing the waters of Tejocotes & Plum Creeks.	
On the Guadalupe, above Gonzales.	
San Marcos, above Gonzales.	
La Vaca Creek.	
San Marcos, above Plum Creek.	
On Tejocotes Creek.	
On the La Vaca.	
On Tejocotes Creek.	
On the Guadalupe, below Gonzales.	
On the San Marcos.	
On Tejocotes Creek, about 20 miles from Gonzales.	
On the head of Tejocotes Creek, 25 miles from Gonzales.	

ABSTRACT OF ORIGINAL TITLES

NAMES OF GRANTEES.	DATE OF TITLES.	Leagues.	Labors.
Abram Zumwalt,	Aug. 12, 1831.	1	-
Adam Zumwalt,	Nov. 23, "		24
"	Aug. 11, "		1
"	May 8, 1832.	1	-
Green De Witt, Empresario, received for his premium, 5 leagues and 5 labors, viz: -			
			1
			1
		1	-
		1	-
			2
		1	-
		1	-
		1	-
			1
Joseph Clements,	July 11, 1835.	1	-
"	" " "	1	-
"	" " "	1	-
J. Antonio Valdez y Gonzales,	Oct. 25, 1833.	1	-

WHERE SITUATED.						REMARKS.
On the San Marcos, above Gonzales.						
" "						
On the Guadalupe.						
On Tejocotes Creek.						
On the Guadalupe.	-	-	{ 621,250	*sq. varas for*	1 *lab.* }	
"	-	-	{ 880,000	"	" }	
"	above Gonzales.					*Concessions by the Gov. of the State.*
"	"					
"	"					
On the Guadalupe.						
"	above Gonzales.					
"	"					
On Berry Creek.	-	-	-	-	-	
Guadalupe, E. side.	-	-	-	-		
" "	-	-	-	-		Different places.
" "	-	-	-	-		
E. side of the Guadalupe, below No 15.						

16

A

LIST OF TITLES

ISSUED BY

JOSE JESUS VIDAURRI,

IN

POWERS & HEWETSON'S COLONY.

ABSTRACT OF ORIGINAL TITLES

NAMES OF GRANTEES.	DATE OF TITLES.	QUANTITY.	
		Leagues.	Labors.
Jose Miguel Aldrete,	Sept. 10, 1834.	1	- -
"	" 22, "	4	- -
"	" " "	1	- -
Jose Ma. Aldrete,	" " "	¼	- -
William Anderson,	Dec. 27, "	¼	- -
Samuel Blair,	Aug. 4, "	¼	- -
Isabella Brien,	" 10, "	1	- -
William Burk,	" 16, "	1	- -
Rosa Brown,	April 25, "	1	- -
Mary Byrne,	Oct. 8, "	1	- -
James Bray,	" 12, "	1¼	- -
Elkanah Brush and his sons, Gilbert, Russell & Bradford,	Oct. 31, " " 1, "	1 ¼	- - - -
Solon Bartlett,	" 30, "	¼	- -
Caleb Bennet,	Nov. 13, "	1	- -
John Bowin,	" 15, "	1	- -
James Brown, for himself, L. Brown, and Wm. Hews,	" " " " " "	1 1	- - - -
William Bartels,	Nov. 20, "	¼	- -
Jose Manuel Blanco,	" 21, "	1	- -
James Burk,	" 25, "	¼	- -
Thomas Banuelos and his two sons-in-law,	" 24, "	1½	- -
Joseph Bartlett,	" 20, "	¼	- -
John Coughlin,	Sept. 2, "	1	- -
John Clarke,	" 5, "	1	- -
James Colleyer,	" 26, "	1½	- -
Thomas Connor,	" 28, "	1	- -
Robert Carlisle, for his two sons,	" 30, "	½	- -
Jose Maria Cobarrubias,	Oct. 28, "	1	- -
Jose Maria Cobian, & Gegorea and Andrew Devereux,	" 30, " " " "	¼ ½	- - - -
Robert Carlisle,	" 31, "	1	- -
Juan Cameron,	" " "	2	- -
Ignatio Castro, for himself, and the Orphans of Jerome Huizar,	Nov. 12, " " " "	1 1	- - - -
John Cassidy & James H. Mullen,	" 24, "	½	- -
Phebe Crain,	" 29, "	1	- -
Dolores Carbajal,	Dec. 17, "	1	- -
Jose Maria Castilla,	" 25, "	1	- -
Joseph Coffin,	Oct. 7, "	¼	- -
Andrew Devereux,	" 30, "	¼	- -
Joshua Davis,	Aug. 9, "	5¼	- -
John Dunn,	Oct. 8, "	1	- -
Guad. Careaga de Cobian, and her two sons,	" 25, " " " "	¼ 1¼	- - - -
Catalina Dugan,	" 21, "	1	- -
Benjamin Dale,	" 30, "	1	- -
Patrick Downey for his sons, Richard, John and Patrick,	Nov. 25, "	¾	- -
James Douglas,	" 28, "	1	- -
John Daly,	" 20, "	¼	- -
Patrick Downey,	Sept. 15, "	1	- -
Francis Dieterich, Juan Andres Baumacker, and Wm. Langenheim,	Nov. 24, "	¾	- -
Robert Eyles,	" 20, "	1	- -

WHERE SITUATED.	REMARKS.
Aransas, lower line.	
" commencing on the River at M. De Leon's Ranch.	
Reference to a map of land for Miguel Aldrete, for description.	
" " "	
Aransas, joins the lands of O. Reilly.	
Agua Sarca, E. side.	
" " joins Scott's.	
Aransas, next to Jeremiah Toll's Sons.	
Aransas.	
On the San Antonio.	
Junction of Blanco Creek, and Agua Sarca.	
Sarca Creek. joins E. with P. Villas, S. C. Winchester, and Smily.	
" joins S W. with Murphy, S. E. with C. Winchester, and N. E. with C. Brush.	
Sarca Creek, joins Sarah Hall, Devereux and Bewett.	
Is the forfeited league granted Elliot Ward, and joins Thos. Holden.	
Papalote Creek.	
Melon Creek, joins with the lands of Malone.	
On Middle Creek.	
Aransas, joins James Douglass, the Germans, and others.	
San Antonio, joins the lands of James Power.	
Aransas, joins the Germans and Wm. Quinn.	
" joins Holden, Robinson and Hart.	
Coleto, joins the lands of E. Townsend & Co.	
Agua Sarca, E. side, joins Scott's half league.	
On Middle Creek.	
One league on San Antonio, low down; half a league on the Saus or Willow Creek.	
On Saus Creek,	
" - - - - -	One-fourth each.
On the Coleto.	
Sarca and a Creek which runs into the same above the Blanco Creek.	
Saus Creek.	
Papolote Creek, joins Benj. Dale and B. Quinn.	
On the San Antonio.	
"	Renounced in favor of Dona Iginia Estrade.
" - - - - -	
On the Aransas, joins the Germans,	
" joins the land of James Coffin.	
On the San Antonio, joins Mrs. Y. Nez Rene.	
Middle Creek, joins the land of Maximo Gomez.	Transferred to P. Scott.
On the Agua Sarca Creek. - - - -	
Sarca, and a creek which runs into the same, above the Blanco Creek.	Concession to J. V. Campos,
On the San Antonio. - - - -	
"	
Saus Creek, joins Aldrete.	
" on Chocolate Creek.	
Magerero Creek, joins N. E. with C. Murphy's.	
Papalote Creek.	
Aransas, joins Lambert's lands.	
Papalote, joins the Germans, and Felix and Thos. Hart.	
Coleto, joins the lands of Joseph Bartlet.	
Aransas, next Garret Roach's Sons.	
On Aransas, joins lands of Hart, Douglas, Quin & Co.	
Middle Creek, joins the lands of Juan Rene, Mrs. Huizar, & M. Knight.	

ABSTRACT OF ORIGINAL TITLES

NAMES OF GRANTEES.	DATE OF TITLES.	QUANTITY.	
		Leagues.	Labors.
Patrick Fitzsimmons,	Sept. 26, 1834.	1½	-
Miguel Fox,	Nov. 25, "	1	-
Nicholas Fagan, for himself,	Sept. 22, "	1	-
for his son James,	" " "	¼	-
for his son John,	" " "	¼	-
Thomas Galan,	Oct. 4, "	1¼	-
Juan Gonzales,	" 15, "	1	-
Jacinto Maria de La Garza,	" 23, "	1	-
Carlos de la Garza, himself, for his son Rafael,	" 28, "	1¼	-
Pedro Gallardo,	Oct. 30, "	1	-
Julian de la Garza, for himself, for his daughter and 3 sons,	Nov. 15, "	2¾	-
Cayetano Garza,	" " "	1	-
Maximo Gomes,	Dec. 20, "	1	-
Jose Maria Galban,	Oct. 30, "	1	-
Francisco Gonzales,	" 13, "	1	-
John Haynes & Peter Haynes,	Sept. 9, "	1¼	-
Robert Patrick Hearn, himself and son James,	Oct. 24, "	1¼	-
Sarah Hall,	" 31, "	1	-
John Hart, for himself and his three sons,	" 10, "	1¾	-
Timothy Hart as heir,	Nov. 20, "	1	-
for his mother and himself,	" " "	¼	-
James Hewetson,	" 19, "	¼	-
"	" " "	1	-
Thomas Holden,	" 22, "	1	-
Felix Hart, himself,	" " "	1	-
his son Timothy,	" " "	¼	-
Thomas Hay, himself, and his son Cornelius,	" 27, "	1¼	-
Manuel Hernandes,	" 28, "	2	-
Elizabeth Hart,	Dec. 29, "	1	-
George H. Hall, William Holly, Wm. D. Crane, and Edward Townsend,	Nov. 20, "	1	-
John James,	Oct. 25, "	1	-
Peter Kehoe,	Dec. 29, "	1	-
Charles Kelly,	Sept. 27, "	¼	-
John Kelly,	" " "	¼	-
John Keating,	Oct. 10, "	1	-
"	" 2, "	½	-
Estavan Lopes,	Sept. 3, "	1	-
Martin Lawler,	Nov. 20, "	¼	-
Victor Loupy,	" 26, "	1	-
Walter Lambert,	" 27, "	1	-
William Lavery,	" 25, "	1	-
John Malone,	Sept. 6, "	1	-
Michael Martin & John Tool,	" 12, "	¾	-
Thomas Mullen,	" 18, "	1	-
James M'Geehans,	" 21, "	1	-
Edward M'Donough,	Oct. 15, "	1	-
Miguel Musques,	" 23, "	1	-
George M'Knight,	" 18, "	¼	-
George Morris,	" 27, "	1	-

WHERE SITUATED.	REMARKS.

On Saus Creek.
Middle Creek.
On the San Antonio.
  "
  "
Saus Creek.
On the Guadalupe.
On the Aransas.
On the San Antonio, both sides, joins N. E. with C. Murphy's.
On the Coleto, joins Francisco Gonzales on the S. E.
Ramirena Lake, joins Cayetano Garza's land.
Nueces, joins Julian de la Garza.
Middle Creek, joins Mrs. Y. Nez Rene.
On the Coleto, joins the land of Francisco Gonzales.
  "   joins Jose Maria Galban.
On the San Antonio.
Melon Creek.
Agua Sarca.
Ramirena Lake, joins Laurenade de la Cruz, and Julian de la Garza.
Aransas and Papalote, joins Wm. Quin & Douglas.
  "   joins the lands of his nephew, Timothy Hart, and son Felix, and the Germans.
On Melon Creek, joins lands of the Empresarios.
  "   touches Copano Creek on the N. E. side.
On the Aransas, joins lands of Robertson, Boyle and O'Bryan.
On the Papalote, joins lands of Robertson & Duylan.
Aransas, joins the lands of Timothy Hart.
On Blanco Creek, joins lands of C. Moga.
San Antonio, joins lands of J. Davis, and Wm. Robertson.
Aransas.
On the Coleto, joins lands of Joseph Bartlet, Huizar Quin, & Rene.
Blanco Creek.
On the Aransas.
  "   below, joins Rosa Brown.
On the Blanco.
On the San Antonio.
On the Blanco Creek, contiguous to M'Donough's.
Saus & Mission Creeks, at the junction.
On the San Antonio, joins lands of Juan Rine, Mrs. Huizar, and M. Night
Papalote Creek, joins lands of O'Connor, Power & Boyle.
On the Aransas.
On the Blanco Creek, joins lands of Murphy.
Arroyo Trevino, joins J. Scott.
Aransas, J. Tool, above.
On Blanco Creek, next Roach's.
On the Blanco.
On the Guadalupe and Coleto.   } Refer to map for description.
On the San Antonio.
joins N. with C. Peland, E. with the same, and S. with C. Fitzsimmons.

NAMES OF GRANTEES.	DATE OF TITLES.	QUANTITY. Leagues.	Labors.
Edward Murphy and his sons, William & James,	Oct. 28, 1834.	1½	-
Malcom M'Auly,	" 30,. "	1	-
James Henry Mullen,	Nov. 24, "	¼	-
Sam. W. M'Camley,	" 30, "	1	-
James M'Cune,	" " "	1	-
Juan Moya,	Sept. 20, "	1¼	-
Augustin Moya,	Nov. 30, "	¼	-
Marcos Marchand,	Dec. 30, "	1¼	-
Domingo Morris,	Oct. 30, "	1¼	-
James O'Reily,	Sept. 11, "	1	-
Miguel O'Donnell,	Oct. 15, "	1	-
James O'Connor,	Nov. 15, "	¼	-
Hugh O'Brien,	" 22, "	1	-
Dan'l & John O'Boyle,	" 24, "	1	-
"	" " "	¼	-
Michael O'Donnel,	Sept. 26, "	1	-
James Power,	" 5, "	1	-
Martin Power,	" 29, "	1	-
Edward Perry,	" 22, "	1	-
James Power & James Hewetson, as Empresarios, received the following lands:	" 15, "	4	-
	" " "	2	-
	" " "	1	-
	" " "	¼	-
John Pollan,	Oct. 30, "	1	-
James Power & James Hewetson,	" 12, "	2	-
" "	" " "	2½	-
Rouge Felipe Portilla,	" 23, "	1	-
" for his 4 sons,	" " "	1	-
Juan Caliste Francisco, & Encarnacion,	" " "	4	-
Same, for his sons, Jose, Maria, & Felipe,	" " "	½	-
James Power & James Hewetson, as Empresariss, received the following lands:	Oct. 30, "	5½	-
	" " "	2½	-
	" " "	1	-
	" " "	1	-
Juan Pobedano,	Sept. 10, "	1	-
James Power & his son James,	Oct. 20, "	1	-
James Power for himself and Partner, James Hewetson,	Nov. 22, "	2½	-
	" " "	1¼	-
	" " "	1	-
James Power,	" 28, "	11	-
James Power & James Hewetson, Empresarios,	Dec. 20, "	5	-
James Power and his Partner, James Hewetson,	Nov. 20, "	6	-
	" " "	5	-
Bridget Quinn,	Oct. 12, "	1	-
Edmund Quirk & Son,	" 30, "	1¼	-
William and Patrick Quinn,	Nov. 20, "	½	-
William Quinn,	" 22, "	¼	-
Thomas Quirk,	Oct. 25, "	¼	-
William Quinn,	Dec. 25, "	1	-
Anastacia Reojas,	Sept. 1, "	1	-
Garret Roache,	" 13, "	1	-
John Roache,	" 16, "	¼	-
William Redmund & William M'Gill,	" " "	½	-
Maria & Ann Roache,	" " "	1	-

IN THE GENERAL LAND OFFICE. 73

WHERE SITUATED.	REMARKS.
Mugerero Creek, joins S. E. with Dugan.	
Joins Peland and Fitzsimmons' lands.	
Aransas, joins lands of the Germans, and Casidy.	
San Antonio, joins lands of M'Cune.	
San Antonio, joins Sam'l W. M'Camley.	
Blanco Creek, joins lands of J. Hays, M. Fox, and E. Quirk.	
Joins lands of his father, Juan Moya - - -	{ Included in the above title.
On Copano Bay.	
On Sarca Creek.	
On the Aransas, joins J. Tool's land.	
Sarca Creek.	
Papalote Creek, joins Quin, Boyle and Loupy's lands.	
" joins lands of Brown, Holden and Robinson.	
On Cruz Lake, joins lands of Victor Loupey, O'Connor and Morris.	
On the Aransas, joins lands of O'Brien and Holden.	
Blanco Creek.	
Agua Sarca, joins J. Sinnot.	
Saus Creek.	
San Antonio.	
At Live Oak Point.	
Melon Creek.	
" lies on Copano Harbor.	
Between the Rio Blanco and Refugio Village.	
On Aransas, joins Morris & Malcom.	
San Antonio, joins land of Keating and Serna.	
" "	
Aransas.	
"	
"	
"	
"	
" joins N. with that river and Felipe Rouge Portillas' lands.	
Mission Creek, joins N. with the Mission Village, E. with Melon Creek.	
Melon Creek, joins N. with lands of same proprietors, S. with C. Hearn.	
" joins N. with C. Hearns, S. with lands of same proprietors.	
On the Aransas	
Almeto, or Copano Creek, joins Hewetson's lands.	
On the lakes which are on the Aransas, joins Gallen and Aldrete.	
On the Aransas, joins lands of Loupy and Portilla.	
On the Chiltepin, joins with lands of Boyle, Pollan and Portilla.	
Corpus Christi Lakes, joins lands of John Hart, & Live Oak Point Tract.	{ Purchased of Francisco de la Penas.
On the San Josefa Island and Part of Matagorda Island.	
On the Nueces, joins lands of Jeremiah Villareal.	
On Chiltepin Creek, joins lands of Polland and M'Auly.	
On Papalote Creek.	
On Blanco Creek.	
On Papalote.	
On the Aransas, joins lands of Burk, Hart and the Germans.	
On middle Creek, joins E. Quirk, Michael Fox and O'Donnell.	
On the Aquilla Creek, joins N. with settlers on the Papalote Creek.	
On Mission River, below Refugio, joins Antonio Vina.	
On the Aransas, joins Wm. Burk.	
On the Aransas.	
Agua Sarca, joins Sam'l Blair.	
On Mission River, joins Thos. Mullen.	

17

ABSTRACT OF ORIGINAL TITLES

NAMES OF GRANTEES.	DATE OF TITLES.	QUANTITY.	
		Leagues.	Labors.
Florentine Rios,	Aug. 28, 1834.	1	-
Michael Reiley,	Sept. 10, "	1	-
William Robertson,	" 24, "	1	-
Leonardo Rodrigues & D. Nira,	Oct. 15, "	2	-
Maria Josefa Rios,	" 12, "	1	-
Francisco Ramon,	" 20, "	1	-
Juan Rener and his son,	" 28, "	$1\frac{1}{4}$	-
Y. Nes Rene,	Sept. 16, "	1	-
Isaac Robinson,	Nov. 20, "	1	-
James Reynolds,	" 30, "	$\frac{1}{4}$	-
Leonardo Rodrigues, for his sons Francisco and Jose Maria,	Dec. 4, "	$\frac{1}{2}$	-
John Sinnott,	Aug. 6, "	1	-
Thomas Scott,	Sept. 2, "	$\frac{1}{4}$	-
John Scott,	" " "	1	-
Edmund St. John,	" 3, "	1	-
Patrick Shelly,	" 13, "	$\frac{1}{4}$	-
John Shelly,	" " "	1	-
John Scott,	" 16, "	$\frac{1}{4}$	-
James and William St. John,	" 29, "	$\frac{1}{2}$	-
Santiago Serna,	Oct. 29, "	1	-
"	" 16, "	3	-
Santiago Serna, as agent for Juan Flores & M. Menchaca,	" 20, "	2	-
Anthony Sideck,	" 27, "	1	-
John B. Sideck,	" 28, "	1	-
Charles Smith, James Walmsley, John Smiley, and H. Winchester received the following lands:	" 30, "	$\frac{1}{4}$	-
	" " "	$\frac{1}{4}$	-
	" " "	$\frac{1}{4}$	-
	" " "	$\frac{1}{4}$	-
John M. Sherry, for his son Joseph Lewis Sherry,	Oct. 28, "	$\frac{1}{4}$	-
Charles Shearn, for himself and son John,	" 31, "	1	-
	" " "	$\frac{1}{4}$	-
Miguel de los Santos,	Dec. 20, "	1	-
Jeremiah Tool,	Sept. 11, "	1	-
Josefa Maria Traviezo,	Oct. 8, "	1	-
Peter Teal,	" 13, "	1	-
John Toole,	Nov. 24, "	$\frac{1}{4}$	-
Victoriano Tares & P. Villarreal,	" 26, "	2	-
Antonio de la Vina,	Sept. 9, "	1	-
Jose Maria Valdez,	Oct. 8, "	$1\frac{1}{4}$	-
T. Vairin & Augustin L. Fernet,	" 29, "	1	-
Pedro Villa, for himself and his Son,	" 14, "	1	-
	" " "	$\frac{1}{2}$	-
Sacarias Villarreal,	Nov. 26, "	$\frac{1}{4}$	-
Ira Westover,	Sept. 22, "	1	-
Elliott Ward,	" 14, "	1	-

IN THE GENERAL LAND OFFICE. 75

WHERE SITUATED.	REMARKS.
On San Antonio River.	
"	
"	
On the Guadalupe.	
On the Arroyo Sarco.	
On the Guadalupe.	By his Agent, Santiago Serna.
On the Coleto Creek.	
On the San Antonio, joins lands of J. Castro.	
On the Papalote, joins lands of Banuelos, Holden, O'Bryan & Hart.	
On the Coleto Creek, joins lands of Juan Rene, and others.	
San Antonio, joins lands of Valdez, Byrne, and others.	
On the Agua Sarca, joins Edmund St. John.	
On the Agua Sarca, E. side, joins his father, John Scott.	
" E. side.	
" "	
" S. of John Shelly,	
" joins R. and M. M'Gill.	
On the Agua Sarca.	
On Blanco Creek, next John Kelly.	
San Antonio River,	
"	
" joins Galban, M'Donough and others.	
On the San Antonio River.	
"	
On the Sarca Creek.	First piece.
"	
"	Second piece.
"	
" joins Morris and Sarah Hall.	
" joins Dugan, Bray, and Devereux's lands.	
" joins Mrs. Rios' lands.	
On Middle Creek, joins Roache & Tool.	
On the Aransas.	
On the Guadalupe, joins Jose Maria Valdez.	
On the San Antonio River.	
On the Papalote, joins lands of Bowin & Benjamin Dale.	
On the Potrero of Ramirena Lake, joins lands of Hart, the Empresario, and Julian de la Garza.	
On Mission River, below Refugio.	
Between the San Antonio and Guadalupe Rivers.	
On the Guadalupe, joins N. E. with Fernet.	
On Sarca Creek, joins N. W. with C. Brush.	
" joins S. with C. Morris.	
On the Nueces River.	
On the San Antonio River.	
Agua Sarca.	

A

LIST OF TITLES

ISSUED

BY THE COMMISSIONER,

GEORGE W. SMYTH,

IN

VARIOUS PLACES, IN
1835.

ABSTRACT OF ORIGINAL TITLES

NAMES OF GRANTEES.	DATE OF TITLES.	Leagues.	Labors.
Jose Mariano Acosta,	Sept. 14, 1835.	1	-
Durham Avant,	Oct. 26, "	1	-
Adam Byarly,	" 2, "	¼	-
William Brewer,	Sept. 9, "	⅓	-
Stephen Burnham,	" 12, "	⅓	-
Jonathan Bittuck,	Oct. 23, "	½	-
William Charles Brookfield,	" 26, "	⅓	-
William Barnhill,	" 14, "	1	1
Radford Berry,	" " "	⅔	-
Green Berry Brewer,	" 26, "	1	-
Henry Blossom,	" 10, "	1	-
John Bush,	Dec. 5, "	⅓	-
John M. Bradley,	Nov. 22, "	1	-
Milly Berry,	" 20, "	1	-
Juan Comunes,	Aug. 24, "	1	-
Juana Berger de Cadena,	" 28, "	1	-
Maria de los Angelos Carmona,	" 11, "	1	-
Francisco Cordova,	" 26, "	1	-
Francisco Castro,	Sept. 7, "	1	-
John Chism,	Oct. 24, "	⅓	-
Damian Cordova,	Nov. 30, "	1	1
Antonio Calderon,	" 5, "	⅓	-
Robert Clever,	" 21, "	⅓	-
Elizah Clark,	" 4, "	¼	-
James C. Cain,	" 26, "	⅓	-
Jose Cervantes,	" 2, "	1	1
John Cartwright,	" 29, "	-	24
"	" " "	-	1
James Clark,	Dec. 26, "	1	1
Benjamin Clark,	" 16, "	1	1
Jose Sebastian Castro,	" 11, "	¼	-
John Cotton,	Dec. 7, "	1	-
William Creager,	" 16, "	1	1
Obadiah Denman,	Sept. 24, "	⅓	-
John M. Dor,	" 10, "	1	1
Maria Vicente Dias,	Nov. 20, "	1	1
Luvick P. Dikes,	" 11, "	1	1
Augustin Dias,	" 26, "	⅓	-
Paul Dry,	" 4, "	1	1
John F. Dry,	" 26, "	1	1
Daniel Dry,	" " "	1	1
George H. Duncan,	Dec. 5, "	1	-
John B. Dillard,	" 12, "	-	24
Patrick Dougherty,	Oct. 29, "	1	1
John Dry,	Nov. 27, "	1	1
Maria Gertrudis Estrada,	Aug. 11, "	1	-
Haden H. Edwards,	Oct. 28, "	⅓	-
Wilson Ewing,	" 29, "	1	1
Felix Flores,	Aug. 11, "	1	-
Maria Finolia Flores,	Sept. 22, "	1	1
A. M. Fuller,	" 12, "	1	-
Franklin Fuller,	Oct. 12, "	1	-
Sabastian Francis,	" 10, "	1	-
Joshua Fulcher,	Nov. 21, "	1	-
Isaac H. Fishback,	Dec. 15, "	1	1
Clerry Gillet,	Oct. 22, "	1	1

IN THE GENERAL LAND OFFICE. 79

WHERE SITUATED.	REMARKS.

On the Neches, N. of Bean's saline.
W. of the Trinity River, on the Cumanche Trail.
On Sandy Creek, N. side, Bevil's Settlement.
On the Angelina River, joins Juan Baptiste Mansola.
Three miles from the Neches River, and 3 miles from the S. A. Road.
E. bank of Tenneha Bayou, half a mile below Bittuck & Alford's mills.
Twelve miles S. E. of Lake Sodo.
Eight miles N. of Sabine River, joins J. L. Travena.
On Red River, including Sassafras Bluffs.
On the Cumanche Road, 30 miles W. of Kechie Village, and vicinity of Trinity River.
About 14 miles N. E. of Sabine, on the Caddoe Trail.
Thirty-five or 40 miles N. of the Sabine, joins Maria Damacia Ramizes.
Tenneha District.
About 3 miles N. of Sabine River.
On the waters of the Angelina, joins Juan Herminez.
On the waters of the Angelina River, joins Ma. Josefa Pru.
Six miles from the Sabine.
On the waters of the Angelina, joins Ma. Josefa Pru.
On the waters of the Sabine, joins Dinsmore.
South West of Wilson Ewing.
Joins S., M. Mora, about 12 or 13 miles N. of the Sabine.
In the vicinity of the Sabine, about 30 miles from Harris's survey.
W. of the Neches, 15 miles from the Salines.
About 25 miles from the Saline, in the vicinity of the Sabine.
In the vicinity of Red River, S. of the Caddoe Road.
On the waters of the Sulphur Fork, joins Alfred Raymond.
- - - - - -   No description.
On Buckley Creek.
In the vicinity of Choctaw Bayou, on a branch of Red River.
   "   "
In the vicinity of Red. 28 miles from the Sabine.
Mouth of the Sabine, joins Alvey R. Johnston.
On Bayou Palo Amarillo Bois d'Arc.
In the vicinity of Walnut Creek, which runs from the E. into the Neches.
Fifteen miles E. of the Sabine.
A short distance S. W. of Richland Creek, W. of the Trinity.
On the waters of Red River, about 13 miles N. of the main Caddoe Trial.
On Sulphur Fork, 75 miles N. E. of Saline, N. of Sabine.
On the waters of Sulphur Fork, N. W. of John Hillhouse.
  "   joins George Glass's survey.
In the vicinity of Sulphur Fork, joins George Glass's survey.
- - - - - -   A parallelogram.
S. of Quirk's survey.
- - - - - -   A square league.
On the waters of Sulphur Fork, in the vicinity of Red River.
Eight miles from the Sabine.
- - - - - -   No description.
              "
Six miles from the Sabine.
In the vicinity of the Sabine River.
Six miles from Lake Sodo.
Five or 6 miles S. of Sodo Lake.
At the mouth of Mineral Creek, on the S. or W. side of Red River.
Twenty miles S. of Lake Sodo, between Sabine and Red Rivers.
At the head of Saunder's Creek, joins Sublett on Bee Bayou.
Fifteen miles E. of the Sabine, joins John M. Dor.

ABSTRACT OF ORIGINAL TITLES

NAMES OF GRANTEES.	DATE OF TITLES.	QUANTITY.	
		Leagues.	Labors.
Peter Glass,	Nov. 4, 1835.	1	1
George Glass,	" 25, "	1	1
John Grigg,	Dec. 16, "	1	1
James Harris,	Oct. 10, "	1	-
Francis Hamilton,	" 12, "	1	-
David Hoofman,	" 22, "	1	1
Henry Harper,	" 13, "	1	-
Hudson Hall,	" 27, "	$\frac{1}{3}$	-
Seth Hard,	" 14, "	1	-
John Hardison,	" 10, "	1	1
John Humble,	Nov. 20, "	1	-
Allen Hines,	" 28, "	1	-
John Hillhouse,	" 3, "	1	1
James E. Hopkins,	Dec. 17, "	1	1
James Humphreys,	" 4, "	1	1
James L. Houghteling	Nov. 19, "	$\frac{1}{3}$	-
Abraham Ives,	" 17, "	1	-
Alvey R. Johnson,	Sept. 21, "	1	-
Benjamin F. Jones,	Oct. 20, "	1	1
Crawford Jones,	Nov. 26, "	1	1
Lewis Jones,	" 17, "	1	1
Gray B. King,	Sept. 20, "	1	1
James Kirkman,	Nov. 4, "	1	1
Isaac Lee,	Aug. 13, "	1	-
Marcelino Lazarin,	Sept. 17, "	1	1
Aniseta Lumbrera,	" 21, "	1	1
John Laramore,	Oct. 9, "	1	1
Polonio la Vina,	Nov. 26, "	$\frac{1}{3}$	-
Willey Lewis,	" 3, "	1	1
Stephen Lynch,	Dec. 15, "	1	1
Juan Batista Manzola,	Aug. 15, "	$\frac{1}{3}$	-
Estevan Mora,	Sept. 29, "	1	1
John Mathew,	Oct. 26, "	1	-
James M Clain,	" 12, "	1	-
William M'Ilvain,	" 10, "	$\frac{1}{3}$	-
Samuel Monday,	" 12, "	1	-
Samuel Murphey,	" 10, "	1	-
Daniel Martin,	Nov. 18, "	1	-
James Y. Mason,	" 20, "	1	-
Timothy Mohan,	" 21, "	1	-
John Missenham,	" 26, "	1	1
Jacob Missenham,	" 17, "	1	1
William C. M'Kinney,	Dec. 16, "	1	1
James M'Kinney,	" " "	1	1
Joseph Nations,	Oct. 4, "	$\frac{1}{3}$	-
Maria Conception Navarro,	Nov. 4, "	1	1
Nicholas Norbeck,	Dec. 1, "	1	1
Thomas Obar,	Oct. 13, "	1	-
Maria Vilarda Peña,	Aug. 27, "	1	-
Maria Josefa Pru,	" 26, "	1	-
G. H. Patterson,	Sept. 14, "		24
Maria Honoria Polvador,	" 19, "	1	1
John Paterson,	Oct. 28, "	$\frac{1}{3}$	-

WHERE SITUATED.	REMARKS.

On the waters of Sulphur Fork, N. W. of Paul Dry's survey.
" in the vicinity of Red River.
In the vicinity of Red River and Bee Bayou.
About 9 miles S. W. of Lake Sodo.
On Red River, four miles from a point called Cross Timber.
S. of the Sabine, joins Crushman and Powell.
About 13 miles W. from Lake Sodo.
Joins John Boyland.
Red River, opposite the mouth of the False Wachita.
Between Mineral Creek and Cross Timber, on the S. or W. side of Red River.
In the vicinity of the Neches, 12 miles from the Saline.
Joins Henry Whitesides.
On the waters of the Sulphur Fork, joins Peter Glass.
Joins John Gragg's survey.
S. of the Caddoe Trail, from their village to Red River.
N. of the Sabine, joins Frost Thorn's survey.
On the waters of Sulphur Fork.
Ten thousand varas from the Sabine, and 400 from Pecan Point Road.
In the vicinity of Big Cow Creek, joins the surveys of Holme and Jones.
Near the Caddoe Trail, between the Sabine and Red River.
On the waters of Sulphur Fork
League on the Sabine, joins J. Gains; labor joins Felipe Gonzales on the N. E.
On the waters of Sulphur Fork, in the vicinity of Red River.
Joins John Walling.
On the right bank of Red River.
In the vicinity of the Sabine.
In the Vicinity of Red River, joins Daniel Fuller.
About 11 miles E. of the Sabine.
On the waters of Sulphur Fork, joins Jno. Hillhouse.
On Red River.
On Cow Creek, joins Thos. Williams's survey.
In the vicinity of the Sabine.
On Sabine River, joins Francisco Castro.
About 4 miles from the Sabine, joins Lee, Dinsmore & Simpson.
Eleven miles E. of the Sabine,
Fourteen miles from Lake Sodo, joins Wm. Smith.
About eight miles S. W. of Lake Sodo, joins Elihu D. Spain and others.
On Hagan's Creek, on the waters of the Sabine.
Twenty-five miles S. of Lake Sodo, between Sabine and Red Rivers.
W. of the Neches, 5 miles from the Salines.
On the waters of the Sulphur Fork, vicinity of Red River.
" joins Alfred Raymond.
In the vicinity of Bayou Palo Amarillo.
Two hundred and fifty varas E. of Bayou Palo Amarillo.
On the Trammels Road, N. E. from Sabine.
In the vicinity of Red River, N. of Caddoe Road.
League N. of the Sabine, joins Maria Josefa Cordova; labor joins Felipe Gonzales.
On the Sabine River, joins Walling.
On the waters of the Angelina River, joins M. B. de Cordova.
On the Waters of the Angelina River, joins Juan Trimenez.
In the vicinity of the Sabine River.
"
Joins John Roland.

ABSTRACT OF ORIGINAL TITLES

NAMES OF GRANTEES.	DATE OF TITLES.	Leagues.	Labors.
William Patton,	Oct. 10, 1835.	$\frac{1}{3}$	-
Aaron Poe,	" " "	1	-
Pedro del Rio,	Aug. 11, "	1	-
Noel G. Roberts,	Sept. 8, "	1	1
Eligio Roberts,	" 7, "	1	-
Manuel Antonio Romero,	" 16, "	1	1
Bethany Rodgers,	Oct. 15, "	1	-
James Robertson,	" 12, "	1	1
Alfred Raymond,	" 14, "	1	1
Francisco de Rojo,	Nov. 21, "	1	-
John E. Rose,	" 27, "	1	1
José de Jesus Ramierez,	" 4, "	$\frac{1}{3}$	-
John Raymond,	" 26, "	1	1
Michael Sacco,	Sept. 23, "		24
Dinsmore Simpson,	" 5, "	1	-
Phillip A. Sublett,	" 8, "		7,659,972 vs.
Richard Slaughter,	" 3, "	1	-
Elihu D. Spain,	Oct. 10, "	1	-
William Smith,	" 12, "	1	-
Isaac C. Skillern,	" 28, "	1	1
Jose Maria Servantes,	" 4, "	$\frac{1}{3}$	-
Pedro Servantes,	" " "	$\frac{1}{3}$	-
John Strange,	" 26, "	1	1
Jose Sanches,	" " "	$\frac{1}{3}$	-
William Sanders,	" 4, "	1	1
George Sanders,	" 15, "	1	1
Amos Stephens,	Dec. 11, "	1	-
Jacob Sterling,	" 18, "	1	1
Frost Thorn,	Aug. 25, "	1	-
Thomas G. Timmins,	Sept. 22, "	$\frac{1}{4}$	-
Maria del Pillar Tores,	" " "	1	1
Charles S. Taylor,	Oct. 30, "	1	-
John Taylor,	" 12, "	1	-
Josiah Thomas,	Nov. 26, "	1	1
George Tanner,	" " "	1	1
C. F. Thompson,	Dec. 5, "	1	1
Francisco Jacinto Vallanova,	Aug. 25, "	1	-
Manuel Vidales,	Sept. 11, "	$\frac{1}{3}$	-
George Vaughan,	Nov. 4, "	1	1
Daniel H. Vail,	Dec. 12, "	1	-
Richard Williams,	Oct. 22, "	1	1
John Walling,	Aug. 15, "	1	-
Russel Williamson,	Oct. 13, "	1	-
James T. White,	" 18, "	1	1
Alexander White,	Dec. 18, "	1	1
Juan Ximenes,	Aug. 31, "	1	-
Maria Telesfora Ybarbo,	Sept. 21, "	1	1
Miguel Ybarbo,	Oct. 12, "	1	-
John Yancey,	Aug. 11, "	$\frac{1}{3}$	-

WHERE SITUATED.	REMARKS.
Twelve miles E. of the Sabine.	
S. W. of Lake Sodo, N. E., joins Hiram Blossom.	
Seven or eight miles from the Sabine.	
Eight miles from San Augustine.	
E. of San Augustine, joins John Cartwright.	
League on the Sabine, labor on the Angelina.	
Joins H. Whitesides.	
On Red River, three miles from a point called Cross Timbers.	
On the waters of Sulphur Fork, joins the survey of J. F. Dry.	
Twelve miles from the Sabine, W. of the Neches.	
On the Trail from Red River to the Caddoe village.	
Eight or 10 miles N. of the Sabine, about 30 N. E. of Harris, and joins the survey of A Calderon..	
On the waters of Sulphur Fork, joins Abraham Ives.	
On the road from Nacogdoches to Bexar, joins S. Kelton,	
On the waters of the Sabine, joins Isaac Lee.	
Five miles from San Augustine, joins John Cartwright.	
On Patron Creek.	
About 7 miles E. of Lake Sodo.	
About 13 miles from Lake Sodo, joins Henry Harper.	
In the vicinity of the Sabine, joins John Cotton.	
In the vicinity of Red River, about 35 miles N. of the Caddoe Road, and 7 or 8 N. of the Sabine.	
In the vicinity of Red River, joins Mansola's survey.	
In the vicinity of Red River, the Sabine, Lake Sodo, the Caddoe Trail, and the Prairies.	
Twelve miles E. of the Sabine.	
On the waters of Sulphur Fork, in the vicinity of Red River.	
" " " " "	
In the vicinity of Frost Thorn.	
On Gragg Creek. - - - - -	In two surveys.
On the Sabine, joins John Matthews.	
In the vicinity of the Neches River.	
In the vicinity of the Sabine.	
Fifteen miles S. of Lake Sodo, between Sabine and Red River.	
A little below the Sassafras Bluffs	
About 4 miles N. from the Sabine, near the Caddoe Road in the vicinity of Red River.	
Joins Jack Missenham, Sulphur Fork, in the vicinity of Red River.	
About 34 miles from the Saline, eight miles E. of the road from Nacogdoches.	
On the waters of the Angelina River, joins Isaac Kendrick.	
On the waters of the Angelina.	
On the waters of Sulphur Fork, joins John Dry.	
On the Neches, 2500 varas from Bean's Saline.	
On the W. side of the Sabine.	
On the Sabine, 800 varas below John Cotton's house.	
In the vicinity of the Sabine, joins Walling's survey.	
The league is N. of Daniel Pharis, and the labor is S. of William Isaac's survey.	
On the S. W. side of Red River, joins Linch.	
On the waters of the Angelina River.	
In the vicinity of the Sabine.	
On Red River, mouth of Mineral Creek.	
N. of Nacogdoches, joins the 3 leagues of the heirs of J. Cordova.	

A

LIST OF TITLES

ISSUED BY DIFFERENT

COMMISSIONERS AND ALCALDES,

AT NACOGDOCHES,

FROM

1791 TO 1835.

86 ABSTRACT OF ORIGINAL TITLES.

NAMES OF GRANTEES.	DATE OF TITLES.	Leagues.	Labors.
Antonio Arriola,	June 6, 1810.	1	-
Maria Josefa Arriola,	May 11, "	-	-
Juan de Acosta,	" 10, "	-	-
James Allen,	April 25, 1831.	¼	-
Juan Isidro Acosta,	Dec. 20, "	1	-
A. C. & J. K. Allen, Agents for Mariana Acosta,	April 24, 1834.	1	-
John K. Allen, as agent for Francisco Roxa,	Oct. 3, 1835.	4	-
John K. Allen, as agent for Antonio Ribas,	" 2, "	1	-
John K. Allen, as agent for Luciano Navarro,	" 5, "	3	-
John K. Allen, as agent for Jose M. de la Garza,	" 1, "	1	-
John K. & A. C. Allen, as agents for Jose Ign. Arrocha,	Sept. 3, "	1	-
John K. Allen, as agent for Manuel Zepeda,	Oct. 1, "	2	-
Jose Luis de la Bega,	May 31, 1792.	-	-
William Barr,	" 28, 1798.	-	-
Peter Elias Bean,	Aug. 13, 1828.	1	-
William Bean,	Sept. 24, "	1	-
Solomon Barrow,	April 25, 1831.		19,680,000 vs.
Shadrach Burney,	" 24, "	¼	-
Peter Elias Bean,	Sept. 26, 1833.	5¾	-
"	Dec. 14, "	2¼	-
Pierre Blanchet,	July 5, 1834.	2	-
"	" " "	1	-
"	" " 1835.		19,713,000 vs.
"	" " "		5,286,400 vs.
"		1	-
Peter Elias Bean, as agent for Jesus de la Garza,	April 5, 1834.	4	-
Barr & Davenport.	May 21, 1810.	1	-
Jose Luis de la Bega,	June 11, "	1	-
"	" 13, "		720,000 s. vs.
"	" 11, "	1½	-
"	" 13, "	1	-
Manuel Bustamente,	May 26, 1810.		123,750 s. vs.
John H. Cummings,	June 29, 1834.	1	-
Francisco de Santa Cruz,	May 16, 1792.	1	-
Jose Antonio Chirino,	" 21, "		-
Nepomuceno de la Cerda,	" 3, "		-
Mariano Santa Cruz,	Aug. 31, 1794.		-
Jose Caro,	March 22, 1808.	-	-
Jose Cordova,	April 26, 1810.	-	-

WHERE SITUATED.	REMARKS.
On La Nana Creek, half league from Nacogdoches.	
One Rancho, on the Corriza, from N. to S., 1 league, joining F. Vialfando; on the E. one league.	
One Rancho 1½ leagues E. of Nacogdoches, from N. to S. 2500 varas, from E. to W. 3,000 varas, joins Ramon.	
On the Trinity, E., adjoining Jacob Geiger and James Miller.	
Waters of the Angelina, W. side Moral Creek.	Only one witness.
On Red River, 14 leagues below the mouth of the Kiamiche.	
On Sulphur fork.	
On Red River, adjoining Marcos Sanches.	
One league on Red River, and two on Sulphur fork, joins Jose Ma. de la Garza.	
On Red River, below the mouth of Grand Monte.	
On Red River, adjoining F. H. Rivere.	
Between Red River and the Sabine, S. of Lake Sodo.	
One place on the banks of the Angelina, measures on the E. side, 1½ leagues, is called chesnut place.	
Rancho on the Angelina, 8 leagues from Nacogdoches, adjoining Dortolan on the N. W., and S. side 2½ leagues.	
On the Neches, N. side, and Sireto Creek.	
" N. E. side.	
On Trinity, joining Benjamin Winfree.	
On Little Turtle Bayou, joins E. H. R. Wallace, James Miller, & W. Taylor.	
On Galveston Bay, at the mouth of the Trinity.	
One league on Red River, 10 miles below the mouth of the Kiamiche, joining F. Ramires, 1 on the Saline in the vicinity of the Neches, one-fourth of a league on La Nana, joining Jose Cordova.	
On the left bank of the Trinity, above the Little Alabama Village, adjoining ¼ league of T. J. Chambers	
On the left bank of the Trinity, between Aaron Cherry & Joseph Fields.	
On the left bank of the Trinity, joins P. Miller and E. Turner.	
On Davis's Creek, between Trinity and Neches	
Between the Neches and Trinity, 18 miles from Long King's Village.	
On the waters of the Neches, E. side, 4 leagues above the S. A. Road.	
Rancho on the Angelina.	
Called "Botijar" joins Francisco de los Santos, on the W.	
Adjoining and S. of Nacogdoches.	
About one league N. of Nacogdoches.	
On La Nana Creek, near Nacogdoches.	
Half league from Nacogdoches.	Called "Rancho de los Aylitos."
On Carizo Creek, Mustang Prairie.	
On Alason's Creek, measures 1 league on the S. side.	
Grind Stone Creek, tributary of the Attoyac, measures 1½ leagues on one side.	
Rancho on the Angelina, joins Dima Moya and J. T. Guerro.	
Rancho measures on the S. W. and N. side, 1 league, and on the E. side 2 leagues.	
Rancho on the Attoyac.	
Rancho 3 leag's N. of Nacogdoches, joins M. Cruz & Pedro Padilla.	

88 ABSTRACT OF ORIGINAL TITLES

NAMES OF GRANTEES.	DATE OF TITLES.	QUANTITY.	
		Leagues.	Labors.
Martin Cruz,	May 28, 1810.	1	-
Manuel de los Santos Coy,	Dec. 2, 1833	7½	-
Jose de los Santos Coy,	April 30, 1810.	1	-
Christobal Chonca,	May 23, 1810.	1	-
Sántiago Cornichi,	July 7, 1826.	1	-
Rafael Caranza, and	April 10, 1829.	2	-
Ignacio Ramas Valdes, and	" " "	3	-
Ignacto Rodriguez, and	" " "	3	-
Eugenio Furundarena,	" " "	3	-
Jose Coronado,	" 12, 1831.	1	-
Matthew Cartwright, as agent for Carlos Gil,	April 17, 1834.	2	-
Francisco de Campredonde,	March 18, 1829.	2½	-
Manuel de los Santos Coy,	Aug. 20, 1827.	1	-
Thomas Dever,	May 11, 1831.	¼	-
Joseph Dunman,	April 24, "	1	-
Theodore Dorset,	May 4, "	1	-
William Duncan,	April 25, "	1	-
Juan Durst, as agent or purchaser of T. M. Mora,	Oct. 30, 1833.	9	-
Miguel Delgado,	Nov. 9, "	1	1
Jose Durst,	May 15, "	1	-
"	" 18, "	1	-
Andrew Dexter, as agent for Carlos O'Campo,	Dec. 16, 1835.	6	-
Bernardo Dortolan,	March 28, 1797.	1	-
Pedro Jose Esparsa	May 13, 1810.	1	-
Geronimo Equis,	May 22, 1810.	1	-
William Elliot,	March 22, 1829.	1	-
William Everett,	May 12, 1831.	1	-
A. Emanuel & A. Stern, as agents for Jesus Lefton.	Nov. 3, 1835.	1	-
Huden Edwards, as agent for Francisco Durse,	" 9, "	6	-
Jose Flores,	May 4, 1792.	4	-
Vital Flores,	July 15, 1829.	1	-
Pedro Falcon,	March 21, "		
Olago Frasestro,	" " "		-
Pedro Galindo,	" " "		-
Manuel de los Santos,	" " "		-
Antonio Valdes y Franco,	" " "		-
Antonio Rajas,	" 22, "		-
Widow of Rafel Romo,	" 21, "		-
Francisco Galindo,	" " "		-
Jose Maria Garcia,	" " "		-
Victor and Francisco Galindo,	" " "		-
Jose Ignacio Santos Coy and Galindo,	" " "		-
Eusebio Ramas,	" " "		-
Jose Maria Galindo,	" " "		-

WHERE SITUATED.	REMARKS.

Or Rancho 3 leagues N. of Nacogdoches, joins Jose Cordova.   -   { Called Llano, (Great Prairie.)
Four leagues on E. and W. side of the Trinity, 2½ on Sabine Lake, and   } Houston & Sublett
¼ on Red River.   { Agents.
Or place, 7 leag's N. of Nacogdoches, joins Jose Cordova and A. Arriola.
Or Rancho on the Palogacho, measures 1 league on each side.   -   Called Gertrudes.
Or Rancho on Ayish Bayou & Carizo; 3267 vs. on the N. & S. s., 7337 vs. on E., & 6593 on W. side.
One league in the Cove, and ¼ in the Potrero.   -
One & a ½ in the Cove, ½ in the the Potrero, & 1 leag. at the Ridge.   ⎫
One & a ½   "   ½   "   1   "   "   ⎬
One & a ½   "   ½   "   1   "   "   ⎭
On the Trinity, E, side, joining Benjamin W Hardin.

On Red River, 1 below the mouth of Pine Creek, joining G. Aranjo, the other below.

Potrero del Marques.
Or Rancho, on Loco Creek, joins Mariana Sanches.
Between the Trinity and Neches.
On the Trinity, E. side, adjoining Nathaniel Moss.
   "   W. side joining John Smith.
   "   W. s., adjoining L. Mason, E. Munson, and D. Minchey.

Four leagues in the vicinity of Red River, adjoining Carbajal's 5 league tract; 1 on the Neches, E. s., between the Neches and Angelina. two on the Ainai Creek, and one on the E. side of the Neches.

On Lake Sodo.
At his Rrancho, 8 leagues N. of Nacogdoches.
Adjoining and N. of Juan Tovar.

Caney Creek and Carizo.

On Loco Creek, four leagues from Nacogdoches, the Mission, and the Old Presidio.   Certified copy.
Rancho Llano Grande, On the La Nana fm. N. to S. one league, joins A San Miguel and Jose de la Bega.
One place, 1 league from Nacogdoches, on the La Nana.
On the Carizo and Angelina, 8 leagnes N. of Nacogdoches joining F. Williams.
On the Trinity, W. side, joins Richard Green and Wm, Swail.

On Bayou Pierre, about 20 miles from Red River, or Coat's Bluff.

On Cypres Bayou, waters of Red River, joining Frost Thorn.

Four Leagues N. of Nacogdoches, measures on all sides 2 leagues.   -   Certified copy.
On the Carrizo, 2 leagues E. of Nacogdoches.   -   -   { Certified copy of a renewed title.
On lakes fed by two inlets of water.

One piece situated between a pond and its outlet.

Lot 17, 500 square varas.
One lot on 3 lakes, 625 square varas, means, probably, 2 pieces of land.   } See remarks on page 92.
One lot, 750 square varas.
One lot, Five thousand square varas.
Two pieces of land, 16,000 & 5,000.
One piece of land, 7,000.
One piece of land, 4,900.
Two pieces, both, 19,900.

ABSTRACT OF ORIGINAL TITLES

NAMES OF GRANTEES.	DATE OF TITLES.	QUANTITY.	
		Leagues.	Labors.
Francisco Casares,	March 21, 1829.		
Matias Valdes,	" " "		
Eusebio Ramas,	" " "		
Victor Galindo,	" " "		
Pedro Gengle,	May 6, 1792.		
James Gains,	April 3, 1830.	1	
Henry Griffith,	" 25, 1831.	1	
Amos Green,	May 2, "	1	
William and Milton Garrett, agents for Jose Felo. Gonzales,	Oct. 13, 1835.	1	
Francisco Guerero,	June 26, 1810.		
Baltazar de la Garza,	July 27, 1803.		
James A. Hines,	April 7, 1830.	$\frac{1}{4}$	
Augustin B. Hardin,	May 11, 1831.	$\frac{1}{2}$	
William H. Hodges,	" 4, "	1	
William Harris,	" 10, "	1	
Joseph Hertz, as agent for Lewis Lefton.	July 31, 1835.	1	
John W. Haney,	Oct. 20, "	1	1
Renjamin Watson Hardin,	May 11, 1831.	1	
Franklin Hardin,	" 12, "	$\frac{1}{4}$	
Hugh B. Johnston,	" 3, "	1	
Helena Kimble, widow of J. Dill,	July 26, 1828.	4	
James Knight,	May 9, 1831.	1	
Antonio Leal,	Feb. 19, 1810.		
Jose Lucobichi,	June 20, 1802.		
Polonia Matilda Valdes Lopez, " Olays Fraestro, " Manuel de los Santos, and Polonio Rodrigues,	June 29, 1829.	5	
W. G. Logan, Agent for Jesus Cantu,	Sept. 11, 1835.	5	
William G. Logan and Henry Raguet, as Agents for J. A. Stockman,	April 23, 1834.	2	
William G. Logan, as Agent for Anthony Huizar,	Oct. 9, 1835.	1	
Ramon de Legarreta,	Jan. 15, 1804.		
Vicente Micheli,	June 9, 1810.	$\frac{3}{4}$	
Jacinto Mora,	Dec. 10, 1795.	6	
Edward Murphy,	Oct. 18, 1791.		
Nicolas de Mora,	May 11, 1792.		1
Vicente Micheli,	June 20, 1797.	2	
Edward Murphy,	Aug. 20, 1798.		
San Augustin Miguel,	April 28, 1810.		
Tomas Mansola,	" " "		
Jose Maria Mora,	Dec. 10, 1824.		

WHERE SITUATED.	REMARKS.

One piece 6,000.
" 7,800.
" 19,250.
One Ancon, probably measures a piece of land that may easily be irrigated.
One lot, 40 varas front and 71 deep, & adjoining the lot of Juan Flores.
On the W. side of the Sabine.
On Old River, adjoining widow Self and David Minchey.
On the Trinity, adjoining James Robeson.
On Red River, below the mouth of Yellow Stake Creek, adjoining Jesus Cantu.
One place on the Atoyac, 10 leag's from Nacogdoches, on the E. & S. s., 3 leagues, adjoining Theresa Mora, Rafael Richero, and R. Querpens.
One Rancho called Jose San, on the W. & E. half leag., adjoining N. de la Serda & G. Ybarbo.
On the Palo Gacho, N. side.
On the Trinity, E. side, adjoining Franklin Hardin and H. B. Johnston.
On Old River, adjoining Charles Filton.
On the E. side of the Trinity, adjoining widow Self and David Minchey
On Red River, adjoining Mariano and Manuel Lopez's 11 leag. grant.
On Sulphur Fork.
On the Trinity, E. side, adjoining George Orr.
On the Trinity, E. side, above Sam Strong.
On the E. side of the Trinity, adjoining the widow Hardin.
On the Angelina, adjoining Barr & Davenport.
On the Trinity, E. side, joins Amos Green.
One Rancho on Ayish Bayou.
One Rancho, called after duraznos, (peaches) one league on each side. djoining Estevan Gauguete.

On the Potrero Santo Monico.

Three, 9 miles from Lake Sodo, and 25 miles from Coate's Bluffs, and 2 in the vicinity of Sassafras and Williams's Bluff.

On the W. side of Red River, adjoining Pollet and Stiddon.

On Red River.
One place, called after the Sereto, in the vicinity of the Neches, 5 leagues each side.
E. side of the Angelina.
At a place called after Ormigos, 25 leagues from Nacogdoches.
One Rancho on Jundo Creek, which separates the two provinces.
On Cariso Creek, measures on 2 sides, 523 vs., joins Maria Padilla, and Mora.
On the Sabine, measuring on each side, two leagues.
One place on the La Nana, on the Road from Nacogdoches to Natchitoches, about 7 leagues from the Sabine.
One place from N. to S. 3,500 varas, and from W. to E. 4050 varas.
One Rancho five leagues from Nacogdoches, on the Angilina, joining Barr and Davenport, and E. Grogate.
Two Ranchos on Atascoja Creek.

Remarks:
These, and the 14 names on the preceding page, are all included in one title. W. of the Rio Grande.

Certified copy.

Certified copy.
"

ABSTRACT OF ORIGINAL TITLES

NAMES OF GRANTEES.	DATE OF TITLES.	Leagues.	Labors.
Elizabeth Munson, - -	May 3, 1831.	1	- -
James M'Fadden, - -	April 26, 1831.	1	
David Minchey, - - -	May 10, "	1	
Thomas F. M'Kinney, as agent for Joaquin F. de Rumayor,	April 25, "	6	
Martin Murchison, purchased of J. M. Procela,	Feb. 7, 1833.	1	
Pedro J. Menard, as agent for Joaquin F. de Rumayor,	March 15, 1834.	2	
M. B. Menard, as agent for Jose Francisco de Zosa,	Oct. 10, 1835.	1	1 -
for Juan Angel Sequin, and Jose Ig. Arrocha,	April 4, "	1	2 -
for Erasmo Seguin,	Oct. 5, "	1	1
for Joaquin Menchaca,	" " "	1	1 -
for Manuel Flores,	Dec. 15, "	1	- -
for Fernando Cabrera,	Oct. 5, "	1	1 -
Antonio Menchaca, as agent for Anacleto Torres,	" 27, "	1	
Daniel M'Lean, - -	Feb. 20, "	1	
Henry C. M'Neil, as agent for Ramon Bradford,	Sept. 5, "	1	
David C. M'Queen, - -	" 20, 1828.	1	- -
James Martin, - - -	May 12, 1831.	1	
Vicente Michele, (purchaser,) -	" 27 1810.	1	
Regmundo Norris, - -	April 5, 1824.		
G. A. Nixon, agent for A Kanaff, -	Nov. 23, 1835.	1	
George Orr, - -	April 23, 1831.	1	- -
Maria Juan Palacios, - -	May 4, 1792.		1 -
Pedro Padilla, - -	" 31, "		
Juan Ignacio Pifermo, - -	Sept. 13, 1794.	1	
Matias Peña, - -	Nov. 30, 1796.		- -
Pedro Procela, - - -	May 8, 1810.		- -
Xabien Padilla, - -	April 30, "		- -
George Pollitt & Sam Stiddon, agents for J. A. Stockman,	April 22, 1834.	2	
George Pollitt, purchased of Marcelina Zalas,	Nov. 11, 1832.	2	
George Pollitt purchased of Marcelina Zalas,	Feb. 5, 1833.	1	- -
George Pollitt purchased of Marcelina Zalas,	Dec. 2, "	2	- ▴ -
Beasly Prewitt, - -	April 23, 1831.	1	
Edmond Quirk, - -	Dec. 16, 1828.	4	
Antonio Rosales, - -	May 16, 1792.		1 -
Julian Rosales, - -	May 31, 1808.		- -
Melchora del Rio, - -	" 29, 1810.		
Elisha Roberts,	April 26, 1831.	1	

IN THE GENERAL LAND OFFICE. 94

WHERE SITUATED.	REMARKS.
On the Trinity, W. side, adjoining Henry W. Munson and H. G. White.	
On the Trinity, E. side, adjoining Baker M. Spinks and Jacob H. Geiger.	
" " adjoining Wm. Harris and Wm. White.	
On the waters of the Trinity, adjoining Aaron Cherry.	
On the Neches and San Antonio Road.	
Both on Red River, below the mouth of Pine Creek, & adjoining Gabino Araujo.	
Between Red River and the Sabine, S. of the Caddoe Trail.	
Between Red River and Sulphur Fork, adjoining Francisco Ramirez.	
In the vicinity of Red River & Sabine, between Lake Sodo & Caddoe Trail.	
On Caddo Trail, in the Vicinity of Red River and Lake Sodo.	
On Red River, above Coates's Bluff.	
In the vicinity of Lake Sodo.	
Between Red River and Sabine, above 20 miles from Lake Sodo.	
In the vicinity of the San Pedro and the Neches.	
On Red River, adjoining F. H. Revere.	
On the Neches, 1 square of 5,000 varas on each side.	
On the Trinity, E. side, adjoining the Liberty Town Tract.	
On the Neches.	
One Rancho called Nacanichi. - - -	Purchased from Wm. Maculins.
In the Vicinity of Red River.	
On the E. side of the Trinity, adjoining Wm. Hardin.	
On the N. and E. side, 1 league on the W. and S. side, as far as La as La Nana.	
One Ranch on La Nana, a creek on the E. side, 1 league on the N., and W. side half league, joins F. de los Santos.	
On Arroyo Agua, (Water Creek,) measures one league on each side.	
One place on the Naroto, 1½ leagues from Nacogdoches, measures from N. to S, and from E. to W. 1056 varas.	
One Rancho, 3 leagues E. from Nacogdoches, joins Jose Flores and others: N. side 7,500, E. 4,000, S. 3,744 varas, W. 3,000 varas	
One place ½ leagues N. from Nacogdoches, joins Ign. Gonzales and Maria Morin: 700 varas front and 900 deep.	
On the W. side of Red River	
- - . - -	
On San Pedro.	Part of a 11 leag. grant.
On Red River: One league on the same at the mouth of the Kiamichi.	
On the Trinity, E. side, adjoining Jesse Prewet and George Orr.	
On Ayish Bayou.	
1,000 vs. front, & 1974 deep, joining, on N., A. de Acosta & N. F. Sandoval.	
One piece of land on the Carizo.	
One Rancho, 2½ leagues from Nacogdoches, joins P. Procela, B. de la	
On the Trinity, E. side. [Garza, & Jose I. Ybarbo.	

ABSTRACT OF ORIGINAL TITLES

NAMES OF GRANTEES.	DATE OF TITLES.	QUANTITY.	
		Leagues.	Labors.
James Robeson,	May 9, 1831.	1	-
Frco. Ramirez, by his agent, Frost Thorn,	Nov. 30, 1833.	5	-
Joaquin Ferndz. de Rumayor, by his agents, A. C. & J. K. Allen,	Feb. 26, 1834.	2	-
John S. Roberts, agent for Jesus Cantu,	Dec. 20, "	5	-
Juan S. Roberts, as agent for Pias Mici,	March 26, 1835.	1	-
Henry Rueg, as agent for Jose Ramon de Arocha,	" 24, "	1	1
J. A. Rosales,	July 16, 1810.		-
James Samuel,	May 18, 1810.		-
Jose Antonio Sepulbeda,	Dec. 17, 1825.		-
"	March 16, 1826.		-
Ignacio Sartache,	Oct. 24, 1826.		
Baker M. Spinks,	April 26, 1831.	1	-
Samuel Strong,	May 9, "	1	-
Henry Stockman,	Aug. 7, 1833.	1	-
Adolfo Stern purchased of V. Elquezabal,	Nov. 28, "	5	-
Ramon de la Serda,	April 2, 1834.	5	-
Juan Angel Seguin,	Dec. 30, "	1	-
Jacob E. Self,	April 26, 1831.	1	-
William Swail,	May 12, "	1	-
Juan Fernando, Tejerina,	" 7, 1829.	1	-
Juan Tobar,	June 13, 1834.	1	-
Patrick Torris, by his agents, Henry and Lewis Rueg,	Oct. 19, 1835.	1	-
Frost Thorn, agent for J. B. B. Davenport,	Sept. 18, 1835.	4	-
Francisco Villalpando,	" 11, 1810.		-
Leonard Williams,	March 28, 1829.	1	-
Thomas Williams,	" 24, "	1	-
John A. Williams,	April 23, 1831.	1	-
Robert Wiseman,	May 4, "	1	-
William Whitlock,	" 11, "	1	-
Brooks Williams, by J. Bradshaw,	Aug. 15, 1835.	1	-
Matthew G. White,	April 23, 1831.	1	-
L. Williams & Wm. Whitley, agents for P. Bean,	Oct. 20, 1835.	1	-
Jose Ignacio Ybarbo,	July 3, 1800.		
Jose Ignacio Ybarbo,	April 30, 1810.		
Maria Antonio Ybarbo,	June 26, "		

WHERE SITUATED.	REMARKS.

On the Trinity, E. side, adjoining and above Hugh B. Johnston.

Four on Red River, 1 on Trinity, S. W. side, above S. A. Road.

One E. s., Adams' Bayou, W. side of Sabine, and on Pine Island. Bayou.

One S. side River; 1 on same, opposite mouth of Blue River, 2 on Sulphur Fork, and one at the mouth of the Bois de Arc.

On the Apinpani, in the vicinity of the Naches.

On Red River, adjoining F. H. Revere.

One Lot, in the town of Nacogdoches,   -   -   -   Certified copy.
One place on the La Nana, 4 leagues from Nacogdoches—from E. to W. 350, and from N. to S. 650 varas.
One Sitio four or five leagues from Nacogdoches, measures 5,000 varas on all four sides, on the Angelina.
Two Sitios, both on the Cochino.
One Sitio on the Trinity, on each 4,000 varas, adjoining Santiago Tete.
On the Trinity, E. side, joins James M'Fadden.
One-third on the Trinity, E. side, joining widow Coleman and Hardin, and ⅔ on the Trinity, E. side, joins Edward Tanner & James Knight.
On the Angelina W. side.

Four on Red River, and 1 four leagues distance from the same

In two parcels, 4 & 1 leagues, both in the vicinity of Red River.
On Red River opposite the mouth of the Kiamichi.
On the Trinity, E. side, adjoining Joseph Dunman.
"   "   adjoining widow Everett.
Aguaje de Corvalletas, San Pedro las Aminas & Rijos con la Mera.
On Nacosote Creek.

Between Red River and Sulphur Fork.

On the waters of the Sabine.

One Rancho on the Carizo, from N. to S. 1 league, on the E. side ½ league, and on the W. side, 1750 varas.
On the Angelina, adjoining Thomas Williams and Joseph Doste.
"   "   "   "
On the W. side of the Trinity, adjoining Sam Horton.
On Old River, N. side.
On the Trinity, W. side.
On San Antonio Road, joins J. Durst, in Vehlein's Grant.
On the E. s., of the Trinity, adjoining Jno. M. Smith & James Martin.

On the Neches, right bank, below the San Antonio Road.

One Rancho on the Amoladeras (Grindstone Creek,) ten leagues from Nacogdoches.
One Rancho two leagues E. of Nacogdoches.
One place ten leagues E. from Nacogdoches.

ABSTRACT OF ORIGINAL TITLES

ELEVEN LEAGUE AND

NAMES OF GRANTEES.		DATE OF TITLES.	QUANTITY.	
			Leagues.	Labors.
J. K. & A. C. Allen, as agents for Marcos Sanches	-	Sept. 24, 1835.	6	-
J. K. & A. C. Allen, as agents for Vital Flores,	-	Nov. 22, 1833.	5	-
J. K. & A. C. Allen, agents for Manuel Zaragoza,	-	" " "	11	-
J. K, &. A. C. Allen, agents for Jose Justo de Liendo,	-	May 2, 1834.	1	-
J. K. & A. C. Allen, agents for J. A. Sepulbeda,	-	March 3, "	7	-
Andrew Briscoe as agent for Vital Flores,	-	Dec. 14, 1833.	6	-
Pedro E. Bean, as agent for Gavino Araujo,	-	March 17, 1834.	11	-
Andrew Dexter, as agent for Jose Ortega,	-	Dec. 13, 1832.	11	-
Roman Flores & Francisco Careaga,	-	April 4, 1829.	11	-
Geronimo Flores, Maximo Valdes, Mauricio Gonzales Pardes, Atanacio Ybarra, Juan Valdes, Ignacio & Pedro Farias,	-	May 18, 1829.	10½	-
A. Hotchkiss, as agent for Cesario Montano,	-	Nov. 16, 1835.	11.	-
for Miguel de Ocadiz,	-	" 12, "	11	-
for Tomas Quevedo,	-	Sept. 23, "	11	-
for J. A. Chirino,	-	Dec. 27, 1833.	9⅛	-
" "	-	March 11, 1835.	1⅛	-
for Jose Ma. Borrego,	-	Nov. 10, "	11	-
for J. L. Escobar,	-	Sept. 30, "	11	-
for Manuel Elizondo,	-	Oct. 22, "	11	-
for Onofre Fernandez,	-	" " "	11	-
for Jose Maria de la Fuente,	-	Sept. 30, "	11	-
for Ignacio Galindo,	-	" 15, "	11	-
William Hardin, as agent for Jose Dolores Martinez,	-	Nov. 28, 1833.	11	-
William G. Logan, as agent for Manuel & Jose Mariano Lopez, for M. Arceniega	-	Sept. 15, 1835.	11	-
	-	" 22, "	11	-
M. B. Menard, as agent for Mariano Lopez,	-	Dec. 14, "	11	-
M'Farland, as agent ino Mora,	-	" 6, 1833.	11	-
ard, as agent for Ms.				
,	-	" 10, 1834.	5	-
Zarza,	-	Nov. 8, "	1	-
"	-	Dec. 16, 1835.	10	-
Neill, as agent for Anonzales,	-	Sept. 8, "	11	-
Noyret, as agent for io Jose Ybarbo,	-	Aug. 25, "	11	-

IN THE GENERAL LAND OFFICE. 98

OTHER LARGE GRANTS.

WHERE SITUATED.	REMARKS.
On the Waters of Red River, in four parcels.	
On Red River.	
On Red River.	
On Red River.	
Three on Red River, 1 on the Sabine, W. side; 2 on the Potroon, W. side.	
Between the San Jacinto and Trinity Rivers.	
Six on Red River, and 5 on the waters of the Neches.	
Two on Trinity, E. side, below Jose Maria Musques, opposite Gordiano Badilla, and 2 on E. side Trinity, joining G. Badilla; 7 in Mustang Prairie.	
Adjoining Santa Catalina, on S. A. de los Alamos; one in Flore's Potrero.	
Potrero Boca Alocha, in the jurisdiction of the City of Monclova.	
On Sulphur Fork.	
On Sulphur Fork.	
On the waters of the Neches, in three parcels.	
Between the Angelina Atoyac, and Amoladeras, (Grindstone.)	
On the Sabine.	
On Sulphur Fork.	
On the waters of the Sabine, in two parcels.	
On Sulphur Fork.	
On the waters of Red River, in 5 parcels.	
Nine on Red River, and 2 between Sabine and Red River.	
On the waters of Red River, in 5 parcels.	
Nine on the right and one on the left bank of the Trinity, and one on Double Bayou, Galveston Bay.	
In 6 parcels, partly on the banks & partly on the waters of Red River.	
On the waters of Red River, in 6 parcels.	
On Red River, near Blue Bluffs.	
On Red River.	
On Red River, in 5 parcels.	
On Red River.	
On Red River, right hand side.	
Partly on the banks, and partly on the waters of Red River, in 9 parcels.	
Between Lake Sodo and Lake Cass.	

ABSTRACT OF ORIGINAL TITLES

ELEVEN LEAGUE AND

NAMES OF GRANTEES.		DATE OF TITLES.	QUANTITY.	
			Leagues.	Labors.
G. A. Nixon, as agent for J. N. Elizondo,	-	Oct. 4, 1835.	11	- -
John S. Roberts, as agent for Simon Sanches,	-	July 30, 1833.	11	- -
J. S. Roberts & A. Stern, agents for Gordiano Badillo,	-	May 15, 1834. " 18, "	1 1	- - - -
John S. Roberts & A. Stern, as agents for Gordiano Badillo,	-	Nov. 20, 1834.	9	- -
P. A. Sublett & Sam Houston, as agents for Juan Mora,	-	Dec. 3, 1833.	11	- -
Frost Thorn, as agent for Juan Jose Ybarbo, & 3 Brothers,	-	May 5, 1834.	10	23½ -
Frost Thorn, as agent for Jose Paneda,	-	April 4, 1834.	11	- -
J. C. Turner, as agent for J. A. Sepulbeda,	-	" 3, "	4	- -

OTHER LARGE GRANTS.

WHERE SITUATED.	REMARKS.
In the vicinity of Red River, Lake Sodo, and the Sabine, in 3 parcels	
Ten on the right, and 1 one on the left, of Trinity River.	
About 2 leagues distant from Red River.	
Between Red River and Sulphur Fork.	
In 5 parcels, on the waters of Red River.	
On Red River.	
At the junction of the Angelina and Atoyac.	
Four on the Angelina, and 7 on the Neches, in two parcels.	
On Red River.	

A

LIST OF TITLES

ISSUED BY

CHARLES S. TAYLOR,

COMMISSIONER FOR THE FRONTIER

SETTLERS EAST OF

AUSTIN'S COLONIES,

DURING THE YEARS

1835 & 1836.

ABSTRACT OF ORIGINAL TITLES

NAMES OF GRANTEES.	DATE OF TITLES.	QUANTITY.	
		Leagues.	Labors.
Francisco Arriola,	Dec. 5, 1835.	1	1
Edwardo Arriola,	" 6, "	1	1
David Anderson,	Nov. 30, "	⅓	-
James Adams,	Dec. 22, "	1	1
John A. Albright,	Nov. 5, "	1	-
Antonio Andrade,	Sept. 18, "	1	-
John S. Barret,	Oct. 30, "	1	-
Sebastian Basques,	Sept. 10, "	1	-
Messina Brown,	Nov. 2, "	1	-
Thomas Basset,	" 23, "	1	-
James Brown,	Dec. 10, "	1	1
James Blythe,	" 5, "	1	1
Augustin Basques,	Nov. 21, "	1	-
G. B. Brownrigg,	" 23, "	1	-
Jean Batiste Bodin,	Sept. 12, "	1	-
Bentusa Bela,	Oct. 22, "	⅓	-
James Barnet,	" 16, "	1	-
John Bridges,	Nov. 23, "	1	1
Jabes Bradberry,	" 29, "	1	1
Roger Barfield,	" 25, "	1	-
Antonio Barrazo,	Aug. 15, "	1	1
David Brake,	Nov. 29, "	1	-
Margarita Buye,	Sept. 24, "	1	-
Stephen Bowmen,	Oct. 13, "	1	-
Frederick Cooper,	Dec. 5, "	1	-
James Calcote,	Nov. 24, "	1	-
Joseph L. Chambers,	" " "	1	-
Rafael de la Cruz,	Dec. 4, "	1	1
Salvador Castillo,	" 6, "	1	1
Thomas Cartwright,	Sept. 19, "	1	-
William Clifton,	Jan. 15, "	1	-
Reuben Cole,	Nov. 23, "	1	1
John Cherry,	Aug. 14, "	1	-
Allen W. Cunningham.	Oct. 21, "	1	-
John Crowder,	Nov. 23, "	1	1
Timothy Cude,	Sept. 15, "	1	-
Daniel P. Coit,	" 22, "	1	-
William Clark,	" " "	1	-
Juan Cruz,	Nov. 2, "	⅓	-
Adam Carraway,	Dec. 7, "	1	-
Aaron Cherry,	Sept. 5, "	1	-
Elias K. Davis,	Aug. 28, "	1	-
James C. Dewitt,	Dec. 1, "	1	1
Luis David,	Nov. 20, "	1	-
John Downey,	" 19, "	1	-
Robert H. Dixon,	Oct. 17, "	1	-
William Davis, (by D. Brown, agent,)	Nov. 29, "	1	1
John Davidson,	" 28, "	1	1
W. L. Dargan, (by S. Stephens,	Oct. 15, "	1	-
John Faliepe,	July 24, 1836.	1	-
Martin Flores,	Nov. 6, 1835.	1	1
Joseph Faliepe,	Jan. 18, 1836.	1	-
G. W. Furguson,	Nov. 26, 1835.	1	-
Jacob Fulcher,	" 24, "	1	1
Abraham Foirman,	" 14, "	1	-
Joseph Flemings,	Jan. 18, 1836.	1	-

WHERE SITUATED.	REMARKS.
Near Big Alabama Creek.	
Four and a half miles S. of Big Alabama, or Village, Creek.	
Four or five miles S. of the San Antonio Road.	{ J. Bradshaw,
On the E. bank of the Neches, 9 or 10 miles S. of San Antonio Road.	{ Surveyor.
North of Taylor's Bayou—corner in the Prairie.	
Between the Neches and Trinity.	
Seven miles E. of Taylor's Creek.	
S. side of Flores' Creek, and 4½ miles S. E. of Little Pine Island.	{ Wm. Rankin,
On the Trinity.	{ Surveyor.
West of the Neches, below the mouth of Big Alabama.	
Near Big Alabama Creek, 4 miles.	
Near Pine Island Bayou, 15 miles from Liberty and 25 from Beaumont.	
Head of Cow Bayou, near Sabine River.	
On Big Sandy Creek.	
On the W. Bank of the Neches.	
On the Waters of Pine Island Creek.	
Between Turtle Bayou and Galveston Bay—corner in the prairie.	
On the head waters of Pine Island Creek.	
On the waters of Big Sandy, 12 miles W. of the Neches.	
On the prairies of the Trinity, 25 or 30 miles from its mouth.	
On the W. bank of the Neches.	{ Surveyed by
- " " "	{ David Brown.
Pine Island Bayou, 2 miles W. of Wolf Point.	
Taylor's Creek, 7 leagues from the sea beach.	
Near the Town of Big Alabama.	
Near Trinity, 25 or 30 miles from its mouth.	
Between Turtle Bayou and Galveston Bay.	
W. bank of the Neches, about 12 miles from Grant's Bluff.	
One mile and a half S. of the road from Liberty to Beaumont, 12 miles from Liberty and 18 from Beaumont.	{ S. C. Hiroms,
Bounded by John Burgess and S. D. Thomas.	{ Surveyor.
S. of Choctaw Bayou.	
On Big Alabama, 2 leagues from the Neches.	
On the W. Bank of the Trinity.	
Between Turtle Bayou and Galveston Bay.	
Head of Cow Bayou, between the Neches and Sabine.	
On the bank of the San Jacinto, joins N. Martin.	{ G. M. Patrick,
Between Trinity and San Jacinto Rivers.	{ Surveyor.
Between Sabine and Adams's Creek.	
On the Angelina, below John Durst's line.	{ J. A. Veatch,
Near Big Alabama Creek.	{ Surveyor.
W. bank of Trinity, bounded on the southern boundary of M'Kinney.	
W. bank of Trinity, S. W. corner of John Berry.	{ Wm. Robinson,
Near Harmon's Creek.	{ Surveyor.
Neches River, 25 miles from Sabine Bay.	
On a Creek E. of Pine Creek.	
Taylor's Creek, N. E., on two small creeks.	
Lavaca, waters of, commences at a mound.	
Village Creek, 5 miles from Neches.	
Between Turtle Bayou and Galveston Bay.	
Between River Neches and Big Cane Bayou.	
Twelve miles from Liberty and 18 from Beaumont, near the road.	
W. of the Neches, near A. Wilburn.	
Between Turtle Bay and Galveston Bay.	
On the waters of the River Neches.	
On the River Neches.	
On Choctaw Bayou, 6 miles W. of the Neches.	

ABSTRACT OF ORIGINAL TITLES

NAMES OF GRANTEES.	DATE OF TITLES.	Leagues.	Labors.
William Glass,	Nov. 28, 1835.	1	1
Fitz H. Green,	Aug. 26, "	$\frac{1}{3}$	-
Antonio Gordian,	Oct. 1, "	1	1
Francisca Gutierrez,	" 8, "	1	-
John Grisset,	Nov. 23, "	1	1
Samuel Gibson,	" 24, "	1	-
Benjamin M. Green,	Aug. 28, "	1	-
Reason Green,	" 26, "	1	-
John Golightly,	Oct. 13, "	1	-
Antonio Ramon Gutierrez,	" 1, "	1	1
David Gistman,	Nov. 29, "	1	-
George M. Glass,	" 22, "	1	-
Joseph Hunter,	" 25, "	1	-
Augustus Hotchkiss,	Sept. 2, "	1	-
Nathaniel Hodges,	Dec. 9, "	1	-
Wade Horton,	" 5, "	$\frac{1}{3}$	-
Christian Hillibrant,	" " "	1	-
Dan'l Hopkins,	" 23, "	1	-
John Higgins,	Nov. 23, "	1	1
William Howard,	" 29, "	1	-
Archibald Hotchkiss,	Sept. 18, "	1	-
William Herring,	Nov. 23, "	1	1
John Hillis,	" 29, "	1	-
Alexander Hughes,	" 28, "	1	1
Encarnacion Juarez,	Aug. 3, "	1	1
Isaac Johnson,	Nov. 23, "	1	1
George Knox,	" 21, "	1	1
Levy Lusk,	Dec. 9, "	1	-
Guadalupe Lopes,	" 4, "	1	1
Armstead J. Lilley,	Jan. 24, 1836.	1	-
Peter Lacey,	Nov. 23, 1835.	1	1
Lewis F. Lillard,	Oct. 17, "	1	-
Maria Felipa Lazarin,	Sept. 12, "	1	-
Juan Simon Lazarin,	" 17, "	1	-
James Liddle,	Dec. 8, "	1	-
John Lampkin,	Nov. 21, "	1	-
John Lacey,	" 23, "	1	-
John Morehead,	Dec. 16, "	1	-
Peter Mendenhall,	Jan. 18, 1836.	1	-
Jose Ma. Medrino,	Nov. 8, 1835.	1	1
Thomas Meredith,	" 25, "	1	-
Peter Mason,	Oct. 17, "	1	-
William Murell,	Jan. 15, 1836.	1	-
William Mayo,	Nov. 23, 1835.	1	1
Juliana Malley,	Aug. 19, "	1	-
H. T. Metcalf.	Nov. 23, "	1	1
Maria Dolores Menchaca,	" 21, "	1	-
Samuel Maxlen,	Jan. 15, 1836.	1	-
Soto Montone,	" 12, "	1	-
William Mott,	Nov. 27, 1835.	1	1
Pedro Mirando,	Sept. 6, "	$\frac{1}{3}$	-
Jacinto Magano,	Aug. 15, "	1	-
Crecencio Morales,	Dec. 4, "	1	1
Henry Middleton,	Nov. 23, "	1	-
John Mayo,	" 27, "	1	-
Drury M'Gee,	Oct. 30, "	1	-
Patrick M'David,	Nov. 21, "	$\frac{1}{3}$	-

WHERE SITUATED.	REMARKS.
On the W. side of the Neches.	
Near Pine Island Creek.	
On Pine Island Creek.	
Twelve miles from Galveston Bay.	
Cow Bayou Settlement, E. of Platilla.	
Five miles E. of Taylor's Bayou.	
On the W. of Trinity River.	
W. margin of Trinity River.	
On Taylor's Bayou, 7 miles from the sea beach.	
Corner of Survey, No. 2.	
E. side of Trinity River.	
" Neches River.	
Between Village Creek and Pine Island Creek.	
On the waters of Trinity River.	
Near Big Alabama Creek.	
Commences at the S. E. corner of B. Earle's survey.	J. A. Veatch, surveyor.
Between Den and Hillebrant's Creek.	
On the margin of the River Neches.	
On the waters of the River Neches.	
W. side of the River Neches.	
S. side of Flores' Creek.	
On the Lavaca, N. E. corner of John Coles.	
E. side of Trinity River.	
On the waters of Village Creek.	
" Neches River.	
" Lavaca Creek.	
Near Pine Island Bayou.	
On the S. branches of Flores' Bayou.	
On the waters of Pine Island.	
Near the S. branches of Chocolate Bayou, joins P. Mendenhall.	
Between the Neches and Sabine Rivers.	
On the N. E. bank of Taylor's Bayou.	
To the S. of Pine Island Bayou.	
On Big Sandy, E. of the Trinity.	
On Big Alabama Creek.	
"	
On the waters of the Sabine.	
On the waters of the Neches.	
Near the southern branch of Chocolate Bayou.	
On the waters of the River Sabine.	
Near Village Creek, 25 miles from the River Neches.	
Distant 25 or 30 miles from the mouth of the Trinity.	
Near Southern Creek of Bayou, Choctaw.	
On the waters of the River Neches.	
Adjoining the survey of Meredith Duncan.	
Adjoining the survey of Yates.	
At the head of Cow Bayou.	
Between Turtle Bayou and Galveston Bay,	
Near, and to the N. of, Taylor's Bayou.	
On the southern side of Big Alabama Creek.	
On both sides of Camp Creek, at the corner of a survey marked A.	
Between the Angelina and Neches Rivers.	
On the waters of Pine Island Creek.	
On the waters of the Neches River.	
" " W. side.	
Bounding on a survey of Robert Rankin.	
In the Prairie, about 6 miles from Sabine Bay, bounding on T. J. Love.	

ABSTRACT OF ORIGINAL TITLES

NAMES OF GRANTEES.	DATE OF TITLES.	Leagues.	Labors.
Samuel M'Combs,	Nov. 4, 1835.	1	-
Joseph Neilson,	Dec. 5, "	1	-
William Nash,	Sept. 12, "	1	-
William Nichols,	Nov. 20, "	1	-
Jesse Norris,	" 26, "	1	-
Juan Prado,	Dec. 4, "	$\frac{1}{3}$	-
Maria Josefa de Padilla,	Oct. 22, "	1	1
Canderio Perez,	Dec. 4, "	1	1
John Parker,	Nov. 23, "	1	1
Manuel Procela,	" 13, "	1	-
Oliver Peterson,	Sept. 19, "	1	-
Robert Petit,	Nov. 23, "	1	1
Maria Francisco Perez,	Oct. 3, "	$\frac{1}{4}$	-
Wm. Rankin, Jr.,	Nov. 3, "	1	-
Jose Antonio Rodriguez,	Dec. 7, "	1	1
Jose Maria Rodriguez,	Oct. 22, "	1	1
Andres de Rojas,	Nov. 22, "	$\frac{1}{3}$	-
Samuel Rogers,	Sept. 4, "	1	-
Absalom, Reeves,	Oct. 8, "	$\frac{1}{3}$	-
Joseph Reynolds,	" 22, "	$\frac{1}{3}$	-
Pierre Rablo,	Dec. 6, "	1	1
John R. Rogers,	Nov. 27, "	1	-
Jose del Rio,	" 30, "	1	-
Nicolas de la Rosa,	Dec. 7, "	1	-
Stephen Richardson,	Nov. 8, "	1	1
Amos Spring,	Jan. 5, 1836.		6
Thomas Sanders,	Nov. 4, 1835.	1	-
Joseph Sanford,	Nov. 26, "	1	-
Richard Sparks,	Aug. 15, "	1	-
Margil Shurnac,	Oct. 22, "	1	1
Henry Stagner,	" 20, "	1	-
Joseph S. Shackleford,	Nov. 27, "	1	-
Joel Stephens,	" 4, "	1	-
Faustino Shavano,	Oct. 22, "	$\frac{1}{3}$	-
Maria Josefa Sanches,	Aug. 15, "	1	1
John Slattern,	Oct. 13, "	1	-
Adolfo Stern,	" 21, "	1	-
Jose Santiago de los Santos,	Dec. 2, "	1	-
William Spears,	Oct. 17, "	1	-
Peter Striker,	Jan. 21, 1836.	1	-
Wiley S. Thomas,	Nov. 25, 1835.	$\frac{1}{3}$	-
Mary Thomas,	Sept. 23, "	1	-
E. Trumbow,	Nov. 5, "	1	1
Jose Andres Torres,	Dec. 15, "	1	1
Henry Tatum,	Oct. 16, "	1	-
J. D. Thomas,	Sept. 12, "	1	-
Meria de Carmon Triviño,	Oct, 22, "	1	1
John Todd,	Nov. 22, "	1	-
Juan Francisco Fermins Tobar,	Dec. 7, "	1	1
Gaston Underwood,	Oct. 16, "	1	-
Ignacio Villegas,	Nov. 6, "	1	1
Juan Villareal,	Dec. 4, "	1	-
Francisco Valmon,	Sept. 2, "	1	-
H. E. Watson,	" 15, "	1	-
Henrique Webb,	Nov. 6, "	1	1

WHERE SITUATED.	REMARKS.
On the E. branch of San Jacinto.	In 2 surveys of ¼ league, each.
Near Big Alabama Creek.	
Big Sandy Creek.	
On the E. side of the Trinity River.	
About 6 miles E. of Taylor's Bayou.	
On Pine Island Bayou and its waters.	In 2 separat surveys.
W. corner of P. Carrol's survey.	
On the Waters of the Sabine, in separate surveys.	
Three leagues from Neches River.	
On Big Alabama Creek.	
On the E. side of Trinity River.	
On the waters of Big Sandy Creek.	
Near the River Neches, and S. W. corner of Williams's survey.	
On the waters of Trinity River.	
On the E. bank of the River Neches, near Sabine Bay.	Surveyed by J. Veatch.
On the waters of San Jacinto.	
W. side of the Trinity.	
In a prairie E. of the San Jacinto, joining Amelia Wilson.	
On the waters of Big Alabama.	
S. W. of the Angelina, on its margin.	
In the vicinity, and to the N. E. of Taylor's Bayou.	
On Pine Island Creek, near the Gulf of Mexico and Neches River.	
Seven or 8 miles E. of Double Bayon, and 9 N. of Galveston Bay.	
On the S. side of Big Alabama.	
On Big Cane Creek, W. of Neches, bounding with J. Box.	
Eight miles E. of Taylor's Creek.	
Taylor's Creek, 7 leagues from the sea beach,	
On the W. bank of the Trinity River.	
S. W. corner of Phillip Carrol's land.	
On the bank of the Angelina River.	
W. of River Trinity.	
N. of Taylor's Bayou.	
N. W. corner of a survey in a prairie.	Veatch, surveyor.
Southern boundary of Barings.	
Eight or 10 miles from the mouth of Trinity River.	
On the River Neches, bounding on Thompson's lower line.	Surveyed by J. A. Veatch.
Twenty-five or 30 miles from the mouth of the Trinity.	
Southern emmediation of Chocolate Bayou.	
On Big Sandy Creek.	S. C. Hiroms, Surveyor.
" "	
On the waters of Pine Island Bayou. [J. A. Veatch, surveyor.]	Surveyed by B. Tennel.
On Big Atoyac Creek. [In 2 surveys.]	
Between Turtle Bayou and Galveston Bay.	
On the W. Bank of the Trinity. [In 2 surveys.]	
On the waters of Pine Island. [In 2 surveys.]	
On the Neches, and opposite the Town of Santa Anna.	
On the E. bank of the Neches, mouth of Pecan Bayou.	
Between Turtle Bayou and Galveston.	
S. W. corner of Edwardo Ariola.	Veatch, Surveyor.
Pine Island Creek, near the Neches and Gulf of Mexico, S. E. corner of Jose del Rio.	
On the S. bank, and near the head of Navigation of Flores' Creek	
On Big Sandy Creek.	
Four miles from the Neches, and 12 miles from Richardson's Bluffs.	

ABSTRACT OF ORIGINAL TITLES

NAMES OF GRANTEES.	DATE OF TITLES.	QUANTITY.	
		Leagues.	Labors.
Samuel Whiting,	Aug. 18, 1835.	1	-
Seth Ward,	Nov. 24, "	1	1
Isaiah Wooton,	" 25, "	1	
John P. Williams,	Oct. 15, "		
James F. Wiggins,	Nov. 5, "	1	
Joseph Wallop,	Oct. 13, "	1	
Zachariah Williams,	Nov. 21, "	1	1
Benjamin Winfree,	Oct. 7, "	1	-

WHERE SITUATED.	REMARKS.
Eastern margin of Galveston Bay, 6½ m's below m. of Turtle Bayou, & 2½	
Cow Creek, waters of Sabine, 10 m's f'm Neches River. [f'm R'nd Point.	
Near the Trinity, and 25 to 30 miles from its mouth.	
E. of Double Bayou, and about 6 miles N. of Galveston Bay.	
N. of Taylor's Bayou.	
In the prairie, near Taylor's Bayou.	
Between Big Alabama Creek and Pine Island Bayou.	
On the margin of Cotton Creek, near Galveston Bay.	

27

A

LIST OF TITLES

ISSUED BY

GEORGE A. NIXON,

COMMISSIONER FOR THE COLONIES

OF

BURNET, VEHLEIN, AND ZAVALA,

IN

1834 & 1835.

ABSTRACT OF ORIGINAL TITLES

NAMES OF GRANTEES.	DATE OF TITLES.	Leagues.	Labors.
Nathaniel N. G. Allen,	April 20, 1835.	1	-
John Arthur,	June 18, "	$\frac{1}{4}$	-
Shelton Alphin,	" 27, "	1	-
George Anding,	July 18, "	1	-
Kinchin Adam,	Sept. 17, "	1	-
Wm. F. Allison,	Oct. 19, "	1	-
John Adams,	" 16, "	1	-
Elihu C. Allison,	" " "	1	-
Casilda Aguilera,	April 30, "	1	-
Henry Bailey,	Nov. 14, 1834.	1	-
Zinn Bennet,	" 29, "	1	-
Henry Brewer,	Jan. 13, 1835.	1	-
Solomon Bowlin,	" 9, "	1	-
Allen C. Bullock,	March 21, "	1	-
Samuel C. Box,	May 8, "	1	-
John A. Box,	" " "	1	-
James E. Box,	" 9, "	$\frac{1}{4}$	-
Reuben Brown,	" 22, "	1	-
Rowland W. Box,	" 12, "	1	-
Larkin Baker,	June 11, "	1	-
Jose Antonio Bontan,	" 4, "	1	-
Taylor S. Barnes,	" 29, "	$\frac{1}{4}$	-
Eli A. Bowen,	" 28, "	1	-
John M. Box,	" 11, "	1	-
Pedro Berma,	July 21, "	$\frac{1}{4}$	-
Gordiano Bardillo,	" 6, "	1	-
John W. Bryan,	" 17, "	$\frac{1}{4}$	-
John Boyd,	" 13, "	1	-
John Beaty,	" 29, "	1	-
William Bartee,	Aug. 26, "	1	-
Isaac W. Burton,	Sept. 18, "	1	-
Hobson Burleson,	Oct. 16, "	1	-
William S. Box,	" 20, "	1	-
Isaac Barnet,	" 16, "	1	-
A. W. Beckham,	" 15, "	1	-
Samuel Boon,	" 7, "	1	-
Crawford Burnet,	" 5, "	1	-
Miguel Cortines,	Oct. 29, "	1	-
Cesario Chamar,	July 16, "	1	-
Mark Copeland,	" 23, "	1	-
John Carroll,	Dec. 30, 1834.	$\frac{1}{4}$	-
Domniquez Cervantes,	" " "	1	-
Elisha Clapp,	Jan. 14, 1835.	1	-
Joseph T. Cook,	Feb. 2, "	1	-
James Cobbs,	April 29, "	$\frac{1}{4}$	-
Jesse H. Chambers,	May 12, "	$\frac{1}{4}$	-
Stephen Crist,	" 21, "	1	-
Jose Agaton Caro,	" 30, "	$\frac{1}{4}$	-
William Clark,	June 17, "	1	-
Jose Antonio Caro,	" 29, "	1	-
Miguel de los Santos Coy,	July 17, "	1	-
William Curry,	" 13, "	1	-
John Chote,	Oct. 18, "	1	-
Redmond Chote,	" 11, "	1	-
Thomas Chafin,	Oct. 26, "	1	-
David Cook,	Nov. 8, "	$\frac{1}{4}$	-
Maria de Canton,	July 19, "	1	-

WHERE SITUATED.	REMARKS.
Joins D. Allen.	
Joins James Gordon.	
On the W. side of the Trinity River.	
Waters of Trinity River, joins Mrs. Groce.	
On the E. side of the Neches River.	Sh'ld be K. Odom; see letter O.
On the Angelina.	
On the E. bank of the Trinity.	
On the waters of the Angelina.	
N. of the town of Nacogdoches.	
On the waters of Bonito, 9 miles from Nacogdoches.	
Joins Joseph Weeks.	
Joins John Durst and Bennett.	
Joins John Little and James Hall.	
Joins James Reiley, San Antonio Road.	
Trinity, E. bank, joins Rowland W. Box.	
Waters of the Trinity, between the two Commanche Traces.	
On the E. side of Trinity, joins Sam'l C. Box.	
Waters of the Trinity, on Box's Creek.	
E. side Trinity, Below the Comanche Trace.	
On the waters of the Angelina, joins I. Kendrick.	
On the waters of the Neches.	
" " joins Sam'l G. Wells.	
Joins M. Maise.	
Joins Hammonds.	
Joins S. E. corner of Henry Masters.	
Waters of the Neches, joins Jno. Adams and Greenwood.	
Joins Wells.	
Joins Lipscomb Norvell.	
On Hurricane Bayou.	
Joins Beverly Pool.	
W. of Neches, 15 miles from Sabine.	
On Amoladeras Creek, W. of Trinity.	
On the Carrizo, E. of the Neches.	
Eight miles E. of the Trinity, and 8 miles from old Kecheye Village.	
Joins Gosset and W. White, on Hurricane Bayou.	
On the Neches, 18 miles W. of Sabine.	
On the waters of the Angelina, joins Simms.	
W. side of the Trinity.	
W. of the Trinity.	
Trinity, E. side, joins M. Murchison.	
Joins Louis Sanches.	
Joins Cummins.	
Joins T. J. Jones, near the Neches.	
Joins Uriah Moore.	
Joins Maria Chinferosa Gonzales.	
Trinity, waters of Parker's Creek.	
On the Waters of the Angelina.	
" "	
Joins Henry Bailey.	
Waters of the Angelina, joins James Hamilton.	
Joins Sarah McNulty.	
On the waters of the Trinity, S. W. side.	
E. bank of the Navasoto.	
W. of the Neches, on a trace from the Sabine to Caddoe village.	
On San Antonio Road, joins J. Durst.	
Betwen Trinity and Navasoto.	

ABSTRACT OF ORIGINAL TITLES

NAMES OF GRANTEES.	DATE OF TITLES.	QUANTITY.	
		Leagues.	Labors.
Allen Dimery,	April 20, 1835.	1	-
Elijah S. Debard,	Jan. 8, "	1	-
Alfred B. Davis,	July 24, "	¼	-
William Davis,	Oct. 14, "	1	-
Matthew M. Dykes,	" 9, "	¼	-
William Elliott,	Jan. 12, "	1	-
John Edoms,	April 20, "	1	-
John Engledow,	June 18, "	1	-
Peter S. Elliott,	Aug. 17, "	1	-
Edley Ewing,	Oct. 15, "	1	-
Wilson Ewing,	" 14, "	1	-
Creed S. Engledow,	July 13, "	1	-
Joseph Ferguson,	Jan. 5, "	1	-
John Ferguson,	" 3, "	1	-
Alston Ferguson,	" 5, "	1	-
Josefa Peres Falcon,	May 9, "	1	-
William Frost,	June 8, "	1	-
Jabez Fitch,	July 12, "	¼	-
Robert Foote,	Oct. 7, "	¼	-
Warwick Ferguson,	" 15, "	1¼	-
Enoch Frier,	" 11, "	1	-
Matthew Golcher,	" 28, "	1	-
Thomas Goss,	" 15, "	1	-
Isaac Greeson,	" 12, "	1	-
Absalom Gibson,	Dec. 30, 1834.	1	-
Zacheus Gibbs,	Feb. 2, 1835.	1	-
Elijah Gossett,	" 7, "	1	-
Garrison Greenwood,	March 5, "	1	-
Alce Garrett,	April 20, "	1	-
Jean Baptiste Gague,	May 25, "	1	-
Romano Gonzales,	" 12, "	¼	-
Maria Sinforosa Gonzales,	" 9, "	1	-
Eli Garrett,	June 3, "	¼	-
Redin Garner,	July 9, "	1	-
William Gates,	June 20, "	1	-
Jesse Gibson,	" 10, "	1	-
Edson Gee,	" 20, "	1	-
Elam W. Gilliland,	July 6, "	1	-
James L. Gossett,	" 24, "	1	-
Thomas H. Gardiner,	" 8, "	1	-
Elizabeth Groce,	" " "	1	-
James Hall,	Jan. 3, "	1	-
Newel C. Hodges,	March 12, "	1	-
Maria G. Henrica,	May 13, "	1	-
Joseph Hertz,	" 22, "	¼	-
Sam Houston,	" 5, "	¼	-
Maria Falcona Huejas,	" 9, "	1	-
Edward C. Harris,	June 26, "	1	-
Edward Hacket,	" 3, "	1	-
James Hamilton,	" 12, "	1	-
Isaac Holman,	Aug. 5, "	1	-
Jonas G. Haile,	" 25, "	1	-
John Hagan,	" " "	1	-

IN THE GENERAL LAND OFFICE. 116

WHERE SITUATED.	REMARKS.
Joins William Johnston.	
On the Neches, joins Saline League.	
Between the Neches and Trinity, joins William Frost.	
S. E. side of Bayou San Pedro.	
Joins William Elliott.	
Joins Little.	
On Alce Creek.	
Rutherland Fork of Angelina, Joins E. Hackett.	
W. side of the Trinity, 12 miles N. of Dexter's Saline.	
One mile S. of Houston Survey, and W. of M'Donald.	
Near the Trinity, joins Edley Ewing.	
Joins Basews.	
On Neches, W. side.	
" "	
Joins John Vaughan.	
On the waters of the Angelina, joins J. Durst.	
On the waters of the Trinity, between Comanche Trail and Parker's Creek.	
S. of road from Ionies Village to Neches.	
W. of the Trinity, near Navasoto.	
One-fourth joins Crawford Burret, and the league joins the 7 league survey of A. Hotchkiss. - - - -	Surveyed by Brookfield
Richland Creek, S. W. of Trinity.	
In the vicinity of the Neches.	
On the W. side of the Neches.	
Three miles E. of the Trinity.	
Joins Uriah Moore, Thos. Timmons, and John Vaughan.	
On the waters of the Neches, joins Levi Jordon.	
On Hurricane Creek.	
Joins John La Rivere.	
On the San Antonio Road, joins Bullock.	
On the waters of the Angelina, joins Wm. Williams.	
On the waters of the Angelina.	
" " joins Josefa Peres Falcona.	
Joins Kerby.	
Joins James Korn.	
On the waters of the Angelina, joins Isaac Reed.	
Joins Jose Maria Mora, near Young Village.	
On the waters of the Angelina, joins John Engledow.	
On the waters of Trinity, 3 miles from San Antonio Road, and 15 from Robbins' Crossing.	
Joins Madera.	
On the waters of the Trinity, 3 miles N. of San Antonio Road, joins Gilliland.	
On the waters of the Neches, 11 miles from Kickapoo Village.	
Joins John Little.	
Hurricane Creek.	
On the waters of the Angelina.	
Between Trinity and Neches, joins Reuben Brown on Comanche Trail.	
On the W. side of Sand Bayou.	
On the waters of the Angelina, joins William Reagan.	
Trinity, E. side, 40 miles from N. Robbins.	
Joins John Engledow and Isaac Read.	
On the waters of the Angelina.	
On the waters of the Trinity and Navasoto, joins Maria Canton.	
Joins Thomas R. Townsend.	
" "	

ABSTRACT OF ORIGINAL TITLES

NAMES OF GRANTEES.	DATE OF TITLES.	QUANTITY.	
		Leagues.	Labors.
Ralph Hunter,	Oct. 10, 1835.	1	-
J. Huntingdon,	" 7, "	1	-
Moses Herrin,	" 13, "	1	-
John Jordan,	Jan. 8, "	1	-
Levi Jordan,	Feb. 4, "	1	-
Jesse T. Jones,	" 3, "	1	-
Frank Johnson,	March 14, "	1	-
William Johnston,	April 24, "	1	-
James Jordan,	May 15, "	1	-
Joseph Jourdan,	June 10, "	1	-
Wiley M. C. Jones,	July 17, "	1	-
Thomas J. Jackson,	Aug. 5, "	1	-
John Jacobs,	Oct. 26, "	$\frac{1}{4}$	-
Adeline Jaques,	May 5, "	1	-
Isaac Kendrick,	June 3, "	1	-
John Kirby,	" 7, "	1	-
William S. Kennart,	July 6, "	1	-
Jesse Korn,	" 23, "	1	-
William Kimbro,	Sept. 17, "	1	-
J. M. Lyon,	July 16, "		23 & 6-10
John Little,	Jan. 5, "	1	-
Martin Lacey,	" 3, "	1	-
Barbara C. Lewis,	" 15, "	1	-
William Luce,	" 2, "	1	-
John La Rivere,	March 5, "	$1\frac{1}{4}$	-
William G. Ladd,	May 22, "	$\frac{1}{4}$	-
Wm. M. Lumpkin,	June 7, "	1	-
Benijah Lafferty,	" 22, "	1	-
James Latham,	" 18, "	1	-
Gertrudis Luna,	July 25, "	1	-
Adolphus D. Lattin,	" 7, "	1	-
Isaac Lindsey,	Aug. 10, "	1	-
Washington Lewis,	Oct. 22, "	1	-
Rachael Leech,	" 27, "	1	-
Jeremiah Latham,	" 12, "	1	-
Martin Latham,	" 5, "	1	-
Lewis Latham,	Nov. 17, "	1	-
Martin Murchison,	Dec. 30, 1834.	1	-
Uriah Moore,	Jan. 3, 1835.	1	-
Jesse B. M'Nealy,	" 8, "	1	-
Daniel M'Lane,	" 31, "	1	-
Jacob Masters, Sr.,	Feb. 14, "	1	-
Jacob Masters, Jr.,	" " "	1	-
Isaac J. Midkiff,	April 21, "	1	-
William Manwaring,	" 30, "	$\frac{1}{4}$	-
Candis Midkiff,	" 22, "	1	-
James Mitchell,	" 2, "	$\frac{1}{4}$	-
Jose Maria Martines,	May 23, "	1	-
Phillip Martin,	" 26, "	1	-
William S. M'Donald,	June 20, "	1	-
George May,	" " "	1	-
Thomas M'Donald,	" " "	1	-
W. K. Merton,	July 18, "	1	-
Henry Myers,	" 22, "	$\frac{1}{4}$	-
Sarah M'Anulty,	" 7, "	1	-

WHERE SITUATED.	REMARKS.

On the Neches, 18 miles from the Saline.
" " "
On the Bank of the Navasoto.
On the Neches, E. S., joins J. Walker.
Joins Jesse T. Jones.
" James T. Cooke.
" John Haggin.
On the San Antonio Road.
On the waters of the Angelina.
" " Trinity, joins Wm. S. M'Donald.
Joins Jesse Karns.
On the waters of the Angelina.
Joins Reuben Phillips.
On the W. side of Trinity, San Antonio Road, joins W. Johnson.
On the waters of the Angelina, 2 leagues W. of the town of Striker.
Joins Henry Baily and E. Gossett.
On Sandy Creek.
Joins W. M. C. Jones.
On the waters of the Neches, 20 miles from the Young Village.
W. of the Trinity Joins Jose Maria Sanches.
Joins William Elliott.
On the San Antonio Road, joins James Bradshaw.
On the E. side of the Neches, joins Bean and Uriah Moore.
Joins Vincent Moore.
" M'Lane.
" Kerly, N. of Nacogdoches.
" Henry Bailey.
On the waters of the Angelina, joins Smith & Reagan.
" " joins Isaac Reed.
" of the Trinity, 10 leagues from the road from Robbins' to San Antonio.
On the waters of the Trinity, 8 miles W. of Kickapoo Village.
On the W. side of the Neches, joins Bean.
Joins Solomon Pickey and John Sheridan.
On Richland Creek, S. W. branch of Trinity.
On Richland Creek, S. W. branch of Trinity.
Waters of the Trinity, S. W. side.
On the E. bank of the Trinity, joins Hugh Morgan.
On the E. side of the Trinity, joins John Carroll.
On the E. side of the Neches, Joins T. Timmons.
Joins John Little.
On the E. side of the Trinity.
Joins J. Masters, Jr.
" " "
Joins Candis Medkiff.
" J. Weeks.
" Bean & Thorn.
Cow-Pen Bayou, Billow's Creek, waters of Nashita, joins Traser.
On the Angelina, joins W. Gates and John Durst.
On the waters of Elkhart Creek, near Comanche Trace, between the Trinity and Neches.
Joins Joseph Jordan.
On the waters of the Angelina.
" "
On the waters of the Trinity, joins M'Donnell.
" Angelina, joins Troutman.
Joins John Boyd.

ABSTRACT OF ORIGINAL TITLES

NAMES OF GRANTEES.	DATE OF TITLES.	QUANTITY.	
		Leagues.	Labors.
James M'Cune,	July 18, 1835.	1	-
John M'Gregor,	" 22, "	¼	-
Robert C. M'Daniel,	" 6, "	1	-
Elias F. Myers,	" 19, "	1	-
Mickam Main,	" 6, "	1	-
Daniel M'Henrie,	" 9, "	1	-
Jose N. Menchaca,	Aug. 4, "	¼	-
Augustus G. Monroe,	Sept. 18, "	1	-
Sam'l B. Marshall,	Oct. 2, "	1	-
James Madden,	" 15, "	¼	-
John Malone,	" " "	¼	-
Vincent Moore,	" " "	1	-
John M'Neal,	" " "	1	-
Robert F. Millard,	Nov. 28, "	1	-
Mariana O. Mariotine,	" 23, "	1	-
Alfred Oliver,	May 30, "	-	22
Kinchin Odom,	Sept. 17, "	1	-
Lipscomb Norvell,	July 13, "	1	-
Jacob Pruett,	Feb. 17, "	1	-
David Page,	" 5, "	1	-
Isaac G. Parker,	May 2, "	¼	-
John Parker,	" " "	¼	-
John Padden,	June 22, "	¼	-
Dickerson Parker,	" 9, "	¼	-
G. W. Price,	July 10, "	¼	-
Jose J. Procela,	" 22, "	1	-
Bernard Pantaleon,	" 7, "	1	-
Beverly Pool,	" 19, "	1	-
Jose Maria Procela,	" 17, "	1	-
Reuben P. Phillips,	Aug. 13, "	1	-
John Peburn,	" 7, "	1	-
Jehu Peoples,	Oct. 11, "	1	-
Daniel Parker, Jr.,	" 14, "	¼	-
Walter F. Poole,	Nov. 7, "	1	-
James Reilley,	March 19, "	1	-
Stephen Rogers,	May 23, "	1	-
William Reagan,	" 4, "	1	-
James Reel,	" 16, "	¼	-
Daniel Reel,	" " "	1	-
Henry Reel,	" 15, "	¼	-
Robert Rogers,	" 23, "	1	-
George Riddle,	" 4, "	1	-
Jacob Roth,	" 18, "	1	-
Isaac Reed,	June 22, "	1	-
Isaac H. Reed,	July 15, "	1	-
Wm. B. Read,	" 9, "	1	-
Eli Russel,	Oct. 16, "	1	-
Thomas J. Rusk,	Nov. 5, "	1	-
Larkin Robeson,	" 5, "	1	-
Simon del Rio,	Oct. 17, "	¼	-
John Shelton,	Oct. 15, 1334.	1	-
Lewis Sanches,	Nov. 26, "	1	-
Mariano Sanches,	" " "	¼	-
Robert W. Smith,	May 13, 1835.	1	-
John Sheridan,	June 11, "	1	-
Manuel Skinner,	July 13, "	1	-
Sidney A. Sweet,	" 9, "	1	-

WHERE SITUATED.	REMARKS.

On the waters of the Angelina, joins Henry Stockman.
E. of the Neches, near the Comanche Trail.
On the waters of the Trinity, joins G. Simpson.
Two miles from the Sabine.
Between the Neches and Trinity.
Joins Sidney A. Sweet.
On the waters of the Angelina.
On the Trinity.
On the W. side of the Trinity, joins Gosest.
On the N. E. side of the Trinity.
On the waters of the Neches.
Joins Wm. Luce, E. bank of the Neches.
On the waters of the Trinity, S. W. side.
W. of the Trinity.
Six miles from Shawney Village, 10 or 12 from the Sabine.
And 838,300 square varas, 20 miles N. of Nacogdoches. - - - - { Printed Adam on Page 113.
E. side of the Neches.
Joins John Boyd.
W. side of the Neches.
E. " " joining John Walker.
On La Nana Creek, W. side.
On Parker's Creek, 1¼ leagues from Stephen Chirst.
Joins John Bryant.
Joins Myers.
Joins James Sparks,
On Elkhart Creek, joins Sheridan.
On the waters of the Trinity, joins R. M'Daniel.
On the road from Nacogdoches to the Salines.
On the waters of the Angelina, joins Edson Gee.
Joins John Jacob.
On the waters of the Angelina.
On Richland Creek, S. W. of Trinity.
On the E. side of the Trinity.
On the W. bank of the Neches, S. E. of Thomas Goss' survey.
On the San Antonio Road, joins Bullock.
On the waters of the San Pedro, joins Edom & Murchison.
" " Angelina, joins Maria Falcon Huijas.
" " " " Dan'l Reel.
" " " " James Reel.
Joins James Reel.
Joins Mark Copeland,
On the W. side of the river Neches.
On the waters of the Angelina.
" " joins G. Hendrick.
Joins Reden Gardner.

Near Waugh's Creek, W. of Trinity.
Joins Crawford, Burnet, and Reed.
E. Bank of the Navasoto.
Near the Angelina, on the E. boundary of Burnet's Colony.
On the San Antonio Road.
Joins Maria Sanches.
Joins Henry Bailey.
Joins J. H. Chambers.
On the waters of the Neches.
" Trinity, Boggy Creek.
Joins James Sparks.

ABSTRACT OF ORIGINAL TITLES

NAMES OF GRANTEES.	DATE OF TITLES.	QUANTITY.	
		Leagues.	Labors.
John Scritchfield,	July 24, 1835.		24
Polly Scritchfield,	" 18, "	1	
William T. Smith,	" 2, "	1	
Isaac Simpson,	" 8, "	1	
James Sparks,	" " "	1	
William Skinner,	" 12, "	1	
W. G. L. Scott,	" 6, "	1	
Jose M. Sanches,	" 16, "	1	
Jacob Snively,	" 25, "	$\frac{1}{4}$	
Hugh Shepherd,	" 9, "	.1	
Wm. H. Steel,	Aug. 10, "	$\frac{1}{4}$	
Michael Shire,	Oct. 12, "	1	
Maria Trinidad Sanches,	" 15, "	1	
Thomas Timmons,	Dec. 24, 1834.	1	
Thomas R. Townsend,	Feb. 7, 1835.	1	
Hiram B. Troutman,	May 3, "	1	
John Taylor,	Oct. 12, "	1	
Ventura Tejeda,	" 17, "	1	
James F. Timmons,	" 22, "	$\frac{1}{4}$	
Montgomery B. Thomas,	July 10, "	$\frac{1}{4}$	
Zachariah S. Thomson,	" 25, "	$\frac{1}{4}$	
John Vaughan,	Jan. 20, "	1	
Juan Vargas,	May 13, "	1	
Joseph Weeks,	Nov. 21, 1834.	1	
John Walker,	Jan. 8, 1835.	1	
William White,	March 9, "	1	
Benjamin F. Whitaker,	June 4, "	1	
James G. Webb,	" 7, "	1	
W. R. Wilson,	March 12, "	1	
Henry A. Ward,	Oct. 11, "	1	
George W. Wilson,	" 15, "	1	
W. Williams,	" 30, "	1	
David R. Winchester,	" 18, "	1	
Hiram Walker,	" 5, "		19

WHERE SITUATED.	REMARKS.
On the San Antonio Road, joins Gaines.	
On the waters of the Trinity, joins Anding.	
On the waters of the Angelina.	
On the waters of the Trinity, ½ mile from Anding.	
Joins George W. Price.	
Joins James Lyon.	
On the W. bank of the Neches.	
W. of the river, Trinity.	
Between the Neches and Trinity, joins Arhcrough.	
Joins Reden Gardner.	
Joins Ferguson.	
On Richland Creek.	
On the E. side of the Neches.	
On the waters of the Trinity.	
On tho Angelina, joins W. Gates.	
On Richland Creek.	
Head waters of the Angelina.	
W. bank of the Neches, joins J. Ferguson.	
Waters of Trinity, joins Robins.	
Joins Elisha Clark.	
On the E. side of the Neches.	
On the waters of the Angelina.	
" "	
Neches, E. side, joins Saline.	
Joins Elijah Gosset.	
San Antonio Road, W. of the Trinity.	
Waters of Trinity, S. of the Neches, joins Wm. M'Donald.	
On Comanche Road, 4 miles from Ironeyes Village.	
On the Amoladeras Creek.	
On the San Pedro, joins Wm. Davis.	
Joins Henry Stockman.	
Ten miles W. of the Delamaw Village.	
W. of the Trinity, joins Shelton Alphin.	

ABSTRACT OF ORIGINAL TITLES

VEHLEIN'S COLONY.

NAMES OF GRANTEES.	DATE OF TITLES.	QUANTITY.	
		Leagues.	Labors.
Elijah Anderson,	April 30, 1835.		24
Ransom Alphin,	May 22, "	1	
Ethan Allen,	" 11, "	1	
William S. Allen,	June 2, "	1	
Jesse A. Aughinsbaugh,	July 9, "	1	
George Allen,	Aug. 27, "	1	
Jacob Armstrong,	" 12, "	¼	
Uriah Anderson,	Oct. 24, "	¼	
Henry W. Augustin,	" 13, "	1	
Nathaniel Amory,	" 5, "	¼	
John W. Adams,	March 25, "	1	
Colin Aldrich,	Feb. 14, "	1	
James Blunt,	March 20, "	1	
Warren Birdsell,	Nov. 14, "	1	
Thomas Burrus,	Feb. 5, "	1	
Burrel Blackman,	March 21, "	1	
Genereaux Benard,	" 16, "	¼	
Nelson Box,	" 15, "	¼	
M. L. Bodin,	April 13, "	1	
Stephen Box,	" 6, "	1	
William Burditt,	" 28, "	1	
David Beers,	May 2, "	1	
John Bush,	" 13, "	¼	
Pliny Blanchard,	" 30, "	1	
Juan Nicolas Bodin,	June 29, "	1	
Juan Lorenzo Boden,	July 30, "	1	
Joab J. Blackman,	" 24, "	1	
Andres Bermea,	" 29, "	1	
Maria Josefa Borsoly,	" 3, "	1	
John S. Blunt,	" 18, "	1	
Pierre Blanchet,	" 7, "	¼	
Samuel Burress,	" 24, "	¼	
John Box,	" 30, "	1	
Gilbert Brooks,	Aug. 17, "	1	
James H. Blount,	Nov. 5, "	1	
John D. Burks,	Aug. 27, "	1	
Stephen Box, Jr.,	" 15, "	¼	
Stilwell Box,	" " "	1	
James Boulter,	" 18, "	1	
John Berger,	" 27, "	1	
William Bloodgood,	" " "		18
Bennet, Blake	Aug. 27, 1835.	1	
Rafael Bicera,	Sept. 15, "	1	
John Bland,	June 18, "	1	
William Beasley,	Sept. 30, "	1	
William Busby,	Oct. 22, "	1	
Berry Beasly,	" 28, "	1	
Maria Theresa Boden,	" 9, "	1	
Antonio Chavana,	Oct. 17, "	1	
Jose R. Chavana,	" 15, "	1	
John Caruthers,	Nov. 13, "	1	
John H. Cummins,	Jan. 5, "	1	
John Crippin,	Feb. 14, "	1	
Hillary M. Crabb,	" 10, "	1	

VEHLEIN'S COLONY.

WHERE SITUATED.	REMARKS.
On Bead Eye Creek.	
W. of the Trinity.	
"	
On the E. side of San Jacinto.	
" " Trinity.	
On Woods' Creek, [a branch of Big Sandy.]	
On the E. side of Cedar Bayou.	
Joins James Martin.	
On Big Sandy Creek, adjoining John Nash.	
Eight miles from Long King's Village, joins James Garner.	
On the W. side of the Trinity, joins Thos. J. Chambers.	
On the E. side of the Trinity.	
On Cyprus Bayou, joining Jane Taylor.	
On Nelson's Creek, waters of the Trinity, joins H. M. Crabb.	
On the E. bank of the Trinity.	
In the vicinity of Cyprus Creek, joins widow Jane Taylor.	
Joins John Cummins.	
Joins Stilwell Box.	
On the waters of White Rock Creek, joins Juan Cruz.	
On the Carrizo, joins Maria Jacinto Charmar.	
On the waters of the Trinity, joins Edinburg.	
On the W. branch of the San Jacinto.	
On the waters of the Neches, joins Bean and M. Garret.	
Trinity, E. side, joins Moses Gragg.	
Joins B. Williams.	
Joins Marmon and Mancus.	
In the vicinity of Cyprus Creek.	
Near Bean's Mill, S. of Nacogdoches.	
On the waters of the Neches, Joins Brooks Williams.	
Joins John Welsh.	
On a branch of the San Jacinto.	
On Walnut Bayou.	
On the E. bank of the San Jacinto.	
Joins William Williams.	
Joins Lindsey on Long King's Bayou.	
On the E. side of the Trinity.	
On Haw Bayou, joins Hodge's.	
On Long King's Bayou, joins Miles Dykes.	
On Kickapoo Creek.	
Cedar Bayou, S. E., joining Griffith are 7 labors, and 11 joins the Walnut League.	
Adjoining James Clarkson.	
Neches.	
On the waters of Long King Creek.	
On the E. bank of the Trinity, joining James S. Garner.	
On the San Jacinto, joining J. Rankin, Jr.	
San Jacinto, joining T. J. Rankin.	
Six miles from Galveston Bay, E. of Double Bayou.	
Adjoining Jose Anselmo Prado.	
On moral Creek and San Antonio Road, joins Lavega and Morin.	
On a branch of Harmond's Creek, waters of Neches.	
On the bank of the Trinity.	
On the W. bank of the Trinity.	
Joins Warren Birdsell, Nelson's Creek, waters of the Trinity.	

VEHLEIN'S COLONY.

NAMES OF GRANTEES.	DATE OF TITLES.	QUANTITY.	
		Leagues	Labors
Moses L. Choate,	Feb. 7, 1835.	1	
Thomas Caro,	Nov. 22, 1834.	1	
Francis B. Conner,	March 14, 1835.	1	
W. A. Cook,	" " "	1	
John Crane,	" 5, "	1	
Ann D. Criswell,	" 25, "	1	
Juan Cruz,	April 10, "	1	
John Crist,	" 13, "	1	
Joseph Carriere,	" 6, "	1	
Elijah Collard,	" 29, "	1	
Barton Clark,	" 3, "	1	
William Cruz,	May 18, "	1	
Job S. Collard,	" 28, "	1	
Francisca Castaneda,	" 27, "	1	
Rafael de los Santos Coy,	June 4, "	1	
Lewis Cox,	July 4, "	1	
Henry H. Cone,	Aug. 27, "	1	
Thomas Colwell,	" 30, "	1	
Lemuel M. Collard,	" 27, "	1	
Julio Cevalles,	" 28, "	1	
Pedro Jose Caro,	" 7, "	1	
David Choate,	" 12, "	1	
Ignacio Chapa,	" 7, "	1	
Macedonia Carmona,	" 27, "	1	
Patrick Carnal,	Sept. 17, "	1	
J. S. Collard,	" 27, "	¼	
James H. Collard,	" 28, "	¼	
Maria B. Cruz,	Oct. 12, "	1	
Isaac S. Conaway,	" 14, "	1	
Moses A. Carroll,	" 3, "	1	
Juan Carmona,	" 2, "	1	
Phillip Carrol,	" 14, "	1	
Ma. Guadalupe de Castro,	" 13, "	1	
Ignacio de los Santos Coy,	" 15, "	1	
Na. M. S. de Cazanova,	" " "	1	
John Colvin,	July 20, "	½	
Maria Jacinto Chamar,	" 30, "		23,166,800
John Davis,	March 18, "	1	
Amos Donovan,	April 13, "	1	
Jacob Duncan,	May 16, "	¼	
Levi B. Dikes,	" 28, "	1	
Sarah Ann Duncan,	June 16, "	1	
Jesse Devore,	" 20, "	1	
John M. Dikes,	" " "	1	
Meredith Duncan,	July 25, "	1	
George P. Dikes,	" 28, "	1	
Edward B. Davis,	Aug. 27, "	¼	
Luis Davi,	Sept. 11, "	1	
Daniel Donaho,	" 3, "	1	

VEHLEIN'S COLONY.

WHERE SITUATED.	REMARKS.
On Long King's Creek, on the road from the village of the same, joins J. Morgan.	
Joins Joseph de La Baume.	
On Walnut Creek.	
On Harmon's Creek.	
On Long King's Creek, joining Dan. Wilburn.	
White Rock Creek, branch of.	
On San Antonio Road, joins Young & Mitchell.	
Menard's Mill Creek, joins James Erie.	
On the E. bank of the San Jacinto.	
" " Trinity.	
On the waters of the Trinity, joining James S. Ward.	
On the waters of Bead Eye's Creek, joins John Talbot.	
On Sandy Creek.	
On the waters of the Trinity.	
Adjoining M'Donald.	
On Big Sandy Creek, adjoining Benj. F. Ellis and Joseph Ellis.	
On Big Sandy Creek.	
On the waters of the San Jacinto, joins Cameron.	
On the waters of White Rock Creek.	
Waters of the Trinity, joins Ignacio Chapa and Jose Leonso Lopez.	
N. of Pine Island, Bayou, and on a road leading from the same to Bevil's Settlement.	
Between the Little Neches and Trinity, on Cummin's Road, joins Pedro Jose Caro.	
On the waters of the Neches, joins John S. Roberts.	
On Menard Creek, joins E. Davis.	
Adjoining Ruth Miller.	
Adjoining Jonathan S. Collard,	
On the waters of White Rock Creek.	
Adjoining Thomas Williams.	
On Turtle Bayou and Galveston Bay, joins La Badia.	
On the Neches.	
On the W. side of the Neches.	
" " "	
" " of Little Neches.	
Menard's Creek, E. of the Trinity.	
Joins Stephen Box, on the Carrizo.	
Seventeen labors on the W. bank of the Trinity, and the remainder at the mouth of Nelson's Creek.	
On White Rock Creek.	
Two leagues from the Angelina, joins D. Nowlan.	
On the waters of the Trinity, joins James S. Ward.	
On the waters of Sorrel Creek, between the Neches and Angelina, joins John Durst.	
Ten miles E. of the Trinity, joins Philip P. Dever.	
On the waters of Long King's Creek, joins Moses L. Choate.	
On the N. bank of Cedar Bayou, about 2 miles above the commencement of the salt water.	
On Long King's Creek, adjoining John Watts.	
Nine miles from the Trinity.	
On Old Trinity, joining Welsh.	
Adjoining Moses Donaho,	

ABSTRACT OF ORIGINAL TITLES

VEHLEIN'S COLONY.

NAMES OF GRANTEES.	DATE OF TITLES.	Leagues.	Labors.
William Donaho,	Sept. 3, 1835.	1	
Moses Donaho,	" 7, "	1	
Jose Alfonsa Domingues,	Oct. 21, "	1	
Jose Maria Duran,	" 10, "	1	
Ma. Gertrudas Dias,	" 9, "	1	
Lewis Duel,	" 26, "	1	
James Erie,	Nov. 21, "	1¼	
Bartolo Escobeda,	June 22, "	1	
Christopher Edinburgh,	" 12, "	1	
George Ellis,	Aug. 17, "	1	
Benjamin F. Ellis,	" 27, "	¼	
Joseph L. Ellis,	" " "	¼	
Ma. Trinidad Equis,	Oct. 9, "	1	
James L. Ewing,	" 11, "	1	
Albert Emanuel,	Nov. 25, "	1	
Antonio Flores,	Oct. 17, 1834.	1	
Juan Falcon,	April 24, 1835.	1	
John Forbes,	May 26, "	1	
Francis Fulcher,	" 14, "	1	
Isaiah Field,	June 12, "	1	
J. R. Faulk,	July 6, "	1	
Juan Flores,	Aug. 7, "	1	
Harmon Frazer,	Oct. 23, "	1	
Jose Maria Games,	Aug. 4, "	1	
Thomas B. Garret,	March 12, "	1	
Milton Garret,	May 15, "	¼	
B. B. Goodrich,	July 22, "	1	
Pleasant Gray,	" 12, "	1	
John George,	" 29, "	1	
Arthur Garner,	Sept. 30, "	1	
James A. Garner,	" 30, "	½	
James S. Garner,	" " "	1	
John Gates,	Oct. 3, "	1	
John Gregery,	Nov. 4, "	1	
T. J. Golightly,	" 3, "	¼	
Moses Gragg,	May 28, "	1	
David Huffman,	Oct. 25, 1834.	1	
Joseph Hodges,	March 16, 1835.	1	
Benj. F Harper,	" 4, "	1	
Samuel C. Hiroms,	April 30, "	1	
Lowry T. Hampton,	" 10, "	1	
Arthur Henrie,	May 16, "	1	
William Heath,	June 7, "	¼	
Milton A. Hardin,	" 17, "	¼	
Manuel Herrera,	July 6, "	1	
Harvey M. Henry,	Aug. 26, "	1	
George William Hallmark,	" 15, "	1	
Francis Hill,	" 3, "	¼	
Thos. S. Haggerty,	Sept. 17, "	1	
James Hanley,	" " "	1	
William Hardin,	" " "	1	
Matthew Hurbert,	Oct. 22, "	1	

VEHLEIN'S COLONY.

WHERE SITUATED.	REMARKS.
On the W. side of Trinity, joins Fauks.	
Adjoining Daniel Donaho.	
On Taylor's Bayou.	
On the head waters of Taylor's Bayou, near Pine Island.	
E. of Double Bayou, 6 miles from Galveston Bay.	
Adjoining John Crane's.	
Four hundred varas from Jos. La Baume's corner, in the vicinity of the Neches.	
On Big Sandy Creek, joins Lawry S. Thompson.	
On the waters of the Trinity, joins William B. Burditt.	
On Cedar Bayou, joins William Bloodgood.	
On Big Sandy Creek, joins Henry H. Cone.	
" " "	
On the W. side of the Neches.	
On the road from Nacogdoches to J. Durst's place.	
In the vicinity of Big Sandy Creek, joins H. H. Cone.	
Joins Antonio Chavana.	
On Sandy Creek.	
On the waters of White Rock Creek.	
Adjoining Robbins and Madera.	
E. bank of the Trinity.	
Between the San Jacinto and Trinity.	
On the waters of the Trinity.	
Ten miles W. of the Neches, joins Bean.	
Between the Big Sandy and Little Neches, joins Sanches.	
Joins Hugh Means.	
On the waters of the Neches, joins John Rusk.	
On the waters of the San Jacinto.	
Adjoining Wiley Parker.	
" M. Marmon and Juan Jose Villa.	
On the W. side of the Trinity.	
On the banks of the Trinity, joining Huberts.	
On the W. side of the Trinity, Joins Wm. Beasley.	
Neches, vicinity of the Sabine.	
Six or 8 miles E. of the Trinity.	
E. branch of the San Jacinto, joins Sam M'Combs.	
Russel's Creek, waters of the Trinity, about 10 miles below the San Antonio Road.	
About three miles S. E. of the Shawnee Village.	
San Antonio Road, waters of the Trinity, joins Masters.	
On Long King's Creek.	
E. Bank of the Trinity.	
On the E. bank of Big Sandy.	
Waters of a creek which are supposed to enter into White Rock Creek.	
Adjoining Jacob Masters.	
On a branch of Long King's Creek.	
On the waters of the San Jacinto.	
On the W. side of the Trinity, near the Coshate Village, joins W. G. Logan.	
On the E. side of the Trinity.	
Joins Henry Masters.	
Targleton's Prairie, joins Domingo Ybarbo.	
Between the Little Neches and the Trinity, joining Castro.	
Below the Coshate Village. - - - -	Date uncertain.
Adjoining James Rankin.	

VEHLEIN'S COLONY.

NAMES OF GRANTEES.	DATE OF TITLES.	Leagues.	Labors.
John W. Holman,	Oct. 12, 1835.	¼	-
John Harrison,	Nov. 2, "	¼	-
William Johns,	March 3, "	1	-
James Jordon,	June 3, "	1	-
Henry A. Johnson,	" 16, "	¼	-
Elizabeth Johnston,	" 20, "	1	-
R. A. Irion,	" 13, "	1	-
John W. Ingersoll,	Aug. 27, "	1	-
Isaac Jones,	" " "	1	-
John Johnson,	Oct. 6, "	1	-
David L. Kokernot,	July 23, "	1	-
Edward King,	Oct. 8, "	1	-
Spencer Kirkham,	May 4, "	1	-
Joseph de La Baume,	Nov. 21, "	1	-
Donato Leon,	Feb. 7, "	1	-
Juan Antonio Longorio,	" 9, "	1	-
John Lindsey,	March 13, "	1	-
Wm. G. Logan,	April 30, "	1	-
Jooseph Lindley,	" 6, "	1	-
Daniel Larrison,	May 16, "	1	-
Ignacio Lopez,	" " "	1	-
Benjamin Lanier,	June 20, "	1	-
Bautiste Tessier Lavigne,	July 25, "	1	-
Robert B. Longbotham,	" 24, "	1	-
Maria Carmon Liego,	" 3, "	1	-
Jonathan Lindley,	" 17, "	¼	-
Samuel Lindley,	Aug. 27, "		24
Luterio Lopez,	Sept. 11, "	1	-
Jose Leoniso Lopez,	Aug. 7, "	1	-
Samuel Larry,	Oct. 11, "	1	-
Lewis Latham,	" 15, "	1¼	-
William M. Logan,	Nov. 7, "	¼	-
Walter Little,	" 15, "	1	-
William M'Donald,	" 12, 1834.	1	-
Henry Masters,	Jan. 28, 1835.	1	-
David M'Coy,	" 30, "	1	-
Ralph M'Gee,	March 12, "	1	-
James Mitchell,	April 20, "	1	-
Manuela Montalba,	May 16, "	1	-
Francisco Martinez,	" 18, "	1	-
Stephen Manning,	" 29, "	1	-
John Magennies,	" 4, "	1	-
Phillip Miller,	June 13, "	1	-
Michael B. Menard,	" 3, "	1	-
Isaac N. Moreland,	" 19, "	¼	-
Peter T. Menard,	July 18, "	1	-
Pedro Medina,	" 22, "	1	-
Jose Morin,	" 2, "	1	-
Ma. Bonita Menchaca,	" 26, "	1	-
Joseph Morgan,	Aug. 27, "	1	-
Manuela Morman,	" 5, "	1	-
John Merry,	" 17, "	1	-
Ruthy Miller,	" " "	1	-

VEHLEIN'S COLONY.

WHERE SITUATED.	REMARKS.
On the San Antonio Road, joins L. Ewing, vicinity of Durst's Mills.	
Between the Angelina and Neches, joins Durst.	
In the vicinity of Long King's Creek.	
Joins William McDonald.	
Joins Edward Russell.	
On the waters of Long King's Creek, joins William Johnson.	
On Menard's Mill Creek.	
On Sandy Creek.	
On the W. side of the Trinity, joining Prentiss.	
Between the Little and Great Neches, joins Hanly.	
About 2600 varas from Cedar Bayou.	
On the waters of the San Jacinto.	
Between the Trinity and San Jacinto.	
Four hundred varas from Erie's corner, in the vicinity of the Neches.	
Adjoining Jose Maria Prado.	
On a creek which runs into the Neches.	
On Long King's Creek, joins Hardin.	
On the N. bank of the Trinity.	
On the waters of the San Jacinto.	
Joins John Talbert.	
Adjoining John Durst.	
On Woods' Creek, a branch of Big Sandy, joins James Woods.	
Joins Antonio Solis, on the waters of the Neches.	
Four labors joins Reding Garner and Hugh Shephard, and 21 labors joins Sarah M'Anulty.	
Two leagues E. of the Neches, joins Williams' survey.	
Adjoining James Lee.	
Twenty-three labors joins John Saddler, & 1 joins Joseph Lindley, on the waters of the San Jacinto.	
Two miles S. of the head of Taylor's Bayou, joins Robert and Velise.	
On the waters of the Trinity, joins Pedro Jose Caro.	
On the W. bank of the Trinity.	
On Cedar Bayou, joins Hugh Morgan.	
In the vicinity of Big Sandy, joins William Hardin.	
On Cedar Bayou.	
On the E. side of the San Jacinto.	
On the San Antonio Road, waters of the Trinity, joins T. Hodges.	
In the vicinity of the Neches.	
" . " Trinity.	
Joins John Crist, on the San Antonio Road.	
On the Waters of the Trinity, joins Arthur Henrie.	
On the waters of the Trinity.	
" " " "	
On Dickerson's Bayou, waters of the Neches.	
On the E. bank of the Trinity.	
On the W. bank of the Trinity.	
On a branch of Long King's Creek.	
On the E. bank of the Trinity.	
On the W. side of the Trinity.	
On Moral Creek, joins Ramon Chavana.	
Between the Big and Little Neches, joins Manuela Marmon.	
On Long King's Creek, joins Moses L. Choate.	
Between the Big and Little Neches, joins Mancha and George.	
On the San Jacinto, joins Lynch.	
On the waters of the San Jacinto.	

VEHLEIN'S COLONY.

NAMES OF GRANTEES.	DATE OF TITLES.	QUANTITY.	
		Leagues.	Labors.
Hugh Morgan, - - -	Aug. 30, 1835.	1	-
James S. M'Gahey, - -	" 17, "	1	-
William M'Fadin, - -	" 5, "	1	-
Andrew Morales, - -	" 30, "	1	-
Abner Mardez, - -	Sept. 12, "	1	-
Angus M'Neil, - -	" 15, "	1	-
John E. Mayfield, - -	" 16, "	1	-
William Morris, - -	Oct. 14, "	1	-
John Moore, - -	" 22, "	1	-
George R. Mercer, - -	" 14, "	1	-
James Morgan, - - -	" 8, "	1	-
Hugh Means, - - -	" 15, "	1	-
John W. Moreland, - -	" 27, "	1	-
Juan Jose Medina, - -	Nov. 20, "	1	-
Henry C. M'Neill, - -	" 22, "	¼	-
James M'Daniel, - -	Oct. 6, "	¼	-
Sam'l P. M'Farland, - -	" 16, "	¼	-
Neal Martin, - -	April 13, "	1	-
Daniel Nowlan, - -	May 11, "	¼	-
Thomas Newman, - -	June 20, "	1	-
Stephen Nicholson, - -	July 25, "	1	-
James Neville, - -	Oct. 2, "	1	-
Hannah Nash, - - -	" 9, "	1	-
Baltazar Orset, - -	March 10, "	1	-
Jose Anselmo Prado, - -	Oct. 17, "	1	-
Vicente Padilla, - -	Jan. 3, "	1	-
Jesse Parker, - -	Feb. 11, "	1	-
Wiley Parker, - -	" " "	1	-
John T. Pinckney, - -	April 30, "	1	-
George Pollit, - -	" 10, "		12
Eusebio Pantalion, - -	" 25, "	1	-
William Pace, - -	May 3, "	1	-
Isaac Parker, - -	" 6, "	1	-
James J. Porter, - -	" 5, "	1	-
Jose Martin Prado, - -	" 18, "	1	-
Juan Bautista Palvador, - -	June 2, "	1	-
Joseph Pritchard, - -	" 21, "	¼	-
William Prissich, - -	" 15, "	1	-
Francisco Perez, - -	" 2, "	1	-
Jonathan C. Pitts, - -	Sept. 13, "	1	-
Jose Policarpio Procela, - -	Oct. 12, "	1	-
Moses L. Patton, - -	Dec. 2, "	¼	-
Robert S. Patton, - -	" " "	1	-
Christopher A. Parker, - -	Nov. 20, "	¼	-
George Robbins, - -	Oct. 16, 1834.	1	-
Nathaniel Robbins, - -	" 17, "	1	-
Reuben R. Russell, - -	Dec. 23, "	1	-
Elijah Ratliff, - -	Jan. 30, 1835.	1	-
Wm. Robinson, - -	March 7, "	1	-
Robert Rankin, - -	April 24, "	1	-
Charles S. Roberts, - -	" 10, "	¼	-
Edward Roberts, - -	" 11, "	¼	-
Henry Raguet, - -	May 21, "	1	-
William Roark, - -	June 22, "	1	-

VEHLEIN'S COLONY.

WHERE SITUATED.	REMARKS.
W. of Cedar Bayou, N. of Mrs. Nash.	
Adjoining White.	
On Long King's Creek, joins Harper.	
On Big Sandy Creek, joins Maria Thomas.	
Between Cedar Bayou and Old River.	
E. of the Trinity, joins P. Blanchet and P. Miller.	
Trinity, joins M'Gee.	
Joins Thomas R. Townsend.	
San Jacinto, E. side.	
On Menard's Bayou, Near Menard's House, joins E. B. Davis.	
Targleton's Prairie, W. of the Trinity, joins John Faulk.	
On Menard's Creek, E. of the Trinity.	
On Big Sandy Creek, joins Henry Cone.	
Adjoining Wiley Thomas.	
On the Neches River.	
On the E. side of the Angelina.	
W. bank of the San Jacinto.	
Two leagues from the Angelina, joins R. Miller.	
Between the same and San Jacinto, joins B. Tarkington.	
Between the Trinity and San Jacinto.	
About 12 or 14 miles E. of the Trinity, and the same distance from San Antonio Road.	
On the E. of Cedar Bayou.	
Joins Antonio Chavana.	
In the vicinity of the Neches.	
Adjoining Wiley Parker.	
Adjoining Jesse Parker.	
On the E. bank of Trinity.	
And 498,200 square varas, on Sorrel Creek.	
On White Rock Creek.	
On the E. side of the Trinity.	
On the E. bank of the Trinity.	
On the W. bank of the Trinity.	
On the waters of the Trinity, joining Manuela Montalla.	
Joins Edward Russell.	
About 8 miles from Thomas Townsend.	
On the waters of the Trinity.	
On the San Jacinto.	
On the waters of the Trinity.	
Adjoining B. Ellis.	
On Big Sandy Creek, joins Womack.	
On E. side of the Trinity, joins P. Miller.	
On the N. side of a creek which runs into the Trinity on the E.	
On the W. margin of Trinity River.	
On a creek which runs into the Neches.	
On the banks of the Trinity.	
On the San Jacinto, joins Wm. M'Donald.	
High Lands, W. of the Trinity.	
On the waters of White Rock Creek, joins Cruz.	
On the waters of White Rock Creek.	
On the waters of the Trinity, joins William Cruz.	
Adjoining William Cook.	

ABSTRACT OF ORIGINAL TITLES

VEHLEIN'S COLONY.

NAMES OF GRANTEES.	DATE OF TITLES.	QUANTITY.	
		Leagues.	Labors.
Sina Runnels,	June 22, 1835.	1	-
John Roark,	July 25, "	1	-
Benjamin W. Robinson,	Aug. 18, "	1	-
Edward Russell.	" 21, "	1	-
John R. Rhea,	" 17, "	1	-
James Rankin, Jr.,	Oct. 30, "	1	-
Ashley B. Rozell,	" 20, "	1	-
James Rankin, Sr.,	" 22, "	1	-
R. C. Rodgers,	" 20, "	1	-
Russell Roark,	" 14, "	¼	-
Robert W. Russell,	" " "	1	-
James W. Robinson,	" 6, "	1	-
William Richards,	" 11, "	¼	-
Juan Jose de los Reyes,	" 12, "	1	-
Guadalupe Ricardo,	" 14, "	1	-
William Richardson,	" 20, "	¼	-
Antonio Solis,	Feb. 7, "	1	-
John J. Simpson,	" 5, "	1	-
Jose Maria Soto,	" 9, "	1	-
Thomas Stephens,	March 2, "	1	-
William Smith,	April 30, "	1	-
William D. Smith,	" " "	1	-
Guadaloupe Sosa,	" 11, "	1	-
John Saddler,	" 29, "	1	-
Jeremiah Strode,	May 18, "	1	-
Jose Juan Sanches,	June 18, "	1	-
Joseph W. Scates,	" 21, "	1	-
James Simmons,	" 20, "	1	-
Willafred Stanly,	" 15, "	1	-
John Scott,	July 11, "	1	-
Christian Smith,	" 20, "	1	-
Candido Sanches,	" 30, "	1	-
Jose Antonio Sepulbeda,	Aug. 27, "	1	-
Alexander Smith,	" 17, "	¼	-
Thomas Smith,	" 12, "	1	-
Morris Smith,	Sept. 5, "	1	-
John Stewart,	" 18, "	1	-
Philip A. Sublett,	Oct. 9, "	1	-
Miles G. Stevens,	" 26, "	1	-
Jane Taylor,	March 21, "	1	-
Geraldus S. Thomas,	" 2, "	1	-
Joseph C. Teague,	" 10, "	1	-
Miguel Torres,	" 26, "	1	-
Jacob Townsend,	April 30, "	¼	-
Arnold Thouvenin,	" 24, "	¼	-
John Talbert,	May 27, "	1	-
James T. Thomas,	June 7, "	1	-
Seth Orville Thomson,	" 10, "	¼	-
J. S. Thorn,	" 11, "	¼	-
Peter Teal,	" 4, "	1	-
John B. Tong,	July 24, "	¼	-
Manuel Tascan,	Sept. 17, "	1	-
Maria Josefa Torres,	Oct. 7, "	1	-

VEHLEIN'S COLONY.

WHERE SITUATED.	REMARKS.
On Woods's Creek, joins J. B. Woods.	
Joins David Beers.	
On the E. bank of the San Jacinto.	
Adjoining Briscoe.	
On the E. bank of the San Jacinto.	
Joins Berry Beasley, on the San Jacinto.	
Joins Daniel Donaho.	
On the W. bank of the Trinity.	
On Big Alabama, joins Lancaster.	
Joins David Beers.	
Joins Thomas Williams.	
Joins Thomas Choate.	
On the E. side of the Trinity.	
On Hog Creek, W. of the Neches.	
In the Forks of the two Neches.	
On Menard's Creek, E. side of the Trinity.	
On Long King's Creek, on the Road from the Village of the same, joins Jas. Morgan.	
On the W. bank of the Trinity.	
Joins Vicente Padilla.	
On the E. bank of the Trinity.	Special Grant. No title.
Part on the shore of Galveston Bay, joining Imes; and part on the N. side of Trinity, and part on the E. bank of Cedar Bayou.	
In the vicinity of White Rock Creek, waters of the Trinity.	
Joins Joseph Lindley.	
On San Antonio Road, between the Neches and Trinity.	
On the waters of the San Jacinto, joins A. Jaques.	
On Long King's Creek, joins William McFaddin.	
On Woods's Creek, waters of the big Sandy, joins J. B. Woods.	
W. of the Angelina.	
Joins Birdsoll, who has his lands on Nelson's Creek, waters of the Trinity.	
W. of the Trinity.	
Between the Little and Big Neches.	
On White Rock Creek.	
On the waters of the Trinity, Joins Wm. Hardin.	
On the waters of the Angelina.	
Between the Trinity and San Jacinto, joins Thomas Newman.	
Above the lower Coshate Village.	
Joins P. T. Menard.	
Joins Blanchet.	
On Cyprus Bayou, joins James Blunt and Burrell Blackman.	
On the E. bank of the Trinity, joins Peter T. Menard.	
On the waters of the Neches, joins Reuben R. Russell.	
On White Rock Creek.	
W. of the Trinity, joins Winfree.	
On Long King' Creek, joins McFaddin.	
On the waters of Bead Eeye's Creek, joins Larrison and Collard.	
On the waters of the Trinity.	
" " " joins James Robertson.	
Five miles from the Trinity, joins a survey made by E. Russell.	
On the waters of the San Jacinto, joins B. B. Goodrich.	
Joins Joseph Lindley.	
On white Rock Creek, joins J. S. Ward's Survey.	
On Caney Bayou, W. of the Trinity.	

VEHLEIN'S COLONY.

NAMES OF GRANTEES.	DATE OF TITLES.	QUANTITY.	
		Leagues.	Labors.
Isabella Townsend, - -	Oct. 14, 1835.	1	-
Oliver Mills Vinton, - -	June 10, "	1	-
Juan Jose Villa, - - -	Aug. 4, "	1	-
Anastasio Varela,	Oct. 20, "	1	-
John A. Veitch, - - -	" 26, "	1	-
Leonard Williams, - -	Jan. 13, "	1	-
John Watts, - - -	March 14, "	1	-
William Wilburn, - - -	" 21, "	1	-
William Whiteley, -	" 14, "	¼	-
James B. Woods, - -	April 9, "	1	-
James S. Ward, - - -	" 11, "	1	-
John Welsh, - -	June 20, "	1	-
Daniel Wilburn, - - -	" 2, "	1	-
Henry White, - -	July 6, "	¼	-
Brooks William, - -	" 24, "	1	-
Andrew E. Westall, - -	July 5, "	1	-
William Weir, - - -	Aug. 17, "	1	-
James Winters, - -	" 18, "	1	-
John B. Win, - - -	" 27, "	1	-
Jesse White, - -	" 17, "	¼	-
Andrew Wilkie, - -	" 30, "	¼	-
Mark S. Womack, - -	" 27, "	1	-
Charles C. P. Welch, - -	Sept. 5, "	1	-
Jordan West, - -	" 5, "	1	-
George White, - - -	Oct. 7, "	1	-
William Winters, - -	" 30, "	¼	-
"	" "	½	-
Jefferson Wilson, - -	" 10, "	1	-
Mitchell Wood, - - -	" 29, "	¼	-
Omy Weir, - -	" 17, "	1	-
Thomas Wilson, - - -	" 15, "	1	-
Harrison E. Watson, - -	" 23, "	1	-
David Wilson, - - -	" 20, "	1	-
John A. Wagner, - -	Nov. 20, "	¼	-
John Waugh, - - -	" 12, "	1	-
Willis B. Watson, - -	" 24, "	1	-
Maria Ximenes, - - -	" 2, "	1	-
Thomas D. Yocum, - -	March 2, "		-
Jose Damacio Ybarbo, -	May 4, "		-
Joseph Young,,	June 20, "	1	-
Thomas D. Yocum, - -	Aug. 17, "		-
Anastacio Ybarbo, - -	Oct. 8, "	1	-
Martin Ybarbo, - - -	" 17, "	1	-
Jesse Young, ' - -	Nov. 25, "	1	-
Domingo Ybarbo, - - -	" 14, "	1	-

VEHLEIN'S COLONY.

WHERE SITUATED.	REMARKS.
San Antonio Road, 10 or 12 miles from the Trinity.	
Three miles E. of the Trinity, joins James T. Thomas.	
On the waters of the Little Neches, joins George.	
E. of the Neches.	
Joins W. G. Castro.	
On the banks of the Neches.	
In the vicinity of Long King's Creek.	
In the vicinity of Cypress Creek, joins Burrell Blackman.	
On the S. side of Rosa Creek.	
N. of the Road from Liberty to Nacogdoches.	
On the waters of White Rock Creek, joins Maria Luisa Boden.	
On the E. side of the Trinity, on an old Spanish road, from an old fort, to Nacogdoches.	
On Long King's Creek, on the waters of the Trinity.	
Joins Christian Smith.	
Vicinity of the Neches.	
In the vicinity of the Trinity.	
On the E. side of the San Jacinto, joins N. Martin.	
On the waters of the San Jacinto.	
On the banks of the Trinity.	
On the E. bank of San Jacinto, joins George White.	
Joins Thompson.	
On Big Sandy Creek, joins Ellis.	
On the W. bank of Old Trinity.	
Between the Trinity and San Jacinto, joins Targleton's survey.	
On the E. side of San Jacinto, joins R. White.	
Joins Cameron and Briscoe.	
Joins William Busby and James Rankin.	
Thirteen miles from Nacogdoches, S. of San Antonio Road.	
Joins Matthew Hubert and Robert Rankin.	
S. of the San Antonio Road, joins John Chairs.	
On the E. bank of the San Jacinto.	
On the waters of Long King's Creek, 10 miles E. of the Trinity.	
Eighteen labors joins Wm. Beasley, E. side of Trinity, and 6 joins James Rankin, Jr.	Two surveys
Joins Pollard and Smith.	
On a branch of the San Jacinto, joins R. Miller.	
In the vicinity of Mill Creek.	
In the vicinity of Big Alabama Creek.	
15,250,760 sq. vs., on the E. bank of the Trinity, joins Baker M. Spinks.	
On the waters of the Neches.	
Joins Thompson.	
9,749,240 sq. vs., joins Choate, M'Kinney, and Menard.	
Eight miles from Galveston Bay, E. of Double Bayou.	
Vicinity of the Neches, E. side, joins Chavana.	
Joins Nathaniel Robbins.	
Targleton's Prairie, joins Garret.	

ABSTRACT OF ORIGINAL TITLES

ZAVALA'S COLONY.

NAMES OF GRANTEES.	DATE OF TITLES.	QUANTITY.	
		Leagues.	Labors.
Nathaniel Allen,	April 6, 1835.	1	-
John Allen,	July 23, "	1	-
William B. Anderson,	Sept. 26, "	1	-
Aaron Ashley,	Oct. 4, "	1	-
Hannah Alexander,	Nov. 21, "	1	-
Benjamin Burke,	Oct. 28, "	1	-
Jehu Bevil,	" 29, 1834.	1	-
Jehu Bevil, Jr.	Nov. 10, "	$\frac{1}{4}$	-
Hiram Brown,	Dec. 23, "	1	-
David Brown,	" 15, 1835.	1	-
James W. Bullock,	Jan. 17, "	1	-
Anderson Barclay,	Feb. 18, "	1	-
John Blair,	" 19, "	1	-
Thomas H. Bruce,	" 26, "	1	-
James Burroughs,	June 15, "	1	-
Bennet Blackman,	" 25, "	1	-
Elias Bowker,	" 22, "	$\frac{1}{4}$	-
G. L. Bourland,	July 17, "	1	-
S. P. Bankston,	Aug. 22, "	1	-
Mark M. Bradly,	" 27, "	1	-
George W. Brooks,	" 22, "	1	-
Sam Bates,	Sept. 4, "	1	-
David Baird,	" 30, "	1	-
Oliver P. Bourland,	" 21, "	$\frac{1}{4}$	-
A. A. Burrell,	" 2, "	1	-
Moseley Baker,	Oct. 9, "	1	-
Andrew D. Bateman,	" 12, "	1	-
Lucretia Brown,	" 16, "	1	-
Joseph Butler,	" 17, "	1	-
William B. Burton,	" 22, "	1	-
Richard Ballew,	" " "	1	-
Frederick Bigner,	" 14, "	$\frac{1}{4}$	-
George Butler,	Nov. 5, "	1	-
Ross M. Bridges,	" 21, "	1	-
Henry Binns,	" 27, "	1	-
Robert Conn,	Nov. 3, 1834.	$\frac{1}{4}$	-
James Conn,	Jan. 26, 1835.	1	-
William Coote,	Feb. 4, "	1	-
James A. Currey,	" 24, "	1	-
George S. W. Collins,	March 16, "	1	-
Squire Cruse,	" 4, "	1	-
Andrew Caddell,	April 14, "	1	-
Maria Candida de Chirino,	" 13, "	1	-
Chichester Chaplin,	May 18, "	1	-
Manuel Chirino,	" 27, "	1	-
Armstead Chumney,	June 28, "	1	-
William Carrol,	" 15, "	1	-
William F. Clark,	" 21, "	1	-
Theophilus Cushing,	" 4, "	1	-
Shelby Corsine,	June 16, "		18,625,650
Mishack Cummings,	" 19, "	1	-
Jno. Baptiste Cazenave,	" 13, "	1	-
James Clark,	June 8, "	$\frac{1}{4}$	-

ZAVALA'S COLONY.

WHERE SITUATED.	REMARKS.
Joins Burk.	
On the Sabine, joins Richard Bellew.	
Joins Henry Stagner.	
On the banks of the Angelina.	
On Big Alabama.	
On a tributary of the Neches called Coyote.	
On Sandy Creek, Joins Henry Thompson.	
On Walnut Creek, joins John Bevil and Robert Conn.	
At a marsh on the W. side of the Neches, joins John Grigsby.	
Neches, W. side, joins Noah Tevis.	
Neches, W. side, joins Charles Williams.	
On Coyote or Wolf Creek, a branch of the Neches.	
Twenty miles W. of the town of Santa Anna, in the vicinity of Wolf Point.	
On the Neches, E. side, adjoining Ashworth & widow Nancy Davis.	
On Taylor's Bayou.	
On the waters of the Trinity and Neches.	
On the banks of the Sabine and vicinity of Housan's Creek.	
On the W. side of the Neches.	
" " "	
" " "	
Joins L. S. Waters.	
Joins Creen Cook.	
Joins Joseph Ellery.	
On the E. shore of Galveston Bay.	
On the W. Bank of Ayish Bayou.	
On the banks of the Neches.	
N. W. shore of the Sabine Lake.	
On Flour Bayou, joins Burrell Blackman.	
On the W. side of the Sabine.	
Joins H. Williams.	
Joins Mary Lankford.	
On the W. side of the Neches, joins Bankston.	
Adjoining John Bevil.	
Half a league on Sandy Creek, tributary of the Neches, and half a league on Bullrush Creek,	
On the W. side of Ayish Bayou.	
Joins James M'Quin.	
On the W. bank of the Neches.	
Twenty-one labors on Wolf Creek, joins Anderson Barclay, and 3 labors on Canada del Nogal, (Walnut Pass.)	
On the N. E. bank of the Angelina.	Petitioned for 1 leag.; title made for 5 labors— 767,500 sq. vs.
On the Atascoso Creek.	
On Ayish Bayou.	
Between the branches of Taylor's Bayou.	
On Ayish Bayou.	
On the W. side of the Neches, joins J. Durst.	
Adjoining John Gallion.	
On the W. side of the Neches.	
Varas, adjoining Pevtot and Stephens.	
Joins J. Nelson.	
On the waters of Big Alabama Creek, about 2 leagues from Bartlett.	
Adjoining William Clark.	

ABSTRACT OF ORIGINAL TITLES

ZAVALA'S COLONY.

NAMES OF GRANTEES.	DATE OF TITLES.	QUANTITY.	
		Leagues.	Labors.
William Clark,	June, 1835.	1	-
Levi M. Crow,	June 27, "	¼	-
John Clark,	July 22, "	1	-
David A. Cunningham,	" 23, "	¼	-
Daniel Chesher,	" 2, "	¼	-
Matthew Cartwright,	" 17, "	¼	-
Eligio Clark,	" 13, "	¼	-
Henry Canfield,	Aug. 30, "	1	-
William N. Cox,	" 16, "	1	-
David Cutts,	Sept. 10, "	1	-
S. Crissman,	" 13, "	1	-
Nicholas Coleman,	Aug. 29, "	1	-
"	Oct. 3, "		4
William Colwell,	" 6, "	¼	-
John Caughran,	" 14, "	¼	-
Wright Cooley,	" 15, "	1	-
Alanson W. Canfield,	" 13, "	1	-
William Campbell,	" 15, "	1	-
James Chesser,	Nov. 11, "	1	-
John Childers,	" 23, "	1	-
Elisha M. Collins,	" 15, "	1	-
Nancy Davis,	Feb. 27, "	1	-
William Defee,	" 13, "	⅔	-
Sophia Dean,	" 19, "	1	-
William Dyson,	" 13, "	1	-
James Dyson,	March 13, "	1	-
Wm. M. Davis,	" 26, "	1	-
William Davis,	April 7, "	¼	-
Sam'l Davis,	" " "	¼	-
Cadwalder Davis,	May 13, "	1	-
Obidiah Denmon,	July 27, "	¼	-
James Drake,	" 19, "	1	-
Elisha Duncan,	Aug. 30, "	1	-
Uriah Davidson,	" 24, "	1	-
John M. Dean,	Sept. 12, "	1	-
Wesley Dikes,	Oct. 16, "	1	-
Willis Donahoe,	" 21, "	1	-
William Denton,	" " "	1	-
Delily, Deark	" 23, "	1	-
Willis Donahoe,	Nov. 7, "	¼	-
John Dorsett,	" 18, "	1	-
Daniel Donahoe,	Dec. 4, "	1	-
Stephen H. Everett,	Feb. 28, "	1	-
Daniel Easley,	" 21, "	1	-
George English,	July 29, "	¼	-
F. P. Elliott,	Aug. 27, "	1	-
Alfred Ellis,	" " "	1	-
Joseph Ellery,	" 23, "	1	-
Daniel F. Edwards,	Sept. 7, "	1	-
Nicholas Elliott,	" 6, "	1	-
Stephen Eaton,	Oct. 24, "	1	-
James English,	" 17, "	¼	-
Jose Falcon,	May 28, "	1	-
John J. French,	June 26, "	1	-
Susannah Frassier,	" 4, "		

ZAVALA'S COLONY.

WHERE SITUATED.	REMARKS.

Adjoining James Clark, the field notes say it contains 23,742,000 sq. vs.
Ayish Bayou, E. side.
Joins James Clark.
Joins Wm. Zigler.
On Sandy Creek, adjoining D. C. M'Queen.
On the E. side of the Atoyac, joins Spear.
Joins James Clark.
On the W. bank of the Sabine.
On the W. side of the Neches.
Joins Thomas Williams.
Joins H. Pace.
On the E. side of the Ayish Bayou.
On Sabine Lake.
On the banks of Atoyac.
Adjoining Lefroi Jedrups.
On the N. side of Palogacha.
On the W. side of the Sabine.
On the W. side of the Neches, joins Parker.
Joins George Butler.
Five miles from the Sabine.
On the W. bank of the Sabine.
On the E. bank of the Neches, joins James H. Breece.
On the W. side of the Sabine, near the mouth of the Partroon.
About 15 miles W. of the town of Santa Anna, joins Susannah Horton.
On the W. bank of Cow Creek, joins John Jett.
On Cow Creek, joins William Dyson.
Between the Neches and Trinity, about 5 leagues from Choate.
Adjoining Samuel Davis.
At the marsh of the E. bank of the Neches.
On the waters of the Sabine.
Joins Stephen Williams.
On the Neches. [The field notes say, contains 9,364,371 square vras.]
On the W. side of the Neches.
On the W. side of the Neches, joins A. W. Smith.
Joins Hardy Pace.
On Pine Island Bayou.
" " joins Reuben Wood.
" " joins Stephen Jackson.
On the banks of the Sabine.
On a branch of Pine Island Bayou.
On Sabine Bay, joins Joseph Butler.
On the waters of Pine Island Bayou and Big Alabama.
On Maleroso. a branch of Cow Creek, a tributary of Sabine.
On Pine Island Creek, joins Hezekiah Williams.
Joins Martin White.
On the W. side of the Neches.
" "
" "

N. of Taylor's Bayou, joins Watson Pevetoe, and Burrell.
On the waters of the Sabine, joins Tolly.
On a branch of the Big Alabama, 7 miles from A. Bartlett.
On Flower Creek.
Ten labors and 811,597 square varas, on the waters of the Neches.

ABSTRACT OF ORIGINAL TITLES

ZAVALA'S COLONY.

NAMES OF GRANTEES.	DATE OF TITLES.	QUANTITY.	
		Leagues.	Labors.
John Ferguson,	June 11, 1835.	1	
Benjamin F. Fuller,	" 16, "	1	
Charles A. Felder,	Aug. 29, "	1	
Samuel R. Fisher,	" 16, "	1	
John Fisher,	" 14, "	1	
Nathaniel Grigsby,	Oct. 28, 1834.	¼	
Joseph Grigsby,	Nov. 6, "	1	
Sally Glenn,	" 4, "	1	
James Gerish, Sr.,	Jan. 27, 1835.	1	
James Gerish, Jr.,	Feb. 17, "	1	
Peter Galoway.	April 15, "	1	
Larkin Gross,	May 28, "	1	
Thomas C. Gaines,	June 20, "	1	
Gregoria Garcia,	" " "	1	
Lefroi Gedruf,	" " "	1	
John Gilbert,	" 5, "	1	
Edward Good,	July 6, "	1	
Allen G. Gray,	Sept. 16, "	1	
Marcello Grange,	Oct. 15, "	1	
Walter B. Graham,	" 26, "	¼	
Samuel L. Graham,	" " "	¼	
Shearly Goodwin,	" 18, "	1	
Robert Goodwin,	" 15, "	1	
Henry Goodwin,	" " "	1	
Jose Garcia,	Nov. 15, "	1	
Casimiro Garcia,	" 23, "	1	
John Graham,	" 7, "	1	
Charles Gilchrist,	" 20, "	1	
Jacob Garret,	" 9, "	1	
John Gallion,	June 19, "	1	
Wyatt Hanks,	Oct. 7, 1834.	1	
Augustin Hotchkiss,	Nov. 21, "	1	
Nathaniel Hunt,	" 24, "	1	
James Hoggatt,	Jan. 18, 1835.	1	
Almanza Huston,	Feb. 14, "	1	
Susannah Horton,	" 24, "	1	
Joses Hobdy,	" 18, "	1	
Alexander Horton,	" 24, "	¼	
Pelham Humphries,	" 14, "	1	
Blassingame W. Harvey,	Feb. 20, "	1	
John Haly,	" 25, "		23,198,750
William Hines,	March 15, "	1	
John M. Henrie,	" 30, "	¼	
Anthony Harris,	" 19, "	1	
Charles S. Hunt,	May 15, "	¼	
John Harmon,	" 21, "	1	
Miguel de Herrera,	June 3, "	1	
Joel Edwin Hawley,	" 22, "	1	
Briton Hall,	" 20, "	1	
Norman Hurd,	" 16, "	1	
Thos. B. Huling,	July 30, "	1	
Gustavus Hart,	" 17, "	¼	
T. J. Harrison,	Aug. 26, "	1	

ZAVALA'S COLONY.

WHERE SITUATED.	REMARKS.
On the Angelina.	
On the W. side of the Neches.	
" " "	
" " "	
On Sandy Creek, joins John Bevil.	
At a marsh on the W. side of the Neches.	
On Walnut Creek.	
About 10 miles W. of the town of Santa Anna, joins Houston.	
About 18 miles W. of the town of Santa Anna, joins David Choate.	
On the N. E. bank of the Angelina.	
On Bear Creek, S. E. of Benj. Lindsey.	
Near the head waters of Pine Island Bayou, joins R. D. Woods.	
Head waters of Pine Island Creek, joins Hauley & Donahoe.	
At the upper part of Davis's Prairie.	
Joins T. and E. Clark.	
On Sandy Creek, joins John Bevil.	
On the N. bank of Two Point Bayou.	
Joins Sam. L. Graham.	
On the W. side of the Sabine.	
On the banks of the Sabine, joins E. Shoemaker.	
On the W. bank of the Sabine.	
On the banks of the Neches, joins Perkins.	
In Davis's Prairie, in the vicinity of the principal branches of Pine Island Barou, joins Miller.	
On the E. side of the Neches.	
Twenty labors on the E. side of the Angelina, joins P. Galloway, 5 labors in the Vicinity of Harvey Bayou.	
On Sandy Creek, waters of the Sabine.	
On the E. side of the Neches.	
On the E. side of the Ayish Bayou, joins N. Hunt.	
" " " joins A. Hotchkiss.	
On the head waters of East Bayou.	
Adjoining Savary.	
About 17 miles from the town of Santa Anna, joins Sophia Dean.	
On the E. side of Ayish Bayou.	
In the vicinity of Wolf Point, joins John Blair.	
At the marsh of the W. bank of the Neches, joins Veatch.	
On the E. side of the Angelina.	
On Bayou Housen, a tributary of the Sabine.	
Ten miles S. W. of Wolf Point.	
On the W. bank of Cow Creek.	
On the W. side of Adams' Creek.	
On the waters of the Angelina.	
On Adams' Creek, adjoining Anthony Harris.	
On the W. bank of the Neches.	
Near the head waters of Pine Island Bayou, joins Garcia & Donohoe.	
On Cow Creek, or Hickory Fork.	
On the W. side of the Neches.	
On the banks of the Angelina, joins Ralph.	
On the waters of the Palogacho, joins J. S. Laws.	
On the W. side of the same.	

ZAVALA'S COLONY.

NAMES OF GRANTEES.	DATE OF TITLES.	Leagues.	Labors.
Alexander Hampton,	Aug. 30, 1835.	1	-
Elijah Hunter,	" 20, "	1	-
Peter M. Henderson,	" 2, "	1	-
Jacob Hill,	Sept. 26, "	1	-
P Holland,	" " "	1	-
James L. Howard,	Oct. 15, "	$\frac{1}{4}$	-
Hiram Hughs,	" 13, "	$\frac{1}{4}$	-
Charles Hereford,	" 11, "	1	-
Elijah F. Hanks,	" 15, "	1	-
Chs. S. Horne,	" 4, "	1	-
Nathaniel Hiden,	" 14, "	1	-
John Howard,	Nov. 25, "	1	-
Walter Hughs,	" 9, "	1	-
William Isaacs,	" 26, "	1	-
John Jett,	Feb. 18, "	1	-
Stephen Jett,	" " "	1	-
Joseph S. Johnston,	April 30, "	$\frac{1}{4}$	-
A. E. C. Johnston,	May 18, "	1	-
Stephen Jackson,	June 10, "	1	-
Elijah Isaacs,	" 20, "	1	-
Candler Johnson,	" 26, "	1	-
William Johnston,	" 25, "	$\frac{1}{4}$	-
John D. Johnston,	Aug. 20, "	1	-
Robert B. Irvine,	Sept. 7, "	$\frac{1}{4}$	-
George Jameson,	" 14, "	1	-
John S. Johnson,	Oct. 16, "	1	-
William Jones,	" 15, "	1	-
James Johnson,	Nov. 18, "	1	-
Stephen Jones,	" 25, "	1	-
William Jacobs,	Sept. 12, "	1	-
Albert G. Kellogg,	June 8, "	$\frac{1}{4}$	-
Abraham Kuykendall,	" 27, "	1	-
Edwin P. Le Grand,	May 25, "	1	-
Benjamin Lindsey,	Feb. 21, "	1	-
Pinckney Lout,	" 27, "	1	-
John C. Lanhorn,	March 10, "	1	-
Isaac Low,	June 20, "	1	-
William Lakey,	" 27, "	1	-
Eli Low,	" 9, "	1	-
Owen Lindsey,	July 6, "	$\frac{1}{4}$	-
Patsey Lewis,	" 23, "		4,889,857
Thomas Lindsey,	" "	$\frac{1}{4}$	-
Leman D. Leslie,	Aug. 30, "	1	-
Alford Langford,	Sept. 17, "	1	-
George P. Lawson,	" 21, "	1	-
L. R. Langdon,	Sept. 10, "	1	-
John S. Lane,	" 22, "	1	-
John S. Lacey,	Oct. 15, "	1	-
Archibald Lancaster,	" 20, "	$\frac{1}{4}$	-
Robert Lucus,	" 11, "	1	-
Mary Lankford,	" 8, "	1	-
Patsey Liney,	" 20, "	1	-
John Lucus,	Nov. 20, "	1	-
Richard Linville,	June 30, "	1	-

ZAVALA'S COLONY.

WHERE SITUATED.	REMARKS.

On the W. side of the Palo Gacho, joins Henry M'Gill.
Same, W. side.
Joins L. Dykes, on Pine Island Bayou.
On the W. side of the Neches, joins T. J. Harrison.
On Village Creek.
Joins James English.
On Ayish Bayou and the Angelina.
On the E. side of Ayish Bayou.
Twelve miles W. of the Neches.

On the W. side of Ayish Bayou.
On the E. side of Ayish Bayou.
On Six Mile Creek which receives its waters from the Sabine.
Adjoining Willis Murphy, on Tibo Creek, branch of Palogacho.
On the S. side of Cow Creek.
Between the marshes of Cow and Adams-Creeks.
Joins the league No 1 of the Empresario's premium lands.
On Bear Creek, S. of Benjamin Lindsey.
N. W. of the Sabine Prairie, about 8 miles N W. of Pine Island Creek and David Choate.
Joins Robert Conn.
On Beach Creek, waters of the Neches.

On the E. bank of the Neches.
On the W. bank of Pine Island Creek.
Adjoining H. Pace.
On the waters of the Sabine.
On the banks of the Neches.
On waters of the Attoyac.
Near Ayish Bayou.

On the W. side of Ayish Bayou.
On Peach Creek, waters of the Angelina, joins Joel Walker.
On the E. side of the Neches, joins Wright.
On Bear Creek.
On the E. side of the Neches, joins widow Nancy Davis & M. Palmer.
Not far from David Choate.
On the E. side of the Sabine.
On the E. side of Ayish Bayou.
Adjoining W. Hughes.
Joins Hobdey.

On the W. side of the Neches, Joins Elizabeth Hunter.

On Palogacho, S. side.
On the Natchitoches Road.
W. of the Alabama Village and Creek.
Joins William Campbell.
On Big Alabama Creek.
On the E. side of the Neches.
On the banks of the Angelina.
On the Sabine, joins Richard Sims.

ABSTRACT OF ORIGINAL TITLES

ZAVALA'S COLONY.

NAMES OF GRANTEES.	DATE OF TITLES.	Leagues.	Labors.
Solomon McJohnson,	Nov. 10, 1835.	1	-
Patrick Mullen,	Oct. 2, 1834.	1	-
Leonard Mabbit,	" 29, "	¼	-
James Moss,	Nov. 22, "	¼	-
Solomon Miller,	Nov. 27, "	¼	-
John M'Gee,	" 3, "	1	-
Willis Murphy,	" 26, "	1	-
James M'Kim,	Feb. 26, 1835.	1	-
Thomas S. M'Farland,	March 18, "	¼	-
William M'Farland,	" 17, "	1	-
Leroy Miller,	" 3, "	¼	-
John Moore,	" 7, "	1	-
Donald M'Donald,	May 19, "	1	-
Matthew S. Miller,	June 25, "		5
Mrs. N. Mackey,	" 4, "		17
Charles Morgan,	" 3, "	1	-
Balthasar X. Mudd,	" 25, "	1	-
Horatio M'Hanks,	" 4, "	¼	-
Shadrach Morris,	" 17, "		16
Joseph Mott,	" 20, "	1	-
Thomas M'Galin,	July 24, "	1	-
Shadrach Morris,	" 11, "		8
Henry G'Gill,	Aug. 25, "	1	-
D. C. Montgomery,	" 29, "	1	-
Edward Miller,	Sept. 24, "	1	-
J. F. Middleton,	" 10, "	1	-
John Moore,	" 30, "	1	-
Francis Millon,	" 17, "	1	-
Daniel S. D. Moore,	" 12, "	1	-
Samuel D. M'Mahon,	Oct. 11, "	1	-
Elisha Morris,	" 29, "	1	-
Jesse M'Gee,	" 23, "	1	-
Anthony M'Gee,	" 15, "	1	-
Levi Mann,	" 11, "	¼	-
Thomas M'Donald,	" 22, "	1	-
Maria en Gracia Rios Mascora,	Nov. 23, "	1	-
Charles J. M'Kinza,	" 20, "	1	-
William Means,	" 15, "	1	-
Juana Martinez,	Dec. 4, "	1	-
John M. Neely,	Nov. 21, "	1	-
Samuel Nelson,	Feb. 25, "	¼	-
John D. Nash,	July 25, "		20
Henry Nichols,	" 7, "	1	-
O. C. Nelson,	Aug. 18, "	1	-
Joel Newton,	Sept. 15, "	1	-
Britton Odom,	Nov. 15, "	1	-
Spencer Osborne,	Oct. 5, "	1	-
Peter B. Pry,	Nov. 7, "	1	-
Thomas Payne,	Feb. 18, "	1	-
Martin Palmer,	" 28, "	1	-
F. H. Pollard,	March 5, "	1	-
James Perkins,	April 25, "	1	-
William Pharess,	May 12, "	1	-
William Pamplin,	June 19, "		4

ZAVALA'S COLONY.

WHERE SITUATED.	REMARKS.

N. of Pine Island Bayou.
Between the Neches and Angelina.
On the S. side of (Cayote) Wolf Creek, a tributary of the Neches, Adjoining B. Burk.
On Ayish Bayou, adjoining Zachariah Redmon.
    "   "   Leroy Miller.
On Cow Creek.
On Tibo Creek, Branch of the Palo Gacho, joins Wm. Isaacs.
In the vicinity of Bear Creek.
On Rose Creek, joins John C. Lanhorn.
Joins D. Choate.
On the W. side of Ayish Bayou.
On Bear Creek.
    "

And 881,988 square varas, in Davis's Prairie.
And 302,291 square varas, adjoining Warin.
On the W. side of the Sabine.
    "   "   Angelina.
On the N. W. bank of the Sabine Bay.
And 458,500 square varas, on the W. bank of the Sabine.
Joins Isaacs.
On the W. bank of the Angelina.
And 541,500 sq. varas, on the waters of the Neches, joins Emery Rains.
On the W. side of the Neches.
On the Neches.
Joins Henry Stagner.

On the Sabine joins G. L. Bowland.
In the vicinity of the Trinity, joins Joseph Young.
On the Sabine, joins Delaney & Willer.
Joins William Roberts.
On the E. side of the Neches.
On the waters of Sandy Creek, about 6 miles from Sabine.
On the head waters of Pine Island Bayou.

On the E. side of the Neches.
Joins John Blair, about 20 miles from Liberty.
S. of the Big Alabama, 12 miles from the Neches.
On the Sabine.
On the Sabine Bay, 2 miles from the mouth of the Neches.
On Ayish Bayou, adjoining Nehemiah Sparks.
In the vicinity of Bear Creek, joins James M'Kim.
W. of Big Sandy Creek, near an Indian village.
On Housan's Creek, adjoining Williams.
On the same, W. side.

On the waters of Cow Bayou.

On the E. side of the Neches.
    " " " Ayish Bayou.
    " " " Neches, joins P. Lout.

On the W. side of the Neches.
On the E. bank of the Angelina.
And 574,121 square varas, on Walnut Run, waters of the Neches.

ABSTRACT OF ORIGINAL TITLES

ZAVALA'S COLONY.

NAMES OF GRANTEES.	DATE OF TITLES.	QUANTITY.	
		Leagues.	Labors.
Isham Parmer, - - -	June 28, 1835.	¼	- -
George A. Padillo, - - -	" 7, "	1	- -
Argalus A. Parker, - - -	" 3, "	1	- -
John Pruit, - - -	July 9, "	1	- -
Walter Pettit, - - -	" 22, "	1	- -
Isaac Powell, - - -	" "	1	- -
Daniel Pharess, - - -	Sept. 2, "	1	- -
Johnson Parmer, Sr., - - -	" 3, "	1	- -
R. Prince, - - -	Sept. 30, "	1	- -
L. K. Peters, - - -	" 15, "	1	- -
George F. Payne, - - -	" 1, "	1	- -
Michael Pivetot, - - -	Oct. 15, "	1	- -
Jose F. Pena, - - -	Nov. 21, "	1	- -
Johnston Parmer, - - -	Sept. 16, "	1	- -
John Lewis Quinalty, - - -	April 27, "	1	- -
John L. Quinalty, - - -	Nov. 10, "	¼	- -
Zachariah Redmond, - - -	" 20, "	1	- -
John S. Roberts, - - -	Jan. 12, "	1	- -
Emery Rains, - - -	Feb. 19, "	1	- -
Joel Robinson, - - -	May 6, "	¼	- -
Joseph Richey, - - -	" 12, "	¼	- -
Honere Robleau, - - -	March 18, "	1	- -
James Rowe, - - -	July 24, "		6
Uel Richey, - - -	" " "	¼	- -
James Rafferty, - - -	Aug. 18, "	1	- -
Aurelia Russell, - - -	" 27, "	1	- -
E. Robertson, - - -	Sept. 28, "	1	- -
Joseph Rusk, - - -	" 30, "	1	- -
Robert Rowe, - - -	" 10, "	1	- -
Matilda Runels, - - -	Oct. 3, "	1	- -
Robert Russell, - - -	" 13, "	¼	- -
Jonathan D. Ray, - - -	" 18, "	1	- -
William Roberts, - - -	Nov. 12, "	1	- -
August C. Reddick, - - -	" 4, "	1	- -
William B. Reed, - - -	" 3, "	1	- -
Calvin C. Robinett, - - -	Dec. 8, "	1	- -
John Schrier, - - -	Nov. 5, 1834.	1	- -
John Saul, - - -	Dec. 23, "	1	- -
Maj. Smith, - - -	" 13, "	1	- -
William N. Sigler, - - -	Jan. 3, 1835.	1	- -
William Smith, - - -	" 27, "	1	- -
William Stephenson, - - -	" 29, "	1	- -
John Smith, - - -	Feb. 26, "		23
Sion Smith, - - -	" 24, "	1	- -
Samuel Stivers, - - -	" 21, "	1	- -
Theron Strong, - - -	March 19, "		23
Nimrod Selser, - - -	April 12, "	1	- -
Asahel Savery, - - -	" 13, "	1	- -
Andrew Speer, - - -	May 23, "	1	- -
George W. Smyth, - - -	" 6, "		18
"	" " "		6
Joseph Ship, - - -	June 26, "	1	- -
Henry Stephenson, - - -	" 13, "	1	- -

ZAVALA'S COLONY.

WHERE SITUATED.	REMARKS.

On Ayish Bayou, adjoining Major Smith.
On the waters of the Trinity and Neches.
On the waters of the Neches.
On the E. side of the Neches.
On Pine Island Creek, joins David Choate.
On the waters of Boragus Creek, a tributary of the Sabine.
On a branch of Villar Creek.

On Big Alabama Creek.
Adjoining J. Williams.
" H. Millard and B. Brown.
On Flower Bayou, joins Hillebrant.
In the vicinity of Pine Island Bayou, joins A. Gray.
On the W. bank of the Angelina.
On a branch of the Neches.
On Housan's Creek, joins Smith.
On Ayish Bayou, joins James Moss.
On Orr's Creek, E. side of Galveston Bay.
In 10 miles of the town of Santa Anna, adjoining David Choate.
On Walnut Creek.
On Adams's Creek, joins Strong and Harris.
On the E. bank of the Trinity, joins H. B. Prentiss's 4 league tract.
And 127,500 sq. varas, on Double Point Creek, 4 miles from the San Antonio Road.
Near a marsh in the vicinity of D. Garner's.
On the W. side of the Neches.
" " " Sabine.
Joins Henry Stagner.
On the W. bank of Village Creek.
On Little Alabama, or Wolf, Creek.
On the Sabine, joins Ray.
Joins Harvey Canfield.
On the banks of the Sabine.

On the W. side of the Neches, joins S. Morris.
Five miles from Wolf Point.
On Pine Island Bayou.
On the E. side of the Neches.
Adjoining D. C. M‘Quin.
On Ayish Bayou, W. side, joins John M‘Neely.
On Taylor's Bayou, at a marsh.
Joins Carr.
On the E. side of the Neches, joins Noah Tevis.
And 381,329 sq. varas, on Boragus Creek, a tributary of the Sabine.
Vicinity of Housan's Creek, a tributary of the Sabine.
In the vicinity of Two Point.
Seven labors on the W. and 16 on the E. side of Adams's Creek, joins Thos. F. M‘Kinney.
On Town Creek, (Arroyo del Pueblo.)
Joins the league No. 1 of the Empresario's premium lands.
On the E. side of the Atoyac.
And 194,307 square varas, on the E. side of the Neches.
And 750,000 square varas, on Walnut Creek, branch of the Neches.
On Ayish Bayou, adjoining William Lakey.
N. of Pine Island Creek, joins Stephen Jackson.

ZAVALA'S COLONY.

NAMES OF GRANTEES.	DATE OF TITLES.	QUANTITY.	
		Leagues.	Labors.
Richard Sims,	June 30, 1835.	1	-
Stephen F. Stanley,	" 27, "	1	-
Harvey P. Savery,	July 14, "	¼	-
Corbet Stevens,	" 15, "	1	-
John Spears,	" 10, "	¼	-
Stephen Stanley,	Aug. 10, "	1	-
William F. Slaughter,	" 16, "	1	-
A. W. Smith,	" 18, "	1	-
R. Stone,	Sept. 2, "	1	-
Andrew Stephenson,	" 30, "	1	-
James Scott,	" " "	1	-
Stephen Stockton,	" 28, "	1	-
Jacob Shelton,	" 15, "	1	-
Thomas Speer,	" 19, "	1	-
Gilbert Shields,	Oct. 7, "	1	-
Isaac L. Stout,	Sept. 4, "	1	-
William T. Shannon,	Oct. 12, "	1	-
Evans Shoemaker,	" 17, "	1	-
John Steinson,	Nov. 25, "	1	-
Efraim Thompson,	Oct. 31, "	1	-
Remigio Totin,	Dec. 24, 1834.	1	-
Amos Thames,	" 27, "	¼	-
Patricio de Torres,	Jan. 30, 1835.	1	-
Noah Tevis,	" 16, "	½	-
Timothy Tredwell,	June 25, "		5
Ruffun Turner,	" 23, "	1	-
Jonathan Turner,	Sept. 15, "	1	-
Conrad Todd,	Oct. 3, "	1	-
Ephraim Talley,	" 16, "	¼	-
James Thomas,	Nov. 25, "	1	-
Baptista Andres Vacocu,	June 13, "	1¼	-
S. K. Vanmetre,	Aug. 30, "	1	-
John A. Vickers,	" 27, "	1	-
John A. Veatch,	Oct. 14, "		5
"	Feb. 6, "		19
William Williams,	Nov. 7, "	1	-
Stephen Williams,	" " "	¼	-
Hezekiah Williams, Jr.,	Dec. 24, "	¼	-
Hezekiah R. Williams,	" " "	¼	-
Hezekiah Williams,	" " "	1	-
Henry Williams,	Feb. 20, "	1	-
Joel Walker,	" 14, "	1	-
Sherod Wright,	" 19, "	1	-
Alexander Wright,	" 20, "	1	-
Leonard S. Walters,	March 10, "	1	-
Roderick Wiggins,	April 15, "	1	-
Clairbone West,	May 20, "	1	-
David White,	June 18, "	¼	-
Lewis Warren,	" 9, "	¼	-
Reuben Wood,	" 25, "	1	-
William Webb,	July 16, "	1	-
Martin White,	" 24, "	1	-
Robert Wakefield,	Aug. 29, "	1	-
Joseph Whitcomb,	Sept. 26, "	1	-
Lemuel Watson,	" 3, "	1	-

ZAVALA'S COLONY.

WHERE SITUATED.	REMARKS.

On the Sabine, joins Richard Linville.
On Shawnee, Creek, waters of the Neches.
On the W. side of the Neches.
On the W. side of the Sabine, joins J. Jett and Jno. Spears.
"   "   "   joins William Hines.
On the W. bank of the Angelina.
On the W. side of the Neches.
"   "   "   "

On the banks of the Big Alabama.
On the waters of Sandy Creek, about 4 miles from the town of Jasper.
Joins Ross Bridges.

On a lake W. of the Neches, joins Bevil and Williams.

On the W. side of Ayish Bayou.
On the W. side of the Sabine.
On the head waters of Pine Island Bayou.
On Sandy Creek, joins John Bevil.
On the W. side of the Atoyac.
Adjoining M'Nare.
Forks of the Carizo and Angelina.
On the W. side of the Neches, joins David Brown.
And 844,750 square varas, joins Goodrich.
On Big Cow Creek.

On the W. side of the Neches.
Joins John Gullian.
On a branch of Pine Island Bayou.
On Flores' Creek, S. of Taylor's Bayou.
On the W. side of the Neches, joins Chas. A. Fletcher.
"   "   "   "   Wilson.
And 538,670 square varas, joins S. Jackson.
And 481,003 square varas, Joins Bullock, near the Two Points.
On the W. side of the Sabine.
On Walnut Creek, adjoining Jno. Bevil and Robert Com.
On the W. bank of the Neches, below the mouth of Pine Island Creek.
On the W. side of the Neches.
On Taylor's Bayou, joins Chas. Williams.
On Ayish Bayou, E. side.
On the W. side of the Atoyac, joins Rimigio O. Totin.
Joins Alexander Wright.
Joins Sherod Wright.
On the W. bank of the Angelina.
W. side of the Angelina.
On the E. bank of Cow Creek.
On Bear Creek, joins Benj. Lindsey.
Joins T. Motts.
Head waters of Pine Island Creek, joins Willis Donahoe.
Angelina, W. side.
On Bear Creek, joins Jesse Hobdy.
On Big Alabama Creek.
Between Oyster and Double Bayou.
On the Neches.

ZAVALA'S COLONY.

NAMES OF GRANTEES.	DATE OF TITLES.	QUANTITY.	
		Leagues.	Labors.
Richard Work,	Oct. 4, 1835.	1	-
Devereaux Jerome Woodlief,	" 27, "	$\frac{1}{4}$	-
Joseph Walker,	" 14, "	1	-
William Williams,	" 22, "	1	
Charles Williams,	Dec. 24, "	1	-
John Wade,	Nov. 3, "	1	-
Thomas Watts,	Dec. 23, 1834.	1	-
William W. Young,	Sept. 2, 1835.	1	-
Andrew J. Yates,	Nov. 23, "	1	-

ZAVALA'S COLONY.

WHERE SITUATED.	REMARKS.
Between the Atoyac and Ayish Bayous.	
Adjoining William Clark.	
On the E. side of the Neches.	
On Taylor's Bayou.	
Six and a half miles from Pine Island Bayou.	
Joins John Saul.	
Joins Jackson.	
Twenty-two miles from Liberty.	

A

LIST OF TITLES

ISSUED BY

WILLIAM H. STEEL,

IN

ROBERTSON, OR AUSTIN AND
WILLIAMS' COLONY.

1834 & 1835.

ABSTRACT OF ORIGINAL TITLES

NAMES OF GRANTEES.	DATE OF TITLES.	QUANTITY.	
		Leagues.	Labors.
Harriet Anderson,	Aug. 26, 1835.		1
Samuel S. Allen,	July 29, "		25
Elisha Anglin,	Feb. 28, "		25
David Anderson,	July 12, "		18
George Allen,	" 29, "		25
Daniel Alexander,	" 25, "		6¼
John Burgess,	Aug. 10, "		6¼
Daniel E. Baylis,	Nov. 7, "		25
John Boyd,	March 25, "		25
John M. Barron,	Aug. 10, "		6¼
Seth H. Bates,	" 18, "		24
Thomas Byrd,	March 5, "		25
Seth H. Bates,	Aug. 18, "		1
Margaret C. Bowman,	July 9, "		25
William Berryman,	Dec. 10, 1834.		25
Thomas H. Barron,	March 26, 1835.		24
"	June 10, "		1
Nancy Boren,	Sept. 1, "		25
Wiley Carter,	Jan. 17, "		6¼
Nathaniel Campbell,	Nov. 4, "		6¼
Charles Curtis,	Jan. 12, "		6¼
Lewis L. Chiles,	April 20, "		6¼
Matilda F. Connell,	Feb. 3, "		25
George W. Chapman,	Sept. 4, "		6¼
George W. Cox,	Jan. 21, "		6¼
Calvin Cunningham,	Nov. 4, "		6¼
Jesus Cantun,	Sept. 12, "		25
Daniel H. Campbell,	Aug. 4, "		1
Mary Carnaghan,	Sept. 10, "		25
Isaac Cronch,	May 18, "		25
Thomas Carry,	July 28, "		25
Conception Charles,	" 16, "		25
Henry Clary,	Aug. 15, "		24
Ewing Caruthers,	July 2, "		6¼
John P. Carr,	Nov. 2, "		6¼
Hays Covington,	Dec. 30, "		6¼
R. M. Coleman,	Feb. 1, "		24
Goldsby Childress,	Sept. 10, "		25
Jeremiah Courtnay,	" 17, "		25
Mary Cole,	" 7, "		24
Maria Josefa Curhiel,	" 16, "		25

WHERE SITUATED.	REMARKS.
Commences at the S. W. corner of labor No. 14.	
Commences at the corner of league 3, on San Gabriel.	
Commences at the Corner of Silas Drake.	
On the San Andres, joins Robert Anderson.	
On the Brazos, W. side, above Viesca.	
S. of San Andres, commences at S. W. corner of league No. 3.	
Commences at the N. E. corner of leag. No. 1, about the Tawyash Village.	
Williamson Creek, commences at the N. W. corner of league No. 1.	
Commences at the N. E. corner of league No. 10, on the W. branch of the Brazos, above the mouth of Cow Creek, above the town of Viesca.	
On the margin of San Andres, commences on the bank, and N. E. corner of league No. 9.	
Commences at the N. W. corner of league No. 1; thence, to S. W. corner of league No. 2, and following the meanders of the river upwards.	
On the bank of the River Brazos, begins at the S. W. corner of labor No. 9.	
On the E. bank of the Brazos, opposite the town of Viesca, Adjoining Chambers and labor No. 1.	
Beginning at the N. W. corner of league No. 6, on the bank of the river, and following its meanders upwards.	
Beginning at the N. E. corner of league No. 2, on Elm Creek.	
Waters of the Brazos, W. side, above Viesca.	
Begins at the upper corner of labor No. 1, on the bank of the river, and meandering the river upwards.	
On the San Andres.	
Commences at the upper corner of W. C. Sparks, on the S. W. bank of the San Andres.	
On San Gabriel Creek, commences at the N. W. cor. of quarter No. 6.	
Between Salado and Lampasas Rivers.	
Front on the W. bank of the Brazos, and on San Andres' Creek.	
Above the town tract of Viesca, S. W. of River Leon.	
On the W. bank of the Brazos, joins league No. 24.	
On the San Antonio Road.	
N. E. corner of quarter No. 1.	
On the E. bank of the Brazos, joins league No. 7.	
Begins at the S. E. corner of labor No. 7, E. of the Brazos, bounding with labor No. 7.	
On the S. A. Road, S. E. corner of league No. 2, crosses Spring Creek.	
Commences at the upper corner of league No. 28, on the W. side of the Brazos.	
One league on the San Andres, N. side, joins league No. 6.	
Commences at the upper corner of league No. 18, below, includes Lost creek.	
Crosses Cavitt's Creek, N. of San Andres.	
Commences at the S. E. corner of league No. 2, following the meanders of the River downwards.	
On the E. bank of the Brazos, commences at the mouth of Childress' Creek.	
Bounding with C. M. Matthews.	
S. A. Road, following its meanders, crossing the Yegua.	
On N. bank of San Andres, and below the Three Forks.	
Commences at the S. E. corner of T. J. Chambers and the N. E. corner of S. M'Gary, and bounding with league No. 2, of Thomas Byrd.	
Front on the W. bank of the Brazos, commencing at the upper corner of league No. 18.	
On the E. bank of the Brazos, below Tahuacano Village.	

ABSTRACT OF ORIGINAL TITLES.

NAMES OF GRANTEES.	DATE OF TITLES.	Leagues.	Labors.
Walter Campbell,	Nov. 2, 1835.		6¼
James Caryell,	June 22, "		6¼
Gilbert Cribbs,	March 31, "		25
Mary Cole,	Aug. 21, "		1
William R. Cox,	Feb. 20, "		6¼
Daniel H. Campbell,	July 14, "		25
David W. Campbell,	June 22, "		6¼
David Curry,	July 20, "		6¼
Nancy Chance,	Aug. 13, "		24
William Cooke,	Feb. 3, "		6¼
Napoleon Darneill,	Aug. 20, "		6¼
William Dillard,	March 25, "		25
Matthew Dunn,	Dec. 8, 1834.		6¼
Brinklay Davis,	March 25, 1835.		25
James Dunn,	Dec. 24, 1834.		25
Ansell Darneill,	Aug. 27, 1835.		6¼
Andrew Dunn,	Feb. 15,		25
Robert Davidson,	Dec. 30, 1834.		24
Alexander Duggins,	" 9, "		25
George Dougherty,	March 3, 1835.		25
G. E. Dwight,	Aug. 15, "		25
James Dunn,	July 31, "		6¼
Maria Josefa Delgado,	March 25, "		25
James Day,	Aug. 25, "		25
G. B. Erath,	July 25, "		6¼
John Easely,	Sept. 29, "		6¼
Monroe Edwards,	Feb. 10, "		25
Richard Eaton,	Dec. 22, 1834.		2¼
C. B. Emmons,	July 7, 1835.		6¼
Ashly D. Eason,	March 18, "		6¼
Thomas Eldridge,	April 1, "		6¼
Richard Eaton,	Sept. 17, "		22½
Stephen H. Eaton,	" " "		25
Harmon S. Easton,	March 18, "		6¼
Rains Elum,	Feb. 1, "		6¼
Abigail Fokes,	Nov. 2, "		25
Job Fisher,	Aug. 10, "		6¼
John Fisher,	" " "		6¼
Samuel Frost,	Dec. 22, 1834.		25
Peter Flemming,	March 15, 1835.		25
Reuben Fisher,	Sept. 5, "		25
David Faulkenberry,	March 18, "		25
James Fisher,	Dec. 12, 1834.		25
Henry Fullerton,	" 23, "		25
John Fulcher,	Sept. 12, 1835.		25
Joseph French,	Feb. 8, "		24
Daniel B. Friar,	" 20, "		24
Greenleaf Fisk,	Nov. 7, "		25

WHERE SITUATED.	REMARKS.

Head waters of Brushy Creek, commencing at the W. corner of leag. G.
On Little River, Cavitt's Creek.
Brazos, W. side, below town of Viesca and league No. 9.
S. W. of Viesca, joins labor No. 8.
Commencing at the S. E. corner of W. E. Moss's survey.
" on the N. line of league No. 8., 500 varas from its N. W.
On the W. side of the Brazos, begins at the N. E. corner of No. 5.
Commencing at the N. E. corner, ¼ on San Andres, S. side.
On San Andres, or Leon Creek; joins Town Reserve.
On the Brazos, joins William Marling.
Tahuacano Creek, E. of the Brazos.
Fronts on the bank of the river, bounding with league No. 3.
On the W. bank of the Brazos, meandering it upwards from a stake, and back on a prairie, joins James Walters.
Commencing at the N. W. corner of Seal, in the prairie
On the San Antonio Road.
Front on E. bank of the Brazos, commencing at the N. W. corner of ¼ league No. 3.
Front on the N. bank of Sandres, commencing at the S. W. corner of League No. 24.
On the N. E. side of San Andres, commencing at the lower corner of League No. 1.
On High Prairie, 6,800 varas N., 19 E., from the S. E. corner of M. Reed's league on the San Andres.
On the waters of the San Andres, crosses Donahoe Creek.
On little River and Whitley's Creek, W. of Viesca.
On Peach Creek, bounding Walker's survey.
On the S. side of San Gabriel, N. side of Brushy Creek.
On the San Gabriel Creek, begins at the N. W. corner of league No. 4.
Commences at the N. W. corner of league No. 4, in the prairie.
Commences at the N. W. corner of league No. 4, W. of Brazos.
" " S. E. corner of league No. 15, following the meanders of the river downwards.
On the San Antonio Road and Peach Creek.
On the E. side of the Brazos, above the upper line of ¼ No. 2.
Commencing at the Navasoto, waters of.
Joins league No. 1.
On the waters of the Navasoto.
On the waters of Cedar Creek.
On the Brazos, crosses Alligator Creek, joins No. 1.
On the San Gabriel, opposite Mr. M'Laine's ¼.
On the San Gabriel Creek.
Bordering on the Webbs.
Joins Joseph Webb and league No. 2.
On the W. side of the Brazos, below Viesca, joins league No. 7.
Commences at the upper corner of League No. 2, on the Brazos.
On the W. side of the Brazos, below the town of Viesca.
Commencing at the N. E. corner of the Anglin, touching the S. W. corner of J. Hoadley.
On the waters of Walnut Creek, E. side of Little Brazos.
S. E. corner of George Robertson, on Muddy Creek.
About 7 miles below the Three Forks of San Andres, crossing Darr's Creek.
On the W. side of the Brazos, joins Chambers' tract, which includes the Waco Village.
On the Brazos, below Viesco.
On the San Miguel, joins No. 46.

ABSTRACT OF ORIGINAL TITLES

NAMES OF GRANTEES.	DATE OF TITLES.	QUANTITY.	
		Leagues.	Labors.
William Fisher, - - -	July 4, 1835.		24
Robert B. Frost, - -	March 25, "		6¼
Samuel Frost, - - -	April 1, "		1
Massillon Farley, - -	Nov. 1, "		25
William Fitz Gibbons, - -	March 29, "		24
John Gafford, - -	Sept. 10, "		22
" - - -	" " "		2
Albert G. Gholson, - -	July 8, "		6¼
Thomas A. Graves, - -	Nov. 10, "		6¼
Moses Griffin, - -	July 29, "		25
Jefferson Gafford, - - -	" 31, "		6¼
Clardy Gafford, - - -	Aug. 1, "		25
John M. Grayham, - -	" 26, "		1
Stephen Gafford, - -	July 30, "		25
Samuel Gholson, - -	Feb. 9, "		1
David Galaher, - -	" 1, "		25
William Garrett, - -	March 17, "		6¼
John M. Grayham, - -	July 5, "		25
Samuel Gholson, - -	April 25, "		25
John Harmon, - -	March 12, "		25
Ennis Harding, - - -	" 27, "		25
James A. Head, - -	March 18, "		6¼
William J. Hawkins, -	" " "		6¼
James Hall, - -	Nov. 6, "		25
Joshua Hadley, - - -	Feb. 25, "		25
Dennis Herrald, - -	June 22, "		25
Samuel Humm - -	Dec. 9, 1834.		25
Hugh Henry, - -	" 22, "		25
Jesse Hannor, - -	Sept. 12, 1835.		25
Robert Henry, - -	Dec. 22, 1834.		24
W. E. Harris, - -	Feb. 7, 1835.		25
Sarah Hansley, - -	July 5, "		24
J. L. Hood, - - -	Dec. 23, 1834.		25
Sarah Hansley, - -	Aug. 21, 1835.		1
Robert Henry, - -	Dec. 22, 1834.		24
Charles Hensley, - -	Aug. 7, 1835.		6¼
Isaiah Harland, - -	Feb. 20, "		25
Andrew J. Hensley, - -	Aug. 7, "		6¼
Elijah D. Harmon, - -	Nov. 7, "		25
Joseph P. Jones, - -	Dec. 11, 1834.		25
Samuel Kenney, - -	Feb. 8, 1835.		6¼
Thomas Kenney, - -	" 20, "		25
Garret Low, - -	Nov. 2, 1835.		6¼
Peter L. Loyd, - -	Oct. 2, "		6¼

WHERE SITUATED.	REMARKS.

Beginning at the upper corner of league No. 6, meandering the River upwards, passing mouth of Darrington Creek.
On Frost Creek, N. W. of Elisha Anglin.
Beginning at the corner of R. B. Frost, on the waters of Pierson's Creek, Navasoto.
N. of the San Gabriel Creek.
On the waters of the Navasoto, crossing Sterling Fork, E. line of Juan Vasques.
N. of the San Andres, and S. W. of league No. 19.
Below the town of Viesca, head of Walnut, alias Pierson's Creek, commencing on the line of league No. 1.
Commencing at the N. E. corner of league No. 1, Fish Creek.
On the S. side of the San Andres.
On the N. bank of the San Andres, running upwards on its meanders, from a stake of a corner.
On the N. side of the San Antonio Road, from the S. W. corner of Day's league to the S. E. corner of Eaton's labor.
On the E. bank of the Brazos.
Adjoining labor No. 11.
On the San Antonio, E. of the Brazos.
Commencing at the upper corner of the Town League.
On the W. side of the Brazos.
On the S. side of the San Andres.
Above the town of Viesca, W. bank of the Brazos, following the meanders of the River upwards.
Commencing at the S. W. corner of league No. 2, on the bank of the river, following its meanders upwards, crossing the Aquilla.
On the banks of the Brazos, bounding upper line of league No. 1.
Commencing at the W. bank of the Brazos, above the mouth of Childress' Creek, joins league No. 4.
On the waters of the Navasoto.
Commencing at the S. E. corner of Juan Basques' survey, joins Fits Gibbons.
On Elm Creek, commences at the S. W. corner of league No. 8, N. of San Andres.
Commencing at the N. E. corner of Plummer, in a small prairie.
Commencing on a line of league No. 1, of S. W. White.
On the waters of Elm Creek.
    "   "   Tamarack Creek.
Front on the W. bank of the Brazos, commencing at the N. W. corner of ¼ of league No. 5.
On Pine Oak Creek, S. of R. Henry.
Begins at the S. E. corner of league No. 16, on the river.
Commencing at the upper corner of league 4, up the river.
    "   "   N. E. corner of league 3, crosses Elm Creek.
    "   "   "   "   labor No. 8, S. W. of Viesca.
On Pin Oak Creek, E. bank of.
On Walnut Creek, E. side of the Brazos.
On Harland's Creek, N. W. of Sarah Pillow.
Commencing N. W. corner of league No. 2, George Hunt; crossing Walnut Creek.
On Brushy Creek, N. W. of Tumlinson, and N. E. of Samuel Hazlett.
Between Little River and Cow Creek.
Upon and crossing the Little Brazos, and joins J. B. Webb.
Commencing at the S. W. corner of labor No. 8, running with a road.
Fronts on W. bank of Brazos, commencing at N. W. cor. of leag. No. 5.
At the junction of the Brazos & San Andres, fronting on the W. bank.

161 ABSTRACT OF ORIGINAL TITLES

NAMES OF GRANTEES.	DATE OF TITLES.	QUANTITY.	
		Leagues.	Labors.
Edward Long, - - -	Aug. 31, 1835.		25
Warren Lymon, - - -	" 20, "		25
Lewis Lomas, - - -	Feb. 12,		25
William W. Lewis, - -	July 15, "		25
Thomas Mackay, - -	" 5, "		25
Bridget M'Gary, - - -	" 12, "		25
Laughlin M'Linnan, - -	Aug. 29, "		25
William A. M'Grouse, - -	Sept. 22, "		6¼
Edley Montgomery, - -	Feb. 1, "		6¼
John Marlin, - - -	" 2, "		25
Edward M'Gary, - - -	" 25, "		6¼
Daniel Munroe, - - -	" 15, "		1
Charles M. Matthews, - -	Dec. 26, 1834.		25
George W. Morgan, - -	Sept. 9, 1835.		25
William Marlin, - -	Feb. 2, "		6¼
Neill M'Clelland, - -	July 28, "		25
Rebecca Moore, - -	Nov. 2, "		25
William M'Lain, - -	Feb. 9, "		6¼
Daniel Monroe, - -	March 20, "		24
William L. Moss, - -	Feb. 15, "		25
John S. M'Coy, - -	June 22, "		6¼
David Mumford, - - -	March 20, "		25
George Morgan, - -	Sept. 7, "		25
Samuel Moore, - - -	March 8, "		6¼
John Montgomery, - -	Feb. 2, "		6¼
Henry W. Moss, - -	March 18, "		6¼
Robert Moffit, - -	July 29, "		25
Francis Maylon, - - -	" 31, "		25
Andrew Montgomery, - -	" 30, "		18¾
" - - -	Feb. 2, "		6¼
Morris Moore, - -	Aug. 17, "		6¼
Jesse Munford, - -	Feb. 25, "		25
Shedrick Meness, - -	Sept. 9, "		25
William M'Farlin, - -	Aug. 17, "		24
Lewis Moore, - - -	" 20, "		6¼
James M'Laughlin, - -	Sept. 4, "		25
Samuel Nelson, - -	" 16, "		25
John Needham, - - -	Dec. 30, 1834.		6¼
George Antonio Nixon, - -	Feb. 9, 1835.	11	
Frederick Neebling, - -	July 27, "		25
William Neill, - -	Sept. 1, "		25
Hardin Nevill, - - -	June 1, "		25

WHERE SITUATED.	REMARKS.
Commencing at **N. W.** corner of league 18.	
Fronts on the **N.** Bank of the San Andres.	
N. bank of the San Andres, above league 23.	
N. side of the San Andres, begins at S. E. of league No. 2.	
Fronts on the E. bank of the Brazos.	
Fronts on the W. bank of the Brazos, commences at the upper corner of League No. 4.	
On Cow Creek, commences at N. W. corner of league No. 5.	
Corners in a prairie.	
Beginning at the S. W. and lower corner of league No. 1, meandering the river downwards.	
Beginning at the N. E. corner of labor No. 1, on the lower line of T. J. Chambers, crossing Mussulman Creek.	
Beginning at the N. E. corner of W. Martin's quarter.	
Commencing 12 varas W. of league No. 1, meandering a stream.	
Corners in timber and prairie.	
Brazos, E. side, commences at the N. W. corner of league No. 2.	
Commencing at the N. E. corner of John Malin, on the lower line of Thomas Jefferson Chambers.	
Commences on the line of No. 4, crosses Cow Creek.	
On the S. side of the San Andres, commencing on the S. E. corner of league No. 4, below T. J. Chambers' survey.	
Commencing at the mouth of the San Gabriel, 8½ miles above the mouth of Brushy Creek.	
Commencing on the N. bank of the San Andres, and passing the S. W. corner of league No. 1.	
On Hutt's Creek, adjoining Joseph Ferguson.	
Mouth of Childress' creek, below No. 28, and above league No. 29.	
On Donahoe's Creek.	
E. of the Brazos, beginning at N. W. corner of T. J. Chambers, and touching N. E. corner of Chambers' 5 league survey.	
Beginning at the S. W. Corner of league No. 8.	
Brazos, Begins at the S. W. corner of league No. 2	
On the waters of Spring and Cedar Creeks.	
On the E. side of the Brazos, below Viesca, and below the 5 leagues surveyed for Robertson.	
Joins labor No. 9, on the W. side of the Brazos.	
On the W. side of the Brazos, above Viesca.	
On the E. side of the Brazos, commencing S. W. corner of T. Byrd.	
Joins ¼ No. 1, fronting on the E. side of the Brazos, above Waco Village.	
On the S. Bank of the San Andres, crosses Donahoe's Creek.	
On the E. bank of the Brazos, following its meanders upwards, commencing at the S. W. corner of league No. 2.	
On the E. bank of the Brazos, above the mouth of Childress' Creek, following the meanders of the river.	
On the E. bank of the Brazos, above the Waco Village.	
Jone's creek bank, and W. bank of the Brazos.	
Commencing at the S. W. corner of league 4, on the N. bank of San Andres.	
Commencing on the San Andres, N. E.	
On the E. side of the Brazos, beginning 1½ miles above Tenoxticlan, and following the meanders upwards, crosses Little Brazos.	
Front on the W. bank of the Brazos, next above league No. 10.	
Fronts on the W. bank of the Brazos, running upwards from the mouth of Childress' Creek.	
On the W. side of the Brazos, begins at the upper corner of league No. 6., above the mouth of Childress' Creek.	

ABSTRACT OF ORIGINAL TITLES

NAMES OF GRANTEES.	DATE OF TITLES.	QUANTITY.	
		Leagues.	Labors.
William Neill,	Dec. 7, 1834.		25
Archibald Powel,	Aug. 31, 1835.		24
Henry Purdom,	Sept. 17, "		24
William Peterson,	July 30, "		25
Harriet E. Perry,	March 12, "		1
A. G. Perry,	" 18, "		25
Niels Peterson,	Feb. 20, "		25
H. & L. Punchard, heirs of Joseph Punchard,	July 6, "		24
John H. Pierson,	Feb. 25, "		6¼
Henry Purdum,	March 18, "		1
Jacob Prichett,	Jan. 21, "		6¼
Luther T. M. Plummer,	April 1, "		25
James W. Parker,	" 1, "		25
William Punchard,	Sept. 11, "		25
James Powel,	Dec. 16, 1834.		25
Sarah Pillow,	Feb. 26, 1835.		25
Mary Pryor,	Dec. 20, 1834.		25
Silas M. Parker,	April 1, 1835.		25
J. G. W. Pierson,	Dec. 10, 1834.		25
O'Neill Perry,	Aug. 10, 1835.		25
William S. Parker,	Nov. 1, "		6¼
M. K. Robinson,	June 2, "		25
Michael Reed,	Dec. 29, "		25
J. W. Robertson,	Feb. 20, "		6¼
Wilson Reid,	Dec. 15, 1834.		6¼
Jefferson Reed,	Nov. 3, "		6¼
Sterling C. Robertson,	March 18, 1835.		25
"	July 31, "	5	
"	March 18, "	1	
"	June 22, "	1	
"	Feb. 27, "	5	
"	July 31, "	1	
"	" 30, "	1	
"	April 1, "	4	
"	Jan. 12, "		1
Lavina Robertson,	Feb. 8, "		25
George Rippley,	Jan. 21, "		6¼
Euphema L. Robertson,	Dec. 1, 1834.		25
G. Robertson,	" 11, "		25
Henry Read,	Jan. 1, 1835.		25
Joseph Ritherford,	" 21, "		25
Daniel Robertson,	Oct. 1, "		25
William Reed,	Feb. 25, "		6¼
Balden Robertson,	Dec. 3, 1834.		24
Fieldin Ruble,	" 27, "		24
Elijah S. C. Robertson,	July 29, 1835.		6¼
Clement Raney,	March 18, 1835.		6¼

IN THE GENERAL LAND OFFICE 164

WHERE SITUATED.	REMARKS.

On the W. side of the Brazos, above the mouth of Cow Bayou.
On the waters of the Little Brazos.
On Elm Creek, commencing at the N. W. corner of league No. 15.
W. of the Brazos, above Cow Creek, above the town of Viesca.
Commencing at the corners of labors No. 19 and 20.
Commencing at the S. E. corner of league No. 17, and fronts on the Brazos River.
On the S. A. Road, commencing at the S. W. corner of leag. No. 2.
Commencing at the upper corner of league 2, above the mouth of Chester's Creek
Commencing at the N. E. corner of $\frac{1}{4}$, No. 3, on the back of line No 4.
Bounding with the W. line of Viesca town tract to its N. W. corner.
Bounding with James Dunn's N. E. line, and the San Antonio Road.
Sterling's Fork, waters of the Navasoto.
On the waters of the Navasoto.
Back of league No. 9, waters of Cow Creek.
W. bank of the Brazos, lower corner of league No. 1.
On the Brazos River, Sterling's Fork.
Begins at the E. corner of league No. 4, Brazos River.
On the waters of the Navasoto, Sterling's Fork.
W. bank of the Brazos, lower corner of Viesca town tract, meandering the river from a point below, to the mouth of Walnut Creek.
On the San Gabrel Creek, commencing at N. W. corner of league D.
N. E. corner of league marked H.
Commencing at the W. corner of league No. 16.
N. E. of San Andres, below John Fulcher.
N. W. corner of the line of league No. 1.
On Elm Creek, waters of, and the San Antonio River.
N. E. side of the San Andres, below Needham's quarter.
Bounding S. line of A. Thompson and leag. 4, crossing Davidson's Creek.
Commencing at the S. E. corner of Mrs. Connell, running towards League No. 5 and Lampasso,s and to Salado or Salt Creek.
Commencing at a stake on the S. E. line of league No. 3, 1600 varas S. W. of its S. E. corner, bounding S. W. of league No. 3.
Adjoining the E. line of G. A. Nixon's 11 league survey.
Beginning on the bank of the river, at the S. W. corner of John Montgomery, crossing Alligator Creek, Little Brazos, to a stake on Fish Creek.
Beginning at the N, W. corner of league 5, to the N. W. corner of leag. 6, to S. W. corner of same, S. W. cor. No. 5, crossing Lampassos Creek.
Beginning at the S. E. corner of league 3, Lampassos.
Beginning at the S. W. corner of Henry Walker, bounding front on Little River, or San Andres.
W. line of Viesca Town Tract.
Beginning at the S. W. corner of Jeremiah Tinan.
On the San Antonio Road, and joins Wheelock.
Beginning on the bank of the river at S. E. corner of league 7.
On Walnut Creek, E. of Little Brazos.
Crosses Muddy Creek. joins James Fisher.
Includes the mouth of the Aquilla creek, and crosses the same.
On the N. side of the San Gabriel.
On the S. W. side of the San Andres, joins W. Reed's labor.
On the N. W. side of Lime Creek.
Bounding with leagues No. 2 and 3, near Cow Creek.
S. side of the San Andres, crosses Clay Creek, commencing at the N. E. corner of league No. 10.
Commencing at the S. W. corner of league No. 3.

ABSTRACT OF ORIGINAL TITLES

NAMES OF GRANTEES.	DATE OF TITLES.	QUANTITY.	
		Leagues.	Labors.
James Red,	Sept. 12, 1835.		25
Sterling C. Robertson,	Feb. 10, "		1
"	" 25, "		25
"	March 18, "		25
"	" " "		25
Uriah Sanders,	Nov. 9, "		6¼
Abner Smith,	Dec. 9, "		1
Samuel C. Smith,	Sept. 12, "		6¼
Christopher B. Stubbins,	Aug. 28, "		25
N. Smithwick,	Nov. 4, "		25
Christopher B. Stebbins,	Sept. 17, "		1
Samuel Smith,	June 10, "		6¼
James S. Steel,	Aug. 17, "		25
Eli Seal,	March 18, "		25
Christopher C. Seal,	Feb. 22, "		6¼
Samuel Sward,	Dec. 20, 1834.		25
Niles F. Smith,	" 30, "		25
William Springer,	" 28, "		25
Joshua G. Smith,	March 18, 1835.		6¼
M. B. Shackelford,	Aug. 25, "		6¼
John P. Smithson,	June 27, "		6¼
Pedro Salinas,	May 18, "		25
Francis de los Santos,	Sept. 17, "		25
M. M. Stephens,	Feb. 9, "		25
William C. Sparks,	Oct. 20, 1834.		25
John D. Smith,	March 18, 1835.		6¼
John D. Smith,	Feb. 25, "		1
Narcissa, Slatter,	Dec. 10, 1834.		25
Michael Sessam,	Aug. 3, 1835.		25
William L. Swain,	March 14, "		6¼
Sion Smith,	Feb. 28, "		25
Erastus Smith,	Oct. 5, "		6¼
Edward Tatum,	Aug. 24, "		6¼
John Tucker,	" 12, "		1
Levi Taylor,	" 18, "		25
Pedro del Toro,	Sept. 17, "		25
Jeremiah Tinnan,	March 20, "		25
Orville T. Taylor,	Feb. 27, "		25

WHERE SITUATED.	REMARKS.
Commencing on the banks of San Andres, S. W. corner of leag. No. 1.	
Commences at the upper corner of labor No. 2, on bank of the river, meandering upwards.	
Commences at the S. E. corner of league No. 8, and N. W. and S. W. of league No. 9.	
Commences at the N. W. corner of league No. 2. [Endorsed, N. of San Antonio Road, W. of the Brazos.	
W. line of league No. 1, crossing Davidson's Creek. [Endorsed, N. of the San Antonio Road, W. of the Brazos.	
Commencing N. W. corner of quarter No. 1, fronting on the river, and passing the mouth of Head's Creek.	
S. E. corner, on the N. bank of the San Andres.	
On Sandy and Muddy Creek, commencing at the lower corner of J. D. Smith's ¾ league.	
On the bank of the Brazos, at the mouth of Cow Creek.	
On Deer Creek, beginning at the N. W. corner of league No. 4.	
On the E. bank Brazos, S. W. of labor No. 2.	
On the San Gabriel Creek, joins leagues Nos. 5 and 13.	
Commencing at league No. 8, upper corner, meandering the river upwards, about 2500 varas, touches Darrington Creek.	
Begins at the N. E. corner of Richard.	
Commencing at the S. W. corner of Young, and touching the S. E. corner of W. L. Eason.	
Fronts on the River, and commencing at the lower corner of league 3, on the bank of the river. [Endorsed, on waters of Brazos.]	
Fronts the corners of Dunn, Jones and Walters.	
Commencing at the N. E. cor. of leag. 3, and S. E. side of leag. No. 4.	
On the W. bank of the Brazos, fronting on the river, touching the S. W. line of league No. 2.	
Commences at the S. W. corner of Thos. Mackey's league.	
S. side of Little River, commencing at ¼ No. 9.	
Crosses Little Brazos, begins at a corner of league No. 4.	
On the San Gabriel, bounding with league No. 5, and the N. E. corner of league No. 6.	
Beginning at the N. E. corner of leag. No. 9, and N. E. cor. of No. 10.	
On the waters of San Andres, (Darr's Creek,) bounding on the N. W. corner of Fulcher.	
Beginning at the S. W. corner of league No. 9.	
A quadrangle.	
On the Brazos, beginning at the lower corner of No. 2.	
Commencing at the N. E. corner of Whitesides, and bounding with him and Chambers.	
On the W. bank of the Brazos, beginning at the N. W. corner of league No. 1, following its meanders upwards.	
S. W. corner of No. 3, N. E. of No. 9, fronts on the river, supposed from inference, San Andres.	
On the waters of Walnut Creek, bounding with James Fisher, No. 3, and Fulcher's No. 9.	
Commencing at the N. E. corner of league No. 1, which fronts on the San Antonio Road.	
On the S. side of Town of Viesca.	
Commencing at the S. E. corner of league No. 8.	
Commencing at the S. W. corner of league No. 6, crossing San Gabriel and Willis's Creek, bounding N. E. corner of league 7.	
On the San Antonio Road, stone on the bluff marked J. T.	
Commencing at the upper cor. of Reserve for Town, on S. bank of Leon, running in a direct line to a front above junction of Lampassos or Leon.	

ABSTRACT OF ORIGINAL TITLES

NAMES OF GRANTEES.	DATE OF TITLES.	QUANTITY.	
		Leagues.	Labors.
Alexander Thompson, - -	Oct. 28, 1834.		25
John Tucker, - - -	July 30, 1835.		25
Juan Vasques, - -	March 29, "		25
Manuel M. Valdes, - - -	Feb. 27, "		6¼
William Young, - -	" 12, "		25
Garet Young, - - -	" 25, "		25
E. L. R. Wheelock, - -	Jan. 19, "		25
David Wright, - - -	June 1, "		25
Reuben Woods, - - -	Nov. 3, "		25
John B. Webb, - - -	Dec. 30, 1834.		6¼
Andrew J. Webb, - - -	" " "		6¼
William Welsh, - - -	July 28, 1835.		25
Sam'l W. White, - -	March 10, "		25
William H. Walker, - -	Dec. 16, 1834.		25
B. Wickson, - -	" 28, "		25
Thos. J. Warton, - - -	" 9, "		25
Joseph Webb, - - -	Jan. 12, 1835.		25
Ann Wheelock, - - -	Sept. 20, "		24
Thos. R. Webb, - -	Nov. 1, "		6¼
Jesse Webb, - -	Dec. 30, 1834.		25
John Waugh, - -	" 27, "		6¼
Alexander Whitaker, - -	March 25, 1835.		6¼
W. C. Wilson, - -	Feb. 10, "		6¼
James D. Webb, - - -	" 28, "		1
Sarah Wilhelm, - - -	March 20, "		25
James D. Webb, - - -	" " "		25
William Woodford, - -	Dec. 23, 1834.		25
Thomas R. Webb, - - -	Oct. 26, 1335.		6¼
Skeigh Walker, - -	July 30, "		6¼
John J. Whitesides, - -	Aug. 12, „		25
James P. Warmack - -	Nov. 1, "		6¼

WHERE SITUATED.	REMARKS.
Tillow Prairie.	
W. of Bosque Creek, W. of the Brazos, crosses Bosque repeatedly.	
Commences on Fitz Gibbons' line, crosses Sterling Fork.	
Commencing at league No. 9, and touching leagues Nos 2 and 10.	
On the waters of the Navasoto.	
Stakes in the Prairie.	
On the San Antonio Road, E. of the Brazos, on Cedar Creek.	
Commencing N.W. corner of league 1, San Gabriel Creek.	
E. of the Brazos River.	
Beginning at the upper corner of Jesse Webb, meandering the river upwards, waters of Little Brazos.	
Begins 12 varas from John B. Webb's upper corner.	
On the San Antonio Road. and E. of Brazos, commencing at the S. E. corner of Wheelock, and Joins L. Robertson.	
Commencing at the S. E. corner of J. W. Robinson's survey.	
On the N. E. bank of San Andres, the survey crossing a little creek which runs S. W.	
Commencing at the S. E. corner of league No. 11, on the bank of the river, following its meanders downwards.	
On the San Antonio, making corner at Wilson Reed's S. E. corner.	
On the E. side of the Brazos, above A. J. Webb, at Kesley's Falls, crossing the Little Brazos.	
League 16, on the W. bank of the Brazos, and above the mouth of Childress' Creek.	
Beginning at the S. E. corner of ¼ league No. 2, on the E. bank of the Brazos.	
On the Brazos, opposite the Falls.	
Little River, S. W. side, joins Carter's survey.	
Commencing on Sarah Pillow's W. line.	
On a creek or lake, joins No. 2.	
Joins labor No. 17.	
On the waters of Little River.	
On the Brazos, above the Waco Village.	
Commencing N. E. corner of league No. 1, Elm Creek.	
S. of the San Andres.	
N. of the San Antonio Road, and E. of the Brazos, S. W. of Eaton's lab.	
On the waters of Cow Creek.	
On San Gabriel Creek, commencing on the W. line of league No. 2.	

A

LIST OF TITLES

FOR

SPECIAL GRANTS

IN DE WITT'S COLONY, AND
BEXAR COUNTY,

BY

JOSE ANTONIO NAVARRO,
AND OTHERS.

ABSTRACT OF ORIGINAL TITLES

NAMES OF GRANTEES.	DATE OF TITLES.	Leagues.	Labors.
Anastacio Manzalo,	Aug. 28, 1831.	1	1
Marjila Chirino,	July 1, 1832.	2	-
James Kerr,	" 8, 1831.	1	-
Sarah Seely,	April 15, "	1	-
Benj. & Graves Fulcher,	June 3, "	1	-
Jas. Bowie, for Ant. Ma. Enaurizar,	Nov. 10, "	11	-
Byrd Lockhart,	June 27, 1833.	1	-
"	July 8, "	1	-
"	April 5, 1835.	1	-
"	Nov. 25, 1831.	1	-
Joseph de la Baume,	July 1, 1832.	6	-
Jose Maria Salinas,	Aug. 31, 1831.	4	-
Wm. Pettus. Ag't for Ed. Pettus,	May 15, "	1	-
William Pettus,	" " "	2	-
Elijio Gortari,	Aug. 30, "	1	-
Jesus Cantù,	Nov. 5, "	2	-

IN BEXAR

Jose Delgado,	Dec. 15, 1833.		1
Angel Navarro,	" 4, "	1	-
Maria Francisco Rodrigues,	Feb. 26, 1834.	1	1
Francisco Rivas,	Dec. 4, 1833.	1	1
Francisco Ruiz,	March 16, 1834.	2	-
Gaspar Flores,	Sept. 25, 1835.	6	-
Erastus Smith,	Dec. 25, 1833.	1	-
Francisco Flores,	Jan. 23, 1834.	5	1
Francisco Herera,	Dec. 24, 1833.	1	1
Maria Calvillo,	March 23, 1834.	1	1
Erasmo Seguin,	" 16, "	5	-
Heirs of Simon & Juan de Arocha,	Feb. 18, 1834.	8	-
Francisco Ricardo,	Dec. 3, 1833.	1	-
Josè Maria Balmaceda,	" 25, "	1	-
Eligio Gortari,	Feb. 23, 1834.	1	1
Vicente Gortari,	Dec. 28, 1833.	1	-
Manuel Ximenes,	March 13, 1834.	1	1
Josefa Rodriguez,	Feb. 24, "	2	1
Baron de Bastrop,	June 8, 1824.	4	-
Jose Sandoval,	Nov. 30, "	½	-
"	" " "		1
Jose Antonio Valdes,	June 4, "	4	-
Mariana Roderigues,	March 7, 1803.	2	-
Francisco Farrias,	Oct. 26, 1835.	.1	-
Juan Martin Verimendi,	Nov. 10, 1831.	2	-
"	" 15, "	1	-
"	" 20, "	2	-
Jose Antonio Navarro,	Oct. 6, "	4	-

WHERE SITUATED.	REMARKS.
Guadalupe River and Mill Road.	Special Grant.
Jerome River, between Gaudalupe & St. Marcos, 38 m's from Gonzales.	
On tributaries of the La Vaca, 20 miles above Atascocito Crossing.	
Gaudalupe, opposite Gonzales.	Special Grant.
San Marcos, S. W. S. below San Antonio Road.	"
Gaudalupe, N. E. side, and S. Antonio Road.	"
Gaudalupe, S. W. side, 22 miles from Ganzales.	"
Plumb Creek.	"
San Antonio Road, 20 miles from Gonzales.	"
Plumb Creek.	"
Gaudalupe, S. W. side, from 18 to 25 miles from Gonzales.	"
Junction of the Gaudalupe and San Marcos.	"
San Marcos.	"
"	"
Guadalupe, W. side.	"
" "	"

COUNTY.

Left bank of Leon Creek, 8 miles from Bexar.	Special Grant.
Leon Creek, mouth of the Rosita.	"
" 8 miles from Bexar.	"
Leon Creek, right bank, above Bexar & Rio Grande, labor on left bank.	"
San Antonio River, 60 miles below Bexar.	"
" S. W. side, 50 miles below Bexar.	"
Cibolo, N. E. side, on Gonzales Road, 28 miles from Bexar.	"
San Antonio River, S. W. side, about 30 miles below Bexar.	"
Cibolo, S. W. side, on Gonzales Road, 27 miles from Bexar.	"
San Antonio River, S. W. side, joins Mariana Cavilla's 2 league tract.	"
San Antonio River, S. side.	"
" N. E. side, mouth of Calabazas, 37 miles from Bexar.	"
Medina, N. side.	"
Cibola, S. W. side, below Gonzales Road, and above the Sulphur Springs.	"
Cibolo, W. side, below the Mill Road.	"
" N. E. side, below the Mill Road, 28 miles from Bexar.	"
" E. side, below the Gonzales Road, 29 miles from Bexar.	"
" W. side, " 27 "	"
On the W. side Guadalupe, above the San Antonio Road.	"
On the San Anotonio River, at the junction of the Salado Creek.	"
On the W. bank of San Antonio River, below the Mission of Espada.	"
At the junction of the Guadalupe and San Antonio Rivers.	"
On the Salado.	"
On the W. side San Antonio River.	"
" " Guadalupe, above San Antonio Road.	"
" " " adjoining the above.	"
On both sides of the San Marcos, at Big Spring.	"
About 11 milles S. W. of Bexar.	"

A

LIST OF TITLES

FOR

LANDS SOLD BY THE STATE,

UNDER CONTRACT OF

S. M. WILLIAMS, F. W. JOHNSON,

AND

ROBT. PEEBLES.

ABSTRACT OF ORIGINAL TITLES

NAMES OF GRANTEES.	DATE OF TITLES.	QUANTITY.	
		Leagues.	Labors.
Moseley Baker,	Aug. 15, 1835.	10	-
Spencer H. Jack,	Sept. 20, "	10	-
Adam Kuykendall,	Aug. 15, "	10	-
John York,	Dec. 12, "	10	-
David Wade,	" 8, "	10	-
Matthew R. Williams,	" 10, "	10	-
William Toy,	" 4, "	10	-
John S. Roberts,	" 5, "	10	-
Edward Pettus,	Aug. 12, "	10	-
Stephen Prather,	Nov. 23, "	10	-
Wesley Pace,	Dec. 5, "	10	-
William Pettus,	" 12, "	10	-
John Pettus,	" " "	10	-
		10	
Samuel Pettus,	" 15, "	10	-
William Lightfoot,	Sept. 13, "	10	-
Thomas F. M'Kinney,	Aug. 12, "	10	-
William Moore,	Dec. 24, "	10	-
Robert A. Irion,	Aug. 15, "	10	-
William Kuykendall,	" 12, "	10	-
Gibson Kuykendall,	" 10, "	10	-
Gray B. King,	Dec. 15, "	10	-
Charles C. Givins,	Aug. 12, "	10	-
Absalom Gibson,	Nov. 30, "	10	-
John R. Foster,	Dec. 16, "	10	-
William Dunlavy,	" 16, "	10	-
Walter Dickerson,	Nov. 30, "	10	-
H. Chriesman,	Dec. 12, "	10	-
Stephen Collins,	Nov. 25, "	10	-
Bennet Blake,	Aug. 20, "	3	-
Jackson Bell,	Dec. 14, "	7	-
Thomas Bell,	" 12, "	10	-
James Bell,	" 8, "	10	-
Joseph Baker,	" 4, "	10	-
John P. Borden,	Aug. 7, "	10	-
Anthony G. Smith,	Dec. 2, "	10	-
William H. Smith,	" 12, "	10	-
George Scott,	Aug. 25, "	10	-
William Scott, Sr.,	Oct. 3, "	10	-
William Scott, Jr.,	Aug. 20, "	10	-
Pascal P. Borden,	" 12, "	10	-
Gail Borden, Jr.,	" " "	10	-

WHERE SITUATED.	REMARKS.

On Sulphur Fork, adjoining Ignacio Galindo.
On the waters of Sabine River, joins Jose Luis Escobar.
On the waters of Sulphur Fork, about 4 leagues S. W. of its mouth.
" " Trinity, W. of Middle Fork.
" " Trinity.
" " Sabine, Trinity and Sulphur Fork, near their sources
" " Sabine.
Seven leagues on Sulphur Fork, about 8 leagues W. of Nacogdoches and Kiamechi, joining Francisco Rojo; 3 leagues on the waters of Sulphur Fork, 18 miles S. W. of the mouth of Mill Creek, and near the Shawnee Village, joining Ramon de la Serda.
Between Bois d'Arc Creek and Red River, joins Damien Rodrigues and P. P. Borden.
On the Waters of the Sabine, adjoining John Henrie.
On the waters of the Sabine and Trinity.
" " Trinity, Sabine and Sulphur Fork, near their sources.
" " " and above the junction of the two principal branches of the same.
On the waters of the Trinity, on Cross-timber Fork.
" " Sulphur Fork, joins Luciano Navarro.
Between Bois d'Arc Creek and Red River, & joining Maria Gertrudis Carmona, Meregildo Ramirez and Feliciano Lopez.
On the waters of Sabine, joins John Henrie.
On the waters of Sabine, near their sources, joins Jose Luis Escobar.
On Sulphur Fork, joins Vicenti Ortiz.
On the waters of Sulphur Fork, joins Manuel Hurtado.
" " Trinity.
" " Sulphur Fork, near their sources, joins Jose Luis Escobar and Jose Ma. de la Fuente.
Waters of Sabine and Trinity.
Waters of Trinity and Choctaw Bayou.
Waters of the Trinity.
" " Sabine.
" " Trinity.
" " Sabine.
" " Sulphur Fork, about 20 miles W. of Nacogdoches and Kiamechi Road, joins Patricio Torres.
On the waters of the Trinity.
" " "
" " " Sabine and Trinity.
" " " Trinity.
" " " Sabine, joining Jose Nicolas Elizondo.
" " " Sabine River, W. side.
" " " Trinity, W. of E. Fork.

4¾ leagues between Boi d'Arc Creek and Red River, joins John B. Hickson Thos. F. M'Kinney and Edward Pettus; 3⅓ on the waters of Bois d'Arc, joins Silvera Paquchin, Manuel Carmona, Moseley Baker, and Wm. Scott; 2 leagus near Sulphur Fork, about 4 leagues from its mouth, joins Adam Kuykendall. } 3 Surveys.

On the waters of Trinity.
Between Bois d'Arc Creek and Red River, joins Silvera Paquchin and Thomas F. M'Kinney.
Waters of Bois d'Arc, near their sources, joins Samuel Hornes and William Lightfoot.
On the waters of the Sabine, near their sources, joins Jose Luis Escobar R. A. Irion, and Spencer H. Jack.

A

LIST OF TITLES

For Lands sold by the State

OF

COAHUILA AND TEXAS,

IN

MAY 1835:

ALSO,

SUNDRY MISCELLANIES.

ABSTRACT OF ORIGINAL TITLES

NAMES OF GRANTEES.	DATE OF TITLES.	QUANTITY.	
		Leagues.	Labors.
John Noblitt,	Jan. 26, 1836	10	-
David Rusk,	Jan. 30, 1836.	10	-
Francis J. Anthony,	Jan. 29, 1836.	10	-
Leander Smith,	Feb. 19, 1836.	10	-
John A. Veitch,	Feb. 12, 1836.	10	-
George H. Duncan,	Feb. 15, 1836.	10	-
Ornan M. Logan,	Feb. 14, 1836.	10	-
Albert Emanuel,	Jan. 28, 1836.	10	-
John K. Allen,	Jan. 27, 1836.	10	-
Augustus C. Allen,	" " "	10	-

IN THE GENERAL LAND OFFICE 180

WHERE SITUATED.	REMARKS.
Four leagues N. W. of Lacey's Saline, on the waters of the Neches; 1 league on the S. W. branch of the Trinity; 1 league on Richland Creek, and 4 about 25 miles N. W. of Lacey's Saline, on waters of Neches.	Four surueys.
Four leagues on the waters of the Neches, 8 leagues N. and 5 W. of the Saline; 4 leagues on the same, 6 leagues N. and 5 W. of the Saline; 1 league 30,000 varas N. of N. W. corner of Bean's Saline, on E. branch of the Neches; 1 league on the W. side of Trinity, on the W. line of Delor's survey.	Four surveys.
Four leagues on the waters of the Sabine, about 30 miles N. W. of Lacey's Saline; 4 leagues on the waters of the Sabine, 10 leagues N. and 5 W. of Lacey's Saline; 1 league on the waters of the Sabine, about 12 or 15 miles S. W. of the point where the road from Nacogdoches to Pecan Point, crosses said river; 1 league on the waters of the Sabine, about 30 miles N. and 5 W. of Lacey's Saline.	Four surveys.
Four leagues on the waters of the Neches, about 39 miles N. W. of Lacey's Saline; 4 leagues on the waters of the Neches, 8 leagues N. of Bean's Saline, beginning at the N. W. corner of J. W. Burton's survey; 1 league on the waters of the Neches, on the S. side of the principal eastern branch; 1 league on the waters of the Neches, 5,000 varas N. of the N. E. corner of Eliphalet Rollin's league.	Four surveys.
Four leagues on the waters of the Neches, about 8 leagues N. and 2 W. of Lacey's Saline; 4 leagues on the waters of the Neches, about 12 or 14 miles W. of the Delaware Village; 1 league on the sources of the Neches, 5,000 varas N. of the N. E. corner of D. H. Vail's league; 1 league about 12½ miles N. W., and 1 league N. of the N. W. corner of Theresa Tumlinson's survey.	Four surveys.
Four leag!s on the Sabine, 10 leag's N. and 7 W. of saline on Neches; Four leag's on the W. side of the Sabine, 12 leag's N. and 5 W. of Bean's Saline; 1 league about 15,000 varas N. of Eliphalet Rollin's survey; 1 league on the waters of the Neches, between the E. and W. branches of the same, 30,000 varas N. of the N. W. corner of Bean's Saline.	Four surveys.
Four leagues on the waters of the Sabine, about 11 leagues N. and 1 W. of Bean's Saline; 4 leagues on the waters of the Sabine, 12 leagues N. and 7 W. of Lacey's Saline; 1 league about 11 miles N. W. of the saline on the Neches, beginning at the N. W. corner of Theresa Tomlinson's survey; 1 league about 11 miles N. W. of the Sabine, beginning at the N. W. corner of Theresa Tomlinson's survey.	Four surveys.
Three leagues on the waters of Cypress Bayou, about 10 or 12 miles W. of where the road from Nacogdoches to Red River crosses the same; 1 league on the waters of the Neches, 10,000 varas N. of the N. W. corner of Eliphalet Rollin's survey; 1 league on the waters of the Sabine, about 10 leagues N. of the Saline on the W. side of the Neches; 1 league on the E. side of the Neches, about 13 miles N. of the Saline; 1 league about 12 miles N. of the Saline, on the waters of the Neches; 1 league on the waters of the Neches, 5,000 varas N. of the N. W. corner of Eliphalet Rollin's survey; 1 league E. of the river Neches; 1 leag. on the waters of the Neches, beginning at the N. E. corner of the preceding survey.	Eight surveys.

On the waters of the Trinity.
" " "

ABSTRACT OF ORIGINAL TITLES

NAMES OF GRANTEES.	DATE OF TITLES.	QUANTITY.	
		Leagues.	Labors.
Pinckney Caldwell,	Sept. 8, 1835.	3	-
Thomas Y. Buford,	" 4, "	10	-
James Clark,	" 3, "	10	-
Moses L. Patton,	" 2, "	10	-
John M. Dorr,	" 3, "	1	-
Guillermo Cruz,	" 25, "	10	-
Antonio Sanchez,	" 3, "	10	-
William Howard,	" 12, "	10	-
Lovic Dikes,	" 21, "	10	-
Luther Smith,	" 4, "	8	-
Nathaniel Norris,	" 1, "	10	-
John K. Taylor,	" 13, "	10	-
John Johnson,	" 30, "	10	-
John Howard,	" 21, "	10	-
Louis Orlando Durst,	" 20, "	2	-
Juan Durst,	April 3, 1834.	3	3
"	" " "		7
"	" " "	1	-
Rafael Peña purchased of Nath'l Townsend,	Oct. 22, "	11	-
Juan Durst purchased of Barr & Davenport,	May 1, 1832.	9	-
Alfred R. Guild,	Jan. 17, 1835.	1	-
Alexander Newland,	" 15, "	9	-

WHERE SITUATED.	REMARKS.
On the waters of Choctaw Bayou.	
On the sources of the Trinity and Choctaw Bayou.	
Six leagues on Sulphur Fork, about 35 miles W. of the road leading from Nacogdoches to the Kiamechi; 4 leagues on the N. side of Sulphur Fork, about 35 miles W. of the road leading from Nacogdoches to the Kiamechi.	Two surveys.
On the sources of Choctaw Bayou.	
On Red River, a little below Williams' Bluff.	
On the Waters of Sulphur Fork,	
On both sides of the Sabine.	
Waters of Red River, above Pinos Creek.	
On the waters of Sulphur Fork.	
On the sources of Choctaw Bayou, joins 6 leagues of Carlos O'Campo.	
On both sides of the Sabine.	
On the waters of Sulphur Fork.	
" " "	
On the sources of Choctaw Bayou, S. W. side of Red River.	
On the waters of Red River, above Pinos Creek.	
E. side of the Trinity.	
" " Angelina.	
Neches, W. side, joins Jose Ma. Procela.	
On the waters of Trinity and Bear Creek, above San Antonio Road.	
On both sides of the Angelina. - - - -	Certified copy.
On Davidson's Creek, W. Brazos.	
On the waters of Sabine and Sulphur Fork.	

www.ingramcontent.com/pod-product-compliance
Lightning Source LLC
Chambersburg PA
CBHW031418290426
44110CB00011B/433